MONTH-BY-MONTH GARDENING

MICHIGAN

D1637327

First published in 2014 by Cool Springs Press, an imprint of The Quarto Group, 400 First Avenue North, Suite 400, Minneapolis, MN 55401. Telephone: (612) 344-8100 Fax: (612) 344-8692

quartoknows.com

Visit our blogs at quartoknows.com

Library of Congress Cataloging-in-Publication Data

Myers, Melinda.
   Michigan month-by-month gardening : what to do each month to have a beautiful garden all year / Melinda Myers.
      pages cm
   Includes bibliographical references and index.
   ISBN 978-1-59186-432-5 (sc)
1. Gardening--Michigan. I. Title.

   SB453.2.M5M95 2015
   635.09774--dc23

Acquisitions Editor: Billie Brownell
Design Manager: Brad Springer
Layout: S.E. Anderson

Printed in USA

MONTH-BY-MONTH GARDENING

MICHIGAN

**What to Do Each Month to Have
a Beautiful Garden All Year**

MELINDA MYERS

COOL
SPRINGS
PRESS
Home and Garden Experts™

Dedication and Acknowledgement

Dedicated to Michigan gardeners, new and seasoned. Thanks for sharing your enthusiasm, experiences, and ideas. And most of all, thanks for inviting me along on your gardening journey.

Acknowledgment

Thanks to the Michigan horticulturist and gardening experts. I appreciate the opportunity to step foot into your horticulture arena and share my knowledge and experiences as a horticulturist and long time northern gardener.

A special thanks to the University and Extension specialists, horticulture educators, horticulturists, master gardeners, greening volunteers, and professionals in related fields, as well as my friends and mentors in the media and garden writers, who so willingly pass along what you know and love. You are a wealth of knowledge and conduit of information that helps us create a more beautiful world and productive gardens.

Thanks to all of you who join me for my live or recorded classes, lectures or via my website. Your questions and ideas keep me fresh and enthused about gardening, teaching and writing. This is especially important during long stretches of travel, delayed flights and snowstorms. And if you haven't visited with me yet, I hope to see or hear from you in the near future.

I want to thank my family and friends for their continued patience, understanding and support. I know I said no more books for a while, but I just couldn't pass up the opportunity. And I promise we will make more time for fun and laughter on the farm, down by the lake or wherever our journeys take us.

Thanks also to Diana, Dawn, and Mark who make up the Melinda Myers team. Your talents, skills and persistence are the reason we can continue to expand our outreach efforts to new and experienced, young and old gardeners.

A huge thanks to my advisory board, Heather, Dave, Dennis, Jim, and Terry. You helped me become a better businesswoman, keep me focused on the mission and continue to help my team and me expand our reach to new gardeners.

Thanks to teachers across the country who made a difference in mine and so many other lives. Please keep inspiring and educating the youth of this country. You have such an important job and need to remember the important role in our future.

A big thank you to my editor Billie Brownell, Tracy Stanley and all the staff at Cool Springs Press for the opportunity to write this and other gardening books.

Contents

Introduction

I have been lucky enough to garden in and call the Midwest my home. In that time, there have been no two years or growing seasons exactly the same. The changing seasons and changeable weather put you and your gardening skills to the test each year.

This is part of the challenge and fun of gardening in the north. It is also why gardeners are such a great group of people. You must be optimistic and perhaps a bit crazy to garden in the north.

Whether you are hoping for a big harvest, a beautiful landscape, or a little stress relief, knowing the "when" and "how" of gardening will help you be successful. Use this book to eliminate some of the guesswork. It is a guide to help, not restrict, your gardening efforts and experimentation.

Always start with a plan. Put your gardening and landscape plans on paper to help you grow and develop a beautiful landscape and productive garden. And don't worry—a landscape plan is meant to change over time, not remain stagnant. Make needed and desired changes along the way to achieve your landscaping goals.

Start or continue a garden journal. It can be as simple as a spiral notebook, as complex as a computer spreadsheet, or as beautiful as a coffee table book. Use this to record planting information, growing records, and pest management strategies. Refer to your garden plan, journal information, and this book to help you get the most enjoyment from your Michigan garden. These tools can help you repeat successes and avoid making the same mistakes.

Refer to *Month-by-Month Gardening in Michigan* throughout the year. Each chapter features monthly tips on the time to plant, water, prune, fertilize, and manage pests. Use these general guidelines as your starting points.

Consult with local experts to fine-tune these recommendations to fit your specific backyard growing conditions and gardening style. Michigan State University (MSU) has long been a leader and known world-wide for its excellence in horticulture education and research. Visit the MSU Horticulture Gardens for ideas and inspiration for your own landscape. And don't overlook all the plantings and information available from your nearby public gardens. These are great places to observe and evaluate plants growing in similar conditions to yours. We have all killed a few plants along the way. This is part of the learning process. Most important, just get started, relax, and have fun.

Michigan is a horticulture paradise filled with great diversity and a few gardening challenges. The Great Lakes and reliable snow cover help buffer the weather extremes in some parts of the state. The milder winters and longer growing season in Michigan are contrasted by the shorter growing season and colder winters of the northern regions.

Always select the hardiest plant available. Locate your county on the hardiness map. Hardiness ratings reflect a plant's ability to survive the average minimum winter temperature. Select plants rated for this or colder climates (the lower number). Remember, hardiness is just a cold-tolerance rating. You must also match the plant to its growing conditions. Healthy plants that get the proper growing conditions and care have better chances of surviving unexpected weather extremes.

Use the average frost dates to help with planting dates. The map on page 220 gives you the average number of frost free days in Michigan. These averages are based on 100 years of data. This does not take into account any late spring or early fall frosts that commonly fall outside these averages.

Consider both the air and soil temperatures when planting. The last spring frost is just one factor to consider. Areas near the Great Lakes are often frost-free sooner than nearby inland spaces, but the soil and air stay cooler into spring and summer. Planting too soon can delay growth and harvest. Wait to plant tropical plants, such as tuberous begonias and tomatoes, until after all danger of frost has passed and both the air (day and night) and soil temperatures have warmed.

Use the weather information, the month-by-month planting guides, and your own experience to time both planting and care.

PLANNING AND IMPROVING YOUR GARDEN

An attractive, healthy landscape starts with a plan. Draw a base map of your existing landscape. Locate the house, trees, shrubs, gardens, and other elements on the plan. Use this as a basis to make future additions, deletions, and changes.

Gather ideas from friends, neighbors, botanical gardens, garden tours, and professionals.

Use trees as the long-term framework of your landscape. They provide structure, screen views, shade the house, and add year-round beauty. Place large shade trees on the east and west sides of the house. They will shade the windows from the summer sun and reduce cooling costs. Avoid growing large shade trees on the south side of your home because they block winter sun, reduce solar heating, and increase winter fuel costs.

Include shrubs to screen views, highlight focal points, and attract wildlife. Look for hardy plants with attractive bark, colorful flowers, and bird-attracting fruit for winter interest. Select plants that fit the available growing space. This will save you time spent pruning the plant down to size and hauling away the debris.

Include flowers, vines, and groundcovers for splashes of color, as focal points, and to attract wildlife. They can be planted in beds, grown in containers, or mixed with your trees and shrubs. Use them as short-term accents or long-term additions to your plan.

Use color in the landscape to create mood and interest. Warm colors of orange, red, and yellow attract attention, brighten the location, and make large spaces appear smaller. It only takes a few warm-colored annuals to steal the show.

Cool colors of green, blue, and violet make a small area appear larger and give hot spots a cooler feeling. So a basket of blue pansies or a planter filled with green foliage plants can transform a small, south-facing patio into a cool and roomy spot.

Use contrasting colors—warm with cool, such as yellow with blue or red with green—for an attractive, eye-catching blend.

Combine similar, related colors to hold a design together. Mixing bold colors of red, orange, and yellow, for example, have equal weight and interest in the flower garden. Mixing cool colors creates a subtle and soothing blend.

■ *Roll up a ball of soil and gentle press the ball until a ribbon begins to form. If a ribbon more than one inch long forms before it breaks, you have silty soil (top). If a ribbon 1–2 inches long forms before it breaks, you have clay soil (middle). If a ribbon greater than 2 inches forms before it breaks, you have very heavy and poorly drained soil (bottom).*

Use color echoing—repetition of a color from one plant to another—to provide a sense of unity in your flower gardens and landscape. Repeat the color from one flower to the next plant's flower, flower part, or foliage. This type of repetition is subtle but as effective as repeating the same plant.

A monochromatic garden uses the same color flowers throughout. This style can be quite dramatic. Some gardeners find this style boring, while others like the elegant, more formal appearance.

Consider the plant's texture in your design. Use fine-textured plants—those with spiky flowers and grass-like leaves—as filler and background. A backdrop of fine-textured plants adds a sense of depth to the garden. Use bold-textured plants—those with large, round flowers and wide leaves—for focal points and accents.

Photograph and videotape your progress. It is fun and helpful to see where your landscape started and the changes you make along the way.

Stuck or overwhelmed? Consider hiring a professional. Some of the best landscapes come from a cooperative effort between a landscape designer and an avid gardener. A designer can offer guidance on plant and bed placement and may save you time and money by helping you avoid some mistakes.

SOILS

Soil, like the weather, presents challenges to gardeners. Selecting plants best suited to the growing conditions will decrease effort and increase your success. Michigan's soils vary from acidic (low pH) great for growing blueberries to high pH alkaline soil. These alkaline soils make it difficult to grow rhododendrons, blueberries, red maples and other acid loving plants.

It is difficult to change the soil pH, and it takes years to repair the damage caused by misapplication of lime (which makes soil more alkaline) and other pH-altering materials. Test your soil and follow the recommendations whenever you attempt to change the soil pH. Reduce your stress and increase success by growing plants suited to the soil, including pH.

Soil type varies throughout the state from poorly drained clay to fast-draining sandy soil. The agriculturally rich regions are filled with loam while the glacial deposits created pockets of gravel-filled soil.

INTRODUCTION

Most urban sites have poor soil due to construction and years of misuse. Proper preparation and care of all these soils improve your gardening results. Adjust watering and fertilization to fit the soil and plant requirements.

Soil is the foundation of your gardening success. Time and effort spent preparing and managing your soil will be rewarded with years of gardening success.

Start with a soil test. This is a good idea when starting a new garden or trying to resolve problems. The results will help you determine how much and what type of fertilizer to add for the plants you grow and may uncover the cause of poor plant growth. Contact the Michigan State University Extension website or local office for a soil test kit.

Perform a soil test anytime the ground is not frozen and has not been recently fertilized. Collect separate samples for each gardening area. You need separate reports for the lawn areas, flowerbeds, and so on. Start with new areas and any spots with problems. Stagger testing to spread out the cost and the time involved.

Remove 4- to 6-inch-long plugs of soil from five or more scattered spots within the garden. Mix these together to create a representative sample of the garden soil. Send 1 cup of soil to the Michigan State University soil testing lab or other state certified soil-testing lab. Allow two weeks for the results.

After you receive the recommendations, incorporate fertilizer and organic matter at the rate and time specified on the soil test report. Like water, too much or not enough fertilizer can influence the health and vigor of your plants. Overfertilizing, fertilizing at the wrong time, or using the wrong product can injure plants, harm the environment, and waste time and money. Follow fertilization recommendations for specific plants if the soil test information is not available.

Soil preparation varies by location, conditions, and the plants you grow. Almost every soil benefits

from the addition of compost, well-rotted manure, or peat moss into the soil. Organic matter is an amazing additive that improves drainage in clay soils and the water-holding capacity in sandy soils. Incorporate a 2- to 4-inch layer into the top 6 to 12 inches of the garden soil.

Do not add sand unless you are prepared to bring it in by the semi-truckload. You must add 1 inch of sand for every 1 inch of soil you plan to amend. This is a large expense and a lot of work. Adding less than this will produce something akin to concrete, not well-drained soil.

Work the soil when it is moist but not wet. Grab a handful of soil and gently squeeze it into a ball. Tap the ball with your finger. If it breaks into smaller pieces, it is ready to work. Otherwise, go back inside and wait for the soil to dry. Patience now will eliminate clods, cracking, and frustration caused by dealing with damaged soil.

Work the fertilizers and amendments into the top 6 to 12 inches of soil. Sprinkle the garden with water long enough to moisten the top 2 to 3 inches of soil or wait a few days for the soil to settle.

Use one of these methods to convert grass into a planting bed. Lay out the boundaries of the garden with a hose. Experiment until you have the desired size and shape. Use curved edges for a more informal look and to make mowing easier. Avoid tight angles that are hard to reach and will require hand trimming.

Edge the bed with an edger or sharp, flat shovel. Remove the sod with a sod cutter and amend the soil as described above. For weedy areas consider using a total vegetation killer to eliminate perennial weeds like quackgrass before establishing a new garden. Several applications may be needed. Be sure to read and follow label directions.

Consider leaving the dead layer of grass intact if soil does not need amending. It acts as an additional layer of mulch and will help prevent erosion when establishing beds on slopes.

Use mulch, newspaper, or cardboard for a non-chemical approach. Edge the bed, cut the grass very short, and cover with several layers of newspaper or a sheet of cardboard. Cover with organic mulch. The grass will die and decompose, and paper mulch eventually decomposes, improving the soil below. You can cut openings in the mulch and plant right away or wait a few months when it will be easier to dig.

Or edge the bed and cover the area with clear plastic for six to eight weeks in the hottest part of the season. This will cook the weeds, many of the weed seeds, and pests. Unfortunately you will be sacrificing much of the short growing season.

Avoid tree and shrub roots when digging new beds. Extensive deep tilling can damage tree roots and kill the plant you're trying to accentuate. Modifying the planting hole but not the surrounding area can limit plant root growth beyond the planting hole. And piling as little as an inch of soil over the root system can kill some trees.

Consider physically removing the grass with a sod cutter and mulching, using the newspaper/cardboard method or a total vegetation killer. Or consider leaving the dead layer of turf intact and mulch to minimize root disturbance.

Add perennial groundcovers suited to the growing conditions for seasonal beauty. Space the plants throughout the area. Dig a hole slightly larger than the rootsystem of the groundcover. Amend the planting holes with peat moss, compost, or other organic matter. Plant, mulch, and water. Water new plantings often enough to keep the soil slightly moist. Keep in mind the tree will prevent much of the rain from reaching the roots and the water that makes it to the ground will be absorbed by the trees.

Improve the soil in existing mixed borders and perennials gardens with vertical mulching. Attach an auger bit, like those used for planting bulbs, on your cordless drill. Use it to drill scattered holes and work compost into the soil. You will aerate and improve the soil while leaving the garden intact.

PLANT

Proper planting is important to establishing a healthy, long-lived plant. There is more to it than making sure the green side points up. Preparing the site, digging the hole, and planting at the proper depth and time will increase your transplanting and gardening success.

To remove annual seedlings, gently pop the young plants from their cell-packs by squeezing the bottoms and pushing up. Do not grab plants by their tender stems or leaves.

Plants growing in peat pots can be planted pot and all, but remove the upper edges of peat pots so that the pot will not act as a wick, pulling water away from the roots.

■ *When planting annuals, plant at the same depth they were growing in the containers. If your growing medium is properly prepared, it will be loose enough that you can easily dig shallow planting holes with your fingers. For gallon pots, use a trowel, spade, or cultivator.*

■ *Pinch off any flowers or buds so the plant can focus its energy on getting its roots established rather than flowering, then water well.*

Get a jump on the season by using some of the homemade or commercial season-extending devices. Gardeners have long used glass bottles, plastic, cold frames, and other devices to trap heat and protect plants from frost.

You can start a month or more earlier than normal by warming the soil. Prepare the garden and cover it with clear plastic for two weeks. This warms the soil and helps germinate annual weed seeds. Lightly cultivate to remove weeds without bringing new seeds to the surface.

Plant seeds and transplants in the warm soil. Cover with a row cover fabric, such as Reemay®, Grass-Fast®, or Harvest-Guard. These products let air, light, and water in while trapping heat near the plants.

Leave the row cover in place until both the day and night temperatures are warm. Covering plants through the early weeks of June can keep them warm on those cool nights, speed up growth, and reduce the time until flowering and harvest.

Use these devices to extend your enjoyment a few weeks longer in the fall.

WATER

Summer droughts and spring floods remind us of the value of water and watering properly. A garden hose can be a great help or a terrible detriment to landscape plants. Consider the plants, soils, and weather when watering the landscape.

Water more frequently during the hot, dry days of July and August. Decrease watering during the cool days of spring and fall. Consider rainfall when calculating water needs. Nature often provides regular—sometimes too regular—irrigation for our planting.

Soil types play a crucial role in determining watering frequency. Gardens with clay soil require thorough but less frequent watering than those growing in sandy and rocky soils because clay soil holds moisture longer. Wait until the top few inches start to dry, about every seven to ten days, before watering again. Water thoroughly, wetting the total root zone. With sandy soils, apply water in two applications. Water thoroughly so that the root zone is moist. Wait three to five days and water again if the top few inches have begun to dry.

New plants need more frequent watering to get established. Check them several times a week, and water often enough to keep their roots moist. Gradually decrease watering frequency to encourage deep, drought-tolerant roots. Proper watering helps maintain growth, improves productivity, and minimizes pest problems. The extensive root systems of established plants allow them to find and use water from a large area for most of the season. However, during extended dry periods, they need supplemental watering.

Water plants early in the morning to reduce the risk of disease and foliar burn. Keeping leaves dry at night helps prevent the development and spread of fungal leaf spots and blight. Allowing leaves to dry before the heat of midday reduces water lost to evaporation and damage caused by the bright sun shining on wet leaves.

Use shredded leaves, evergreen needles, and woodchips as a mulch to reduce watering frequency. A thin layer of these materials over the soil surface will conserve moisture, suppress weeds, and gradually improve the soil.

And consider installing a rain barrel. It is an easy way to capture rainwater when it's plentiful to use for irrigating your containers and gardens when rainfall is lacking. And install a rain garden where appropriate to help retain water on your landscape, recharge the groundwater, and reduce the pressure on urban storm sewers.

FERTILIZE

A trip to the garden center and down the fertilizer aisle can be overwhelming. There seems to be a bag and formulation for every plant you can imagine.

HERE'S HOW

TO COLLECT SOIL FOR TESTING

1. Clean a thin garden trowel and gallon bucket with a mild soap mixture. Allow them to dry before gathering the soil.

2. Dig up samples from different areas of the lawn. Half a trowel of dirt or less from each of about five or six locations will be plenty..

3. Collect the soil in the bucket as you go. When you've collected the soil you'll need, use the trowel to thoroughly blend the soil samples.

It is difficult to decide which product is best for your garden situation.

Start with a soil test. Take representative samples, 4 to 6 inches deep, from several areas of the garden. Send it to a state certified lab or contact the Michigan State University Extension local office or website. The results will tell you how much and what type of fertilizer to add.

Add the type and amount of fertilizer recommended by the soil test report provided by the Extension Service office. If soil test recommendations are not available, follow the recommendations in the monthly chapters.

Select the fertilizer formulation (the three numbers on the front of the fertilizer bag) recommended by your soil test, or check the fertilizer recommendations in each chapter for the plant you are trying to grow. These are based on general plant needs for Michigan.

The first of the three numbers is nitrogen. It is essential to plant growth, especially leaves and stems. The middle number is the percentage of phosphorus in the fertilizer. This nutrient encourages root, flower, and fruit development. The last of the three numbers is the percentage of potassium, which plants use to help fight

■ *Use a compost bin to contain and dress up your compost pile.*

disease and increase hardiness. Most of our soils have high to excessive levels of phosphorus and potassium.

Avoid complete fertilizers, such as 10-10-10, and those with high percentages of phosphorus and potassium. Adding more can interfere with the uptake of other essential nutrients and pollute our groundwater.

Your next choice is between liquid or dry fertilizers. Liquid fertilizers can be applied with a sprinkling can, garden hose, or spray tank. Dry fertilizers are spread on the soil surface. Apply dry fertilizers to the soil using a small shaker, hand-held spreader, or push-type spreader.

Look for the words "slow-release" or "fast-release" on the bag. Slow-release fertilizers provide a constant supply of nutrients over a long period of time. Use fast-release fertilizers when you want a quick fix. These need to be applied several times throughout the garden season. Use a slow-release formulation to reduce your workload (you will only apply once or twice a season), encourage slow steady growth, and avoid burn, especially during a drought. Check the label for specific recommendations.

Choose between an organic or inorganic form of fertilizer. Inorganic fertilizers come in a variety of formulations and are in a form ready for the plants to use. Organic fertilizers improve the soil and provide small amounts of nutrients over a long period of time.

Select the fertilizer that best suits your plants, soil, and gardening style. Use a fertilizer recommended by your soil test report. Or try a low-nitrogen, slow-release fertilizer to reduce the risk of nitrogen burn and overfertilization.

COMPOST

Make your own organic matter (compost) by recycling all your pest-free plant debris. It is as simple as putting it into a heap and letting it rot. The more effort you put into the process, the sooner you get compost.

■ *It's a good idea to add thin layers of topsoil or finished compost to a new pile to introduce the decay organisms that create compost. Add water as needed to keep the pile moist but not soggy.*

■ *Build your compost pile as materials become available, layering carbon materials alternatively with nitrogen materials. If you have an abundance of carbon materials, put some of them on the side until more nitrogen materials become available. Too many green grass clippings can mat down and prohibit the composting process. Mix them with looser materials such as straw or dried leaves or allow them to dry in the sun before adding them to the pile.*

Start with green debris. Shred fallen leaves, add herbicide-free grass clippings, and include other plant debris. Avoid meat and animal products that can attract rodents. Make a pile at least 3 feet tall and wide for quicker results. Add soil and enough water to moisten the pile and turn it occasionally to speed up decomposition.

■ *Turn your compost occasionally to speed up decomposition. Turning more often—once a week—will greatly shorten the time to creating finished compost. If you don't turn your pile, you'll still get compost, but it will take a lot longer. If you want to speed up the composting process, turn the pile more often, add more nitrogen-rich materials, and shred or chop the carbon materials before adding them to the pile so they break down more quickly. Ideally, you will have several piles going at the same time so you will always have some finished compost available. You'll know your compost is ready for the garden when it is dark, crumbly, and most of the plant parts are decomposed.*

Start a holding pile. Use the second pile to store plant debris until you have enough to make a new pile. The first pile will decompose faster if fresh materials are not continually being added.

Use finished compost to amend new and existing gardens. Try mixing it with topsoil to create a well-drained potting mix for container gardens. Or, topdress by spreading a thin layer of compost over the soil surface in lawns, perennial gardens, and groundcover plantings.

PRUNE
Keep your plants healthy and attractive with proper pruning. Pruning is helpful for training young plants, developing a strong framework, encouraging flowers and fruiting, and repairing damage. Understand why you are pruning before you make the first cut.

Pruning also includes deadheading, pinching back, and other related grooming techniques. Using a pruner or your fingers, pinch back leggy plants to encourage fuller, more compact growth. Deadhead

Be sure to check the plant guidelines for advice on the proper timing for pruning each type of plant.

faded flowers to encourage rebloom and discourage reseeding. Prune some young perennials to control height and bloom time.

Check each month's Care section to find out when and what to prune for the results you desire. And review the pruning tips starting on page 209 for more details.

PESTS & PLANT HEALTH CARE

Insects, disease, wildlife, and weeds all add to the challenge of growing a healthy landscape. Some are essential to the health of the landscape, while others need to be managed to minimize the damage they cause. To be respectful of the environment while controlling pests, use a "Plant Health Care" approach (the horticulturist's version of "Integrated Pest Management") to manage your landscape. This starts with proper plant selection and care, continues by managing pest problems using a variety of the most environmentally sound techniques, and ends with chemicals as a last resort.

Select the most pest-resistant varieties available and grow them in the proper location. This simple practice can avoid many pest problems, eliminating the need for control. Provide proper care, such as watering, fertilizing, and pruning, based upon the plant's needs.

Monitor the garden throughout the growing season. Finding pests early can mean the difference between picking off a few sick leaves and spraying a plant throughout the season. Look under the leaves, along the stems, and on the ground for signs of insects, disease, and wildlife.

Remove weeds as soon as they appear. Not only do they compete with your garden plants for water and nutrients, but they also harbor insects and disease. Remove them before they have a chance to set seed and infect the soil for the next season. Mulch to prevent weeds.

Follow the planting and care guidelines in this book to keep your plants healthy and more resistant to pests. Prevent many disease problems by keeping water off the leaves. Water early in the morning so that leaves dry quickly, or apply water directly to the soil to minimize wet foliage. Use a watering wand to extend your reach and get the water to the soil, or try a soaker hose or drip irrigation to make the job easier.

Cover the plants to prevent the insects from reaching and damaging them. Continually remove spotted and insect-infested leaves and weeds to reduce insect and disease problems. Remove weeds and debris that can harbor pests. Clean the garden each fall, leaving healthy perennials stand for winter, to prevent disease and insects from overwintering in the garden.

Properly identify all pests before reaching for a pesticide. Sometimes the pest we see is not causing the damage. Other times the damage is done, the pest is gone, and there is no need to treat. Always find out what is causing the damage and if control is needed to maintain the health of the plant.

Consult my website (www.melindamyers.com), Michigan State University Extension website or local office, or your favorite garden center for advice. It is important to use the right product or technique at the right time to maximize effectiveness and minimize any negative impact on the environment.

Consider all control options and their impact on the plant, your health, and the environment. Select the most environmentally friendly method that fits your gardening style and the plant's needs.

Hand pick or trap insects to minimize negative attacks on the good insects, fungi, and wildlife in the environment. Remove small infestations of insects or infected leaves. This can limit damage and still provide a productive harvest. You can use yellow pans filled with soapy water to trap aphids, whiteflies, and other common insect pests. Trap slugs with stale beer in a shallow can sunk into the ground and earwigs with crumpled paper under an overturned pot.

Cover plantings with floating row covers such as Reemay or Harvest-Guard to keep out unwanted insects. This is an effective technique for preventing cabbage-worm damage on cabbage, broccoli, and Brussels sprouts and bean beetle damage on beans.

And consider using some of the environmentally friendly products on the market. Soaps, Neem oil, *Bacillus thuringiensis*, and others control specific pests while reducing the risk to beneficial insects, wildlife, and people.

Always read and follow all label directions before using any product, whether synthetic, natural, or organic, in your landscape. Make sure it is labeled to control the pest on the plant you want to treat. Wear any protective clothing recommended or required by the label. Consider wearing long sleeves, pants, goggles, and gloves as a regular part of your pesticide application gear.

Evaluate the success of control measures used and record this in your journal. Mark next year's calendar and review this book's monthly pest management sections to help reduce and control problems next season.

WINTER CARE
Some plants need a little help surviving our winters. Snow is the best mulch, but it often arrives too late, melts too soon, or comes and goes throughout the winter.

Protect new plantings, borderline hardy plants, or those subject to winterkill and frost heaving with winter mulch. Apply winter mulches of evergreen boughs, straw, or marsh hay over the plants after the ground freezes. The goal is to keep the soil constantly cold throughout the winter. Fluctuating soil temperatures cause early sprouting and frost heaving. Early sprouting results in damaged leaves and flowers when the normal cold temperatures return. Frost heaving causes the soil to shift, damaging roots and often pushing perennials and bulbs right out of the ground.

Use discarded holiday trees, decorative fencing, burlap, or other items to create windbreaks and shade for tender plants and broadleaf evergreens. Place them on the windward and sunny sides of the plant. The screening reduces the wind and sun that reaches the plants and dries the leaves.

See fall and winter months for more ideas on winter protection. A little preventative action in the fall can save a lot of time repairing damage and money spent replacing damaged plants.

WANT TO LEARN MORE?
Use the *Michigan Getting Started Garden Guide* as a companion to this book. It features more details on individual plants and additional gardening techniques suited to our area. My website (www.melindamyers.com) also offers additional audio, video, and written tips as well as answers to your questions.

Contact your local office of the Michigan State University Extension Service or their website. They have excellent publications and Master Gardeners to help with your garden and landscape.

Visit local botanical gardens and arboreta to gather ideas for gardening in your community. And don't forget the library. Check out the many garden books and magazines your community library has to offer. It is a great place to spend your spare time in January, dreaming and planning for the upcoming season.

How to Use this Book

Michigan Month-by-Month Gardening is the "operating manual" for your northern landscape. It is a great companion to my book *Michigan Getting Started Garden Guide*.

Each monthly chapter focuses on the major tasks needed to keep you growing and maintaining healthy and attractive plants in your landscape. It is meant as a guideline to help new gardeners get started and experienced gardeners continue to improve their gardening skills.

The tasks include the basics of gardening: Plan, Plant, Care, Water, Fertilize, and Problem-Solve. Pruning and grooming tips are covered in the Care section, and design ideas are woven throughout the chapters. The major plant groups described below are addressed in each of these categories. The goal is to create an easy-to-use, year-round reference.

Annuals have long been used to add lots of color throughout our short growing season. Learn how to start them indoors, plant them outdoors, manage pests, and keep them looking beautiful throughout the growing season.

Bulbs, corms, rhizomes, and tubers provide color before other plants dare to show their leaves. Summer bulbs can brighten the shade and provide a tropical feel to your landscape. Learn how to use and care for them in the landscape.

Edibles, whether in a traditional vegetable garden or mixed with flowers, provide fun and flavor the whole family can enjoy. Use their texture and color to brighten up the landscape. Find out how to grow a bountiful harvest.

Lawns create a green backdrop for other landscape plants. Whether it is your pride and joy or just something to keep your feet from getting muddy when it rains, proper care will keep your lawn green and growing. Learn the what, when, and how of managing your lawn.

Perennials and ornamental grasses' seasonal interest and potential years of service make them a good addition for most landscapes. Learn how to transplant, when to deadhead, and how to combine perennials for maximum enjoyment with minimal effort on your part.

Roses provide fragrance, beauty, and sometimes frustration for gardeners. Find out how to get all the benefits, reduce the work, and increase your rose-growing success. Learn how to plant, care for, and winter-protect roses for long-term beauty and survival.

Shrubs are diverse plants that help us create privacy, attract wildlife, and add four seasons of interest to your landscape. Keep them looking beautiful by following the monthly tips on proper selection, planting, and care.

Trees create a framework upon which to build the rest of your landscape. Their longevity depends on proper selection, care, and management of the surrounding landscape. Find out how to plant, prune, manage pests, and grow attractive trees for your landscape and for future generations.

Vines and groundcovers soften structures, unify plantings, and add texture and color throughout the landscape. Learn how to select the best plants for your specific needs, manage them for health and beauty, and minimize problems.

Now, let's get started gardening month by month!

USDA Hardiness Zone Maps

COLD HARDINESS ZONES

Plants included are hardy throughout the state unless otherwise noted. Keep in mind there may be hardier or less hardy cultivars within a particular group of plants.

Cold-hardiness zone designations were developed by the United States Department of Agriculture (USDA) to indicate the minimum average temperature in an area. A zone assigned to an individual plant indicates the lowest temperature at which the plant can be expected to survive over a winter. Michigan has zones ranging from 4a to 6b. Cold hardiness is just one factor to consider when selecting plants. Matching plants to their cold hardiness zones will help increase your gardening success.

ZONE	Average Minimum Temperature
4A	-25 to -30
4B	-20 to -25
5A	-15 to -20
5B	-10 to -15
6A	-5 to -10
6B	0 to -5

USDA Plant Hardiness Zone Map, 2012. Agricultural Research Service, U.S. Department of Agriculture. Accessed from http://planthardiness.ars.usda.gov.

January

January is a time for dreams and excitement, rest and reflection, study and plans. There's very little physical labor needed in a Michigan garden during this time, so most of the work should be inside your head.

Planning is integral to this month's chores. Think about your goals and how to achieve them. Create a garden you can easily manage, in the time and effort you want to expend. Good design and a bountiful garden start with good planning.

Place gardens in areas where they can be viewed from inside the house looking out or while enjoying other parts of the landscape. Just ensure their location does not create a maintenance nightmare. For example, avoid building flowerbeds in areas that are hard to reach with tools or hoses. Design gentle curves and avoid narrow or irregular grassy borders that require hand trimming.

Make the garden wide enough to create visual impact. A 3-foot by 6-foot bed offers a greater visual punch than a 1-foot-wide planting area that encircles the yard. Start with this formula: the garden width should be two-thirds the height of its background. For example, if you plant a garden next to a 6-foot-tall fence, the garden should be at least 4 feet wide. Add pathways or stepping stones to gardens wider than 6 feet so you can easily reach the plants for care and maintenance. Leave at least 1 foot of space between the last row of plants and the back of the garden This provides access to the backside of the garden. The extra space also *increases* air circulation, which helps *decrease* disease.

Once you select your garden size, choose a style. For a more formal look, place flowers in straight lines or geometric designs. For an informal feel, try massing flowers and creating sweeps of color with various plants.

January is a perfect time to evaluate what you want to plant. Allow extra time to locate harder-to-find annuals, as you may need to start these from seed indoors. Browse garden catalogs and websites to seek out summer-blooming bulbs, edibles, perennials, ornamental grasses, roses, shrubs, trees, vines, and groundcovers.

January is the time of resolutions; maybe one of yours is to hire someone to care for your lawn. It's also a great time to buy new tools—or refresh the ones hanging in a garage or shed. And finally, it's time to kick back and enjoy a well-earned rest. You're going to need energy in just a few short months.

■ *Snow-capped seedheads of coneflowers provide visual interest in winter.*

ANNUALS

Annuals are plants that grow from a seed, flower, produce seeds, and die within one year. They provide season-long color and may be changed seasonally and yearly for added interest. Use them to provide continuous bloom and to fill in empty spaces reserved for expanding perennials. Select informal, subtle annuals such as 'Blue Horizon' ageratum (*Ageratum* 'Blue Horizon'), creeping zinnia (*Zinnia angustifolia*), and heliotrope (*Heliotropium*) that offer the look and feel of perennials.

A groundcover of pansies makes a nice backdrop of color for spring-flowering bulbs. Annual vinca (*Catharanthus*), *Begonia*, and other annuals can mask the declining foliage of spring-flowering bulbs.

Use annuals in containers to brighten areas that lack planting space or welcome guests to your home. Combine upright and trailing annuals to balance and complement the container. Select a mixture of plants with similar growing requirements. Consider how the foliage and flowers look together.

Tuck a few annuals in tree and shrub planting beds. Never add soil or do extensive digging

PLAN

ALL

The catalogs start pouring in and the wish list keeps growing. Compare the seeds you already have and want to use this season to those you plan to order. Develop a list with plants best suited to your growing conditions that give you a desired look. Order seeds you plan to start indoors.

Review your garden journal, videos, and pictures of last year's landscape. Plan to expand or reduce planting space based on the previous year's experience. Remember that more planting space means an increase in maintenance.

Make and keep a resolution to faithfully write in a garden journal and record details on planting times, techniques, successes, and challenges. Make a list of your favorite plants and those that need to be replaced.

■ *Heliotrope is an annual here that blooms all summer and blends nicely with perennials.*

around the base of trees and shrubs. Instead, dig several holes throughout the planting bed. Sink 8- to 12-inch nursery pots in these holes. Plant a few annuals in slightly smaller containers. Set the potted annuals inside the sunken pots; they will look as if they were always there. This technique saves you a lot of digging while reducing damage to the all-important tree and shrub roots.

For easier care, try lower-maintenance annuals such as alyssum (*Lobularia maritima*), *Torenia*, and wax begonias (*Begonia semperflorens-cultorum*), adding mulch, sharing the workload with family or friends, or decreasing the planting space. If you reduce the size of an annual garden, you can convert it to a perennial, shrub, groundcover, or turf area. Draw a sketch of the proposed changes. Put it aside for a few days to consider the impact on the appearance and maintenance of the landscape.

BULBS
Keep in mind that last year's plants have grown and multiplied, so you also may need to find additional space or new homes for some of them.

EDIBLES
It's time to plan this year's vegetable garden. Make a list of the vegetables to grow again. Adjust the number of rows and plants to include. Reduce the number of those vegetables that were more productive than you needed or not very popular with family and friends. Find a few new and fun things to try in this year's garden.

Plan some kid-friendly features to get your children, grandchildren, or neighborhood kids to share your gardening passion. Have each family member cut out pictures of the vegetables they want to grow and eat. Try a theme garden, such as a pizza garden. Include all the fresh ingredients you need to make your own pizza—except for the cheese and pepperoni, of course!

Plan to grow pole beans on a teepee made of stakes that shades lettuce planted in the center. Include a sunflower maze planted in narrow rows and patterns to create a mazelike walkway through the garden. Use the maze to direct children from planting to planting or from one side of the garden to the other.

■ *Amaryllis and hyacinth can be forced to bloom indoors during the winter.*

Give your children a little gardening space of their own. Let them plan, plant, and harvest their own garden. When my daughter was seven, she chose the seeds and plants for her own plot. Then she asked for a 10-foot-high fence—to keep her parents, not the rabbits, out!

LAWNS
Selecting the right lawn care professional is not just about price. Know what services you want performed. Contact several companies for cost estimates and ask about their staff's training and qualifications. Ask friends and relatives for recommendations. Get a written service agreement that includes information about automatic renewals and penalties for discontinuing the service.

Pesticides, including herbicides, insecticides, and fungicides, should only be applied as needed. Ask what chemicals they plan to use and why. Some companies provide more eco-friendly methods of managing lawns. And make sure the company provides advance notice of chemical applications to allow you to remove pets, toys, and lawn furniture from treated areas.

Hire a company that is a member of a professional organization, such as the Michigan Green Industry Association, or the Professional Grounds Management Association. Ask the company for references from local customers and check with the Better Business Bureau to receive a report about the company, if available.

PERENNIALS

Look for areas in your yard to convert to perennial gardens, as well as locations for adding a few new plants. When selecting perennials, consider color and texture of flowers, foliage, and seedheads, as well as bloom time. Once the plan is completed, consider dividing the number of different perennials in half and doubling the number of each to reduce your maintenance and increase the garden's visual impact.

ROSES

Before you order new roses, make sure the ones you select are suited to your climate and will fit in the available space. Take note of the bloom cycle, as there are one-time, repeat, and continuous bloomers. Whatever roses you choose, select the most pest-resistant varieties available. Consult your local botanical garden for suggestions.

One-time bloomers flower on the tips and new side branches of the previous season's growth. They start flowering the second year after planting. Most species and old garden roses are in this group. Some modern roses and shrub roses are one-time bloomers.

Repeat bloomers flower the summer they are planted. They flower in spring on the tips of new growth or side shoots formed on the previous season's growth. Fall flowers develop on the tips of summer growth or side shoots. Some modern roses and shrub roses are repeat bloomers.

Continuous bloomers produce flowering canes and side shoots all season long. Hybrid tea roses and some shrub roses such as 'Chuckles', 'Nearly Wild', 'Carefree Delight', 'Knock Out', and 'Ballerina' fit in this category.

Consider areas that are suitable for roses. Evaluate growing conditions and your landscape plan. Select and place roses in areas where they will thrive,

add beauty, and serve a function in the yard. Use climbers for vertical accents, large shrub roses for screening, and fragrant species for a little aromatherapy near a patio or screened porch.

Consider adding a native rose to your landscape. Prairie rose (*Rosa setigera*) and Virginia rose (*Rosa virginiana*) are hardy natives. Use prairie rose as a climber on walls, fences, or trellises to brighten your landscape. It boasts single pink flowers in early- to mid-July and small reddish fruit (rose hips) in the fall. The fruits attract birds to your landscape. Try Virginia rose *en masse* on banks or to cover large areas. The plant grows 6 feet tall and features pink flowers in June, followed by an attractive orange to red or maroon color in the fall. The red rose hips last into winter.

Visit your local library and check out the many books on roses. Attend meetings of your local rose society, and contact the American Rose Society, P.O. Box 30000, Shreveport, LA 71130 or www.ars.org and check out Earthkind® Roses for low maintenance roses.

SHRUBS

Consider how friends and neighbors are using shrubs to add year-round interest to their landscapes. Expand your search to include nearby botanical gardens and arboreta. Evaluate the form, color, and fruit of individual plants. Consider how these can help improve your existing landscape. Start a list of plants you would like to add. Evaluate their ultimate size and desired growing conditions to see if they are appropriate for your landscape.

Look for areas that would benefit from some new shrub plantings. Consider the shrub's mature size as it relates to nearby buildings, existing plants, and overhead and underground utilities.

For smaller areas, investigate dwarf varieties, which are smaller than the standard species but not necessarily as small as you might imagine. Select plants suitable for your growing conditions. Matching the shrub to the existing growing conditions results in an attractive plant that requires very little maintenance.

TREES

January is a great time to ponder tree additions to your landscape for screening, seasonal interest, shade, and windbreaks. Begin with a walk around your property, followed by a visit to a library and an arboretum.

Growing a tree into a healthy and attractive landscape asset begins with a plan.

Select trees suited to the area's growing conditions. They should thrive in the light, winds, and existing soil. Make sure that the tree will fit the space available once it reaches its mature size. Oftentimes young trees outgrow the small space we have allotted.

Grow the most pest-resistant trees and cultivars available. Healthy trees will live longer with less care and cleanup from you.

Plant for the future, not just the immediate impact. Fast-growing trees are usually the first to break apart in storms, decline, or die from disease. Use a mix of fast- and slow-growing trees for immediate and long-term enjoyment. The slow growers will take over as the fast-growing trees begin to decline.

As you narrow down your selection, look for trees that provide year-round interest. In Michigan, summer is relatively short and memories of that beautiful summer landscape fade quickly during the long winter months. Select trees with colorful bark or interesting growth habits for the winter landscape and flowers and fruit for added color and for attracting birds and butterflies to your outdoor living space.

Avoid planting too close to buildings, power lines, and other utilities.

Check out *Michigan Getting Started Garden Guide* and the Michigan State University Extension Services' publications for help with selecting trees best suited for your landscape.

Visit botanical gardens, arboreta, and parks to observe the trees appropriate for your climate. Going at this time of year identifies which trees have colorful bark, persistent fruit, or an attractive form for winter interest. Trees worthy of consideration include: 'Winter King' hawthorn and disease-resistant crabapples (*Malus*) for their decorative fruit and bird attraction, or magnolias and the region's native musclewood (*Carpinus*) and serviceberry (*Amelanchier*) for their smooth, gray bark. Visiting mature specimens gives you a better way to evaluate if the size and shape will fit in your yard.

VINES & GROUNDCOVERS

Vines and groundcovers allow you to expand planting options by adding texture and seasonal interest to vertical and horizontal spaces.

Grow vines on trellises to create privacy, screen a bad view, or cover an ugly fence. Use them in both large areas and in narrow spaces where most shrubs won't fit.

Cover an arbor or trellis with vines to create shade for outdoor patios and decks or to shelter shade-loving plants, such as hostas and ferns.

Improve the growing conditions for trees and shrubs by growing groundcovers. Perennial groundcovers keep tree and shrub roots cool and moist throughout the growing season. They also keep harmful mowers and weed whips away from trunks, stems, and surface roots.

Reduce mowing and hand trimming by growing groundcover beds around trees and shrubs so you only have to mow around one large bed instead of individual plants.

Use this time to look for solutions to difficult planting situations for vines and groundcovers.

Remember to minimize root disturbance when planting these under established trees. Avoid deep cultivation, and do not add soil over tree roots. Both practices can damage or even kill some trees.

PLANT

ANNUALS

Prepare your light setup for starting annuals indoors. Select an area that is out of the way but one that you won't forget. When starting seedlings,

Check the back of the seed packet for the recommended time to start that particular seed indoors. Many popular annuals should be sown indoors about six weeks before the last frost in your area. Start pansies at the end of the month to have large transplants ready for your early spring garden.

BULBS

If you have spring bulbs that you didn't plant in the ground last fall, there's still time to force them for spring bloom. Store them in a 35- to 45-degree Fahrenheit location for fifteen weeks to initiate bloom. Plant in a well-drained mix, move to a cool location, water as needed, and wait several weeks for colorful blooms.

You may have received an amaryllis (*Hippeastrum*) as a gift or have one stored in the basement. Now is the time to pot it and get it growing.

EDIBLES

As with growing annual flowers, you should gather and organize seed-starting equipment and supplies for edibles. Find an area where you can place flats near a window or under artificial lights. See the tips in the Plant, Annuals section for greater detail.

LAWNS

Still in our dreams for now—so sit back, relax, and enjoy the peace and quiet!

PERENNIALS

Perennials can be started indoors much like annuals. Some seeds need to be stratified (a cold treatment) for weeks, scarified (the seed coat scratched), or soaked in tepid water overnight prior to planting. Check the label directions for seed treatment, timing, and planting directions.

SHRUBS

Take advantage of this downtime to prepare your tools for the growing season. Clean and sharpen your spade.

TREES

Tree planting season is a mere thought while the ground is frozen. If you're not content to kick back and relax, use a little elbow grease to clean and sharpen your planting tools.

If you want to get a head start on the garden season, or if you want to try more unusual varieties than the ones offered in the garden stores, you will need to start seed indoors.

you need a power source and ample room.

Purchase a seed-starting system from a garden supply catalog or build your own. You need cool fluorescent lights, a light fixture, and a system for keeping the lights 6 inches above the tops of the seedlings.

Build your own system by mounting light fixtures on shelves, creating tabletop supports for the lights, or designing a stand-alone system. Adjustable chains or pulleys allow the lights to be lowered and raised over the growing seedlings. Paint the shelving white or use reflective surfaces under and around the unit to increase the light reaching the young seedlings.

TO POT AN AMARYLLIS

1. Plant the amaryllis in a pot just slightly larger than the bulb. The roots should be crowded.

2. Place the pointed end up, with half the bulb above the soil level.

3. Fill the pot with any sterile, well-drained potting mix.

4. Water and move the pot to a cool, bright location, such as a sunny window in a cool room with temperatures around 60 to 65 degrees Fahrenheit. Keep the soil moist but not wet. New growth will soon appear. If you're lucky, it will be a flowering stem.

5. Remove the flower stem when the plant has finished blooming so the bulb's energy goes to rejuvenating the bulb, not producing seeds.

6. Move the plant to a sunny window. Keep watering and fertilizing with a dilute flowering houseplant fertilizer solution.

7. Move the potted bulb outdoors after all danger of frost. Water and fertilize as needed. Bring it back indoors before the first fall frost. Allow the plant to go dormant by storing it in a cool location and withholding water for eight to ten weeks, then top-dress or repot. It will take four to eight weeks to rebloom.

ALL

Apply winter mulch *after* the ground freezes. In some years the ground freezes by Thanksgiving, while other times it doesn't freeze until January. The goal is not to keep the soil warm but to prevent temperature extremes caused by winter thaws and fluctuating spring temperatures.

Nature provides the best mulch—snow—for parts of Michigan. If the ground isn't covered with snow, you can still add protective winter mulch to planting beds. Cover them with evergreen branches for insulation. This keeps the ground cold and helps prevent bulbs and other plants from sprouting during winter thaws.

Shovel snow before reaching for the plant-damaging deicing salt. Avoid shaking or brushing frozen snow off trees and shrubs. This can cause more damage than if the snow was left in place. Make a note on your calendar to prevent plant damage next season by applying winter protection in late October or November before the heavy snow arrives.

Monitor the landscape for animal damage.

Wait to prune most outdoor plants. Remove hazardous and winter-damaged woody branches as they are found. Wait until the snow melts and the worst of winter has passed to start major pruning.

ANNUALS

Check on any geraniums (*Pelargonium*) you stored in the basement or another cool, dark location. Plant any that started growing. Move them to a warm, sunny location and treat them as houseplants.

Pinch back leggy geraniums, coleus (*Solenostemon*), impatiens (*Impatiens*), and other annuals that you are overwintering as houseplants. Remove the growing tips or pinch stems back to just above a

■ *To keep indoor houseplants flowering, be sure to remove, or "pinch off" older blooms, like this example.*

set of healthy leaves. This encourages branching and stouter stems.

BULBS

Check on non-hardy bulbs such as dahlia species that were tucked away for winter storage. Discard any soft, discolored, or rotting bulbs. Move sprouting bulbs to a cooler (45 to 50 degrees Fahrenheit), dark location. If they continue to grow, you may need to pot them and cope with a few extra houseplants until planting time.

If you had the foresight to plant spring-blooming bulbs last fall to force in containers, stagger the forcing times to extend your indoor bloom. Bring the bulbs out of cold storage after at least 15 weeks. Move them to a cool, bright location. Water when the soil below the surface feels barely dry, and wait for a glorious display. Remove spent flowers, continue to water, and fertilize with a diluted solution of any flowering houseplant fertilizer.

Check on the remaining bulbs you have in cold storage. The soil should remain slightly moist and the temperatures between 35 and 45 degrees Fahrenheit. Gradually reduce the storage temperature or move bulbs to a cooler location if they begin to sprout.

Remove spent flowers on amaryllis (*Hippeastrum*) and other forced bulbs. Leave the leaves intact to restore spent energy if you plan on reblooming these bulbs in the future.

EDIBLES

Harvest herbs from your windowsill herb garden as needed for cooking. You may need to add extra light during the short, dark days of January. Artificial light improves growth and productivity.

Cut back leggy herbs to a set of healthy leaves. This encourages branching and more growth. Dry or use these pieces for cooking.

Harvest carrots and parsnips that were stored in the garden for winter. You may need to wait for a thaw. Dig carefully to avoid damaging these root crops. Enjoy their sweet flavor. Check on

■ *Windowsill herb gardens are a good way to experience fresh edibles in the dark of winter.*

■ *Adding gravel to the saucer will help keep your plants from sitting in water.*

stored vegetables and discard any that are shriveled or rotten.

ROSES

Check roses and make sure winter protection is secure. Locate and replace any rose shelters, rose cones, or mulch that may have blown away during a storm.

Vent rose cones on sunny days or during warm spells. Some cones come with precut or removable vents. If not, cut small holes on the side away from the wind and near the top of the cones.

Monitor the health and growing conditions of miniature and tree roses you're overwintering indoors. Keep plants in a cool room in front of a southern or other sunny window. Place plants on a pebble tray to increase humidity and to eliminate the need to pour excess water out of the saucer. As you water plants thoroughly, the excess water will collect in the pebbles, allowing the pot to sit on the pebbles and not in the water. As the water evaporates, it increases the humidity around the plants.

SHRUBS

Wait until after flowering to prune spring-flowering shrubs if you want to maintain the spring display.

TREES

Trees can be pruned during the dormant season, as it is much easier to see the overall shape of the tree and what needs to be removed. Prune oaks in winter to reduce disease problems.

Prune with a purpose in mind. Strive to maintain the plant's natural shape. Prune young trees to establish a strong framework. Use proper pruning to maintain a strong structure and healthy growth, as well as to improve flowering and fruiting on established trees.

Save branches from flowering trees such as crabapples (*Malus*), *Magnolia*, and pussy willows for indoor bloom. Recut the stems and place in a bucket of water in a cool (60 degrees Fahrenheit), brightly lit location. Mist the branches several times a day until the stems start to bloom. Flowering stems can be used in arrangements with other flowers or by themselves. Prolong the blossoms by storing the blooming stems in a cooler spot (40 degrees Fahrenheit) at night.

VINES & GROUNDCOVERS

Evaluate the winter sun and winds. Both can be drying to evergreen groundcovers and vines. Use a discarded Christmas tree to create a windbreak and shade for pachysandra and other sensitive plants. Make a note to move, shelter, or create a more permanent solution. Check vines, trellises, and arbors to make sure they are securely mounted.

WATER

ALL

The only watering needed this month is indoors. The ground is frozen, so there is no need to break out the hose.

ANNUALS

Adjust your watering schedule to match the needs of coleus, geraniums, fuchsias, and other annuals overwintered as houseplants. The shorter days, less intense sunlight, and low humidity of winter changes the plants' needs. Water the soil thoroughly, and wait until the soil is slightly dry before watering again.

Water seedlings often enough to keep the soil moist but not wet. Overwatering can cause root rot and seedling failure. Allowing the soil to dry stresses seedlings, resulting in poor growth, or even seedling death.

BULBS

Water amaryllis and any other flowering bulbs, keeping the soil moist but not wet.

EDIBLES

Keep the soil slightly moist in windowsill gardens. Water thoroughly, allowing the excess to drain out the bottom of the pot. Check the plantings twice a week and water whenever the top 2 inches of soil start to dry.

ROSES

Water roses growing indoors as needed. Keep the soil slightly moist. Check on container roses stored in the garage. Water them whenever the soil is dry and not frozen.

SHRUBS

Check the soil moisture of all the aboveground planters you have stored in your unheated garage or porch. Water whenever the soil thaws and dries. Water thoroughly so that the excess runs out the bottom of the planter.

TREES

Aboveground planters should be watered anytime the soil is dry but not frozen.

VINES & GROUNDCOVERS

Monitor the landscape for ice buildup and flooding. Consider amending the area or moving the plants in spring to reduce winter damage caused by these conditions.

Water tropical vines overwintering indoors. Water thoroughly until the excess runs out the bottom. Pour off excess water or set on a pebble-filled saucer. Wait until the top few inches dry before watering again. Check hardy vines in planters stored in the garage. Water the soil whenever it is dry. Apply enough water so that the excess runs out the bottom. Avoid letting plants sit in standing water.

FERTILIZE

ALL

Outdoor plants don't need fertilizer while the ground is frozen. Applying fertilizer to frozen soil can pollute the water. Melting snow and winter rains wash the fertilizer off the soil surface and into nearby storm sewers, rivers, and lakes.

ANNUALS

Do not be overanxious to fertilize fuchsias, geraniums, and other annuals you are growing as houseplants. Poor growing conditions indoors during the winter result in slow plant growth that requires very little, if any, fertilizer. Fertilize only actively growing plants with stunted growth, yellow leaves, or other signs of nutrient deficiencies.

Seedlings need to be fertilized once they are sprouted and actively growing. Use a dilute solution of houseplant fertilizer according to label directions.

■ *Use sticky traps to catch whiteflies and other flying insect pests indoors.*

BULBS

Fertilize amaryllis and forced bulbs when they have finished blooming. This restores some of the spent energy. Use a dilute solution of any flowering houseplant fertilizer.

EDIBLES

Watch indoor herbs for signs of nutrient deficiencies. Pale leaves and poor growth may be a result of poor light as well as a lack of nutrients. Try improving the light before fertilizing the plants. Go light on the fertilizer for better flavor.

VINES & GROUNDCOVERS

Monitor the health and growth of tropical vines growing indoors. Use little to no fertilizer on these plants. The low light and low humidity is hard on these plants. Adding fertilizer can add to the stress. Only fertilize actively growing plants with pale or stunted growth. Use a diluted solution of any flowering houseplant fertilizer.

PROBLEM-SOLVE

ALL

Monitor indoor plants for fungus gnats, mites, aphids, and whiteflies. Fungus gnats do not hurt plants, but they are nuisances. Often mistaken for fruit flies, they can be found flitting throughout the house. These insects feed on the organic matter in the soil, such as dead plant roots and peat moss. Keep the soil slightly drier than normal to reduce their populations.

Aphids, mites, and whiteflies suck out plant juices, causing leaves to yellow and brown. Look for poor growth and a clear sticky substance, called honeydew, on the leaves.

Aphids, which are small, teardrop-shaped insects, can weaken plants. Treat outbreaks with insecticidal soap, which is found at most garden centers and floral shops. This soap is effective at killing soft-

TO PLANT CAT GRASS

1. Fill a 6-inch pot with well-draining potting mix. Sprinkle wheatgrass seeds on the soil surface. Lightly rake the surface to ensure good seed-to-soil contact.

2. Water thoroughly until the excess runs out the bottom of the pot. Cover with plastic, or water often enough to keep the soil surface moist.

3. Move to a warm, sunny window. The grass should sprout in one to two weeks. Water less frequently once the grass begins to grow. Water until the excess runs out the drainage hole. Water again when the top few inches of soil begin to dry.

bodied insects such as aphids and mites, but it is safe for plants, pets, and children. Repeat once a week as needed. You will probably need at least two to four applications to keep these pests under control. It is safe for edible and ornamental plants.

Try catching insects with yellow sticky traps. Buy them at a garden center or make your own by coating pieces of yellow paper with a sticky substance. Place them near the plants.

You can also try knocking the insects off. Cover the pot with a plastic bag. Place plants in the shower and rinse with clear water. This helps dislodge many of the insects. Then spray the upper and lower leaf surfaces with insecticidal soap.

BULBS
Check stored bulbs and discard any that are showing signs of mold or bulb rot.

EDIBLES
Make sure cats and other pets are not enjoying more of the indoor herb harvest than you are. Keep tempting plants out of reach of these animals. Consider planting a pot of ryegrass or wheatgraass to give cats their own herbal fix. Be sure to check with your vet first!

LAWNS
Make a note of areas where snow and ice tend to linger. These are prime candidates for snow mold. Damaged turf becomes matted and covered with a gray or pink fungus in spring. Also watch for vole (meadow mouse) activity as these rodents scurry beneath the snow eating seeds,

chewing on bark, and wearing trails in the lawn. Be prepared to do a little raking and overseeding in the spring.

PERENNIALS
Check for tracks, chewed bark, and other signs of vole damage. Voles are mouse-like rodents that travel under the snow, feeding on seeds, roots, cambium, and bark. Snap traps baited with peanut butter and oats can be used to manage these pests. Place traps in pipes or otherwise out of reach of other wildlife, birds, pets, and children.

High vole populations may nibble on the roots of Siberian iris and hostas. Chipmunks and squirrels can also damage perennials by digging up the plants and leaving the roots exposed to cold winter temperatures. There is not much you can do when the plants are buried in the snow. Next year, plan ahead to prevent the damage.

ROSES
Properly covered roses should be safe from rabbits and deer. Try repellents on uncovered roses that are suffering damage.

SHRUBS
This is a good time to spring a surprise attack on many garden pests. A little preventative pest management can reduce plant damage, pesticide use, and your summer workload.

Check for signs of animals. Rabbits, voles, and deer feed on stems and branches. Get busy if you find tracks, droppings, and feeding damage. Secure animal fencing and reapply repellents as needed.

Check ornamental plums and cherries (*Prunus*) for Eastern tent caterpillar egg masses. The eggs look like a shiny glob of mud on the stem. Prune and destroy all that are found.

Watch for black knot cankers on plums and cherries. This fungal disease causes branches to swell, turn black, and crack open, releasing infectious spores. Prune out infected branches below the swollen areas. Burn, bury, or destroy cankered branches to reduce future infections.

Check the bases of *Viburnum*, *Euonymus*, and spirea (*Spiraea*) stems for round, swollen growths called galls. These galls eventually girdle and kill the stem. Prune the infected stems below the gall, and discard. Disinfect your tools between cuts with rubbing alcohol or a solution of one part bleach to nine parts water.

TREES

Walk through the landscape and check for animal damage and overwintering insects. A little prevention now can save lots of headaches and extra work this season. Check and repair fencing and other animal barriers. Reapply repellents or alternate scare tactics to prevent and reduce animal damage. Remove egg masses of tent caterpillars and gypsy and tussock moths as well as black knot cankers described above.

VINES & GROUNDCOVERS

Check outdoor plants for animal damage. Look for tracks, droppings, and other signs of animal damage. Euonymus, junipers (*Juniperus*), and other groundcovers make great winter housing and food for rabbits and voles. Apply commercial or homemade repellents to high-risk plantings.

■ *Rabbits will remove and eat the bark of shrubs, so watch carefully for damage.*

February

Although it's still cold outside, you're probably starting to feel the seasonal changes and nearness of spring. With the amount of daylight increasing, the days may begin to seem noticeably longer. Plus, being the shortest month, February seems to go by faster too.

Use these still-dormant days to continue researching and planning additions to your landscapes. Visit area garden and home shows for landscape and planting ideas and glimpse the spring gardens to come.

Take a winter hike through nearby botanical gardens and arboreta for a bit of inspiration and help beating the winter blues. Then surround yourself with other gardeners, gathering more ideas at garden lectures and workshops.

As always, patience is a virtue, especially for northern gardeners. Planting is still just a dream and nature continues to drop a few white reminders that winter is not yet over. So pull out the wish list and finalize your orders for seeds, bulbs, perennials, and more.

And as you finalize your vegetable garden plan and plant list, keep in mind your families' eating habits. Grow plenty of the things they love and try a few new vegetables for fun. If you are the only one that likes a particular vegetable, just grow a plant or two to take care of your needs.

Use this time to update your landscape plans. Bring out the garden journal and photos, or warm up the computer, and start reviewing last year's garden season. Make a list of changes you want to make; plants to purchase and those that need to be moved, shared, or composted.

Start sketching areas where you would like to add perennial gardens. Locate the garden in spaces that have good soil drainage and the right amount of sunlight for the plants you want to grow.

Then create a planting chart. Use this to record when and what you plant this spring. Keep it handy so you can continue to add to it throughout the season. Include successes and failures to help with future projects.

Continue to monitor your outdoor plantings. Watch for animal and storm damage on existing plants. Then note areas that could benefit from additional winter interest. Use your journal to record any observations and needed actions. Supplement your notes with photos. Your cell phone camera is a convenient tool for capturing your observations.

It takes just a little bit of time to clean your seed-starting trays, but it is important for seedling health.

PLAN

ALL

Visit home and garden shows to get new ideas. The professionals at these shows can give you terrific design and planting tips. Check out landscape books and magazines at the library for ideas and pictures of how to incorporate new plants in your yard.

Make a final wish list and order your seeds as soon as possible, especially those you will start indoors.

Inventory and clean tools. Use a wire brush to remove excess soil. Follow this with steel wool to remove any rust that formed on metal surfaces. Sharpen the soil cutting edge of trowels and shovels with a triangular file. Rub in a couple of drops of oil to prevent further rusting.

ANNUALS

Finish assembling your light setup and seed-starting area. Purchase a sterile potting or seed-starter mix. These mixes increase your success by retaining moisture, providing good drainage, and allowing you to start disease-free.

Gather and clean your planting containers. Use flats and pots purchased at the garden center or recycled from last year's garden. Disinfect used pots in a solution of one part bleach to nine parts water. Or, gather emptied yogurt containers or used paper coffee cups for seed starting. Rinse these containers and punch holes in the bottom.

Buy or make plant labels to label flats and pots with the name of the seeds you are growing. Try wooden craft sticks, discarded plastic spoons, or similar items, labeling with a permanent marker or pencil.

Create a seeding chart for recording plant names, starting dates, and other important information. Use a garden journal or other notebook to record and save the information for next year.

BULBS

Finalize your order for tender bulbs so you can start them inside in mid-March for earlier summer bloom. At the same time, place your order for hardy bulbs to be delivered in the fall, so you take care of both orders at once. Identify potential planting areas for new and stored bulbs.

Seed-starting mix is actually not soil; it is a lightweight sterile soilless mix that may contain peat moss, perlite, and other ingredients that is perfect for starting seeds.

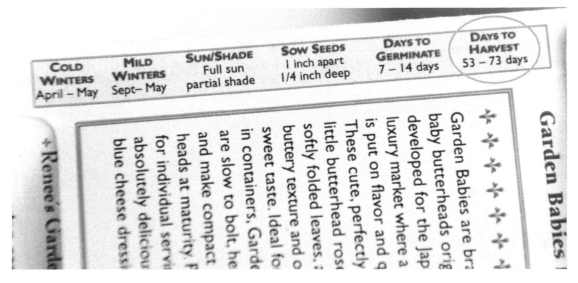

COLD WINTERS April – May	MILD WINTERS Sept– May	SUN/SHADE Full sun partial shade	SOW SEEDS 1 inch apart 1/4 inch deep	DAYS TO GERMINATE 7 – 14 days	DAYS TO HARVEST 53 – 73 days

Garden Babies — Garden Babies are br... baby butterheads orig... developed for the Jap... luxury market where a... is put on flavor and q... These cute, perfectly... little butterhead ros... softly folded leaves... buttery texture and o... sweet taste. Ideal fo... in containers. Garde... are slow to bolt, he... and make compact... heads at maturity... for individual serv... absolutely deliciou... blue cheese dress...

+ Renee's Garde...

■ *When you're ready to start purchasing your seeds, be sure to check the package for the number of days to harvest.*

Note any outdoor bulb beds that have standing water or ice. These conditions can lead to bulb rot and even bulb death. Note the location of any bulbs that sprout during winter thaws. Plan on moving them this year or mulching them next fall after the ground freezes.

Hybrid tulips and hyacinths are generally not long-lasting in the garden. Increase their longevity by mulching the bulbs in summer, removing flower stems after the flower fades, or replacing them with species or tulips that perennialize, such as triumph tulips, Darwin tulips, or species tulips.

EDIBLES

Start finalizing your garden plan. List the vegetables your family likes to eat, and remember to include the ingredients for your favorite recipes. Visit a local garden center to see if they have the seeds you need for starting indoors. Order any unusual or hard-to-find seeds from a reliable company.

Consider the space each plant needs. For example, one tomato plant produces lots of fruit. And while nothing beats the taste of freshly harvested corn, one corn plant only produces one or two ears, and you need at least a 4-by-4-foot block for pollination and fruit production.

Decide how many vegetables and herbs you need for fresh use and preserving. Most vegetables can be canned or frozen for later use. Consider buying a food dryer to dry vegetables and herbs, or let nature, the oven, and microwave dry herbs for later cooking and crafts.

Add a few fun vegetables, such as purple carrots, popcorn, pumpkins, and watermelons, for children. Radishes, Bibb lettuce, and other short-season vegetables provide quick results for young, anxious gardeners.

Make sure the chosen vegetables are suited to your climate and garden location. Vegetables must be able to thrive in our weather and reach maturity within the short growing season. Check the frost maps starting on page 218 for the average number of frost-free dates in your location.

Make a list of herbs you use for cooking, crafts, and gifts. Flavored vinegars and oils are easy to make and great to give as gifts. Consider using bunches of dried herbs for decorations, deodorizers, or potpourri.

LAWNS

Draw a sketch of the lawn. Mark areas where water and ice collect, snow is slow to recede, and deicing salts may cause damage so you can fill low spots later to reduce future drainage problems. Consider using magnesium chloride, calcium acetate, or other more plant-friendly deicing compounds.

PERENNIALS

Evaluate making changes in your perennial beds by planning beds in front of hedges, walls, or buildings. Make sure all parts of the garden can be reached for maintenance chores. Add walkways or steppingstones in large gardens for easier access.

Plan year-round interest by using a variety of perennials that bloom at different times or create several different gardens to peak at various times. Create dramatic impact by planting perennials in large masses and drifts.

Check catalogs for newer and harder-to-find perennials and important information. If you do not currently receive catalogs, explore the Internet, talk to friends, and contact the Michigan State University Extension Service office or visit their website.

ROSES

Select roses that give you the desired flower color, fragrance, and plant size. Always select the hardiest and most pest-resistant variety available. Look for seasonal attributes, such as continuous flowers, and rose hips for fall and winter interest. Also look for added features such as fragrance and flower color.

Plan to use roses in your perennial garden. Shrub roses can be used as informal flowering hedges or backdrops for flowerbeds. Climbers make nice vertical accents and privacy screens.

Proper site selection and care can provide beautiful results. Plant roses in locations that receive at least six hours of daily sunlight, which is important for both flowering and disease control. A south- or east-facing location is ideal because the morning sun dries the dew, reducing disease problems.

Grow roses in well-drained, fertile soil. Incorporate 2 to 4 inches of organic matter into the top 12 inches of soil to heavy clay soils to improve drainage, as well as to sandy soils to improve water- and nutrient-holding capacity.

Proper spacing allows roses to develop a more natural appearance with minimal pruning. The space also increases air circulation and assures that light reaches the plants. This means fewer pest problems. Consult plant tags and rose catalogs for information on the mature size and spread of specific rose varieties.

Many roses are grafted onto hardy rootstocks. A small bud is attached to the roots of another rose. The roots are hardy, but the graft and aboveground growth can be damaged over the winter. Protect the graft by planting it 2 inches below the soil surface.

Bare-root roses are available through garden centers and catalogs. Select Grade 1 roses, which have several long, stout canes and a larger root system. You pay more for these plants, but they produce the best blooms. They are sold as dormant canes and shipped with their roots packed in moist peat moss. Plant these in early spring for best results.

Potted hybrid tea roses are usually bare-root plants placed in containers by the nursery or garden center in early spring. They are often placed in the greenhouse to encourage leaf and root growth. These can be planted during spring through early summer. See the April, Plant section for specific planting information.

TREES

When you discover a tree you'd like to have in your yard, consider the size of trees to purchase. Larger trees (more than 3 inches in diameter) give you bigger trees immediately, but they stay the same size for several years as they adjust to their new locations. Smaller trees adapt faster to transplanting and often outgrow their larger counterparts.

VINES & GROUNDCOVERS

Consider letting a few vines run wild. Use them as groundcovers or let them crawl over stones, onto shrubs, and up tree trunks. Use nonaggressive plants that don't suffocate their neighbors or strangle the stems and trunks.

Make sure the plant and its flower buds are hardy in your area. Chinese or Japanese wisteria plants (*Wisteria floribunda* and *W. sinensis*) survive our cold climate but their flower buds may not. Select Kentucky wisteria (*W. macrostachya*) for wisteria that is both plant- and flower-hardy in northern climates. The cultivar 'Blue Moon' is a hardy selection from Minnesota.

HERE'S HOW

TO START SEEDS

2 Sprinkle seeds in the furrow or drop one or two in each hole. Cover with soil and water with a fine mist. Avoid a strong stream of water that can dislodge the seeds.

3 Keep the soil warm and moist to ensure germination. Use commercially available heating cables or place the flats in a warm location (on top of refrigerators, heating ducts, or other warm places). Cover the containers with a sheet of plastic to help conserve moisture. Check daily and water often enough to keep the soil surface moist, but not wet.

4 Remove the plastic and move the container into the light as soon as the seedlings appear. Place lights 6 inches above the plants and keep them on for twelve to sixteen hours a day. Lighting them longer doesn't help the plants, but needlessly increases your electric bill.

5 Transplant seedlings growing in flats as soon as they form two sets of leaves (seed and true). The seed leaves are nondescript, while the true leaves look like the particular plant's leaves.

1 Fill clean flats or containers with a sterile starter mix. Moisten the mixture prior to seeding. Sprinkle fine seeds on the soil surface and water them. Use a chopstick, pencil, or similar item to dig a shallow furrow or punch a planting hole into the mix for larger seeds. Plant seeds at a depth that is about twice their diameter.

Avoid aggressive vines and groundcovers. They can take over a landscape and require a lot of work to control. Several, such as crown vetch and oriental bittersweet, are invasive and should not be planted.

Select vines that are best suited to climb your wall, trellis, or support structure, understanding that some vines twine and others cling.

Use twining-type vines, such as honeysuckle, clematis, and American bittersweet, for chain-link fences, trellises, and arbors. Cover walls and stones with wires and netting to train twining vines over these types of structures.

Consider using clinging vines, such as climbing hydrangea, on stone and brick structures. These vines use rootlike hairs to grasp the surfaces they climb. Avoid using clinging vines directly on wooden buildings. Their roots can damage the wood, and the excess foliage can trap moisture, causing the wood to deteriorate.

Use groundcovers and vines massed or mixed with other plants. Choose companion plants that are equally aggressive and require the same growing conditions. Mix plants with plain, variegated, or colorful foliage and various flowering times for season-long interest. Mix annual and perennial vines. The annuals provide quick cover and flowers while the perennial vines are getting established.

PLANT

ANNUALS

Start impatiens, petunias, wax begonias, pansies, and gerbera daisies in early February in southern Michigan and two weeks later in northern Michigan including the upper Peninsula. Use pelleted (coated) petunia and begonia seeds to ease planting these small seeds, or mix these and other small seeds with sand to help you spread the seeds more evenly over the soil surface.

Sow ageratum, lobelia, and love-in-a-mist seeds in mid- or late February; two weeks later for those in the north.

HERE'S HOW

TO FORCE PAPER-WHITES

1. Fill a shallow container with sterile pea gravel, pebbles, or marbles. Add enough water to reach the top of the gravel. Place the bulbs on the gravel, and cover with just enough gravel to hold them in place.

2. Or, plant them in a container of any well-drained potting mix. Leave the tops of the bulbs exposed. Keep the planting mix moist but not wet.

3. Move the potted bulbs to a cool 45- to 60-degree-Fahrenheit location for rooting.

4. Place them in a bright location as soon as the leaves start to grow. It takes just a few weeks to get flowers.

■ *This is still a good time to force indoor bulbs into bloom. Check garden centers and catalogs for paper-white narcissus bulbs.*

Seeds can be started in two ways. Sow them in a flat, and then transplant young seedlings into individual containers; or sow one to two seeds directly into the individual pots.

Check the planting dates on the seed packets and in catalogs. Sow seeds according to the label directions. February is the time to start many of the spring-blooming and long-season annuals.

BULBS

You can still purchase, plant, and force amaryllis into bloom. See January, Plant, Bulbs for details. Once the amaryllis flowers have faded, repot any plants that were held over from last year.

1. Remove any bulblets that formed in the past year. Plant these in separate small pots.

2. Plant amaryllis in a pot slightly larger than the bulb. Fill the pot with any sterile, well-drained potting mix. Place the bulb so that the pointed half is above the soil.

3. Water, and move the potted bulb to a sunny location. Allow the soil to dry slightly between watering.

4. Fertilize with any dilute solution of a flowering houseplant fertilizer.

5. Harden off, and move outdoors after the danger of frost.

6. Bring it back indoors for winter and a chance to rebloom.

You can still pot spring-flowering bulbs for indoor forcing. They need about twelve to fifteen weeks of 35- to 45-degree-Fahrenheit temperatures. They flower about the time your outdoor gardens begin to bloom. This makes them perfect to use outdoors in flowerboxes and containers.

EDIBLES

Start onions indoors from seeds. Plant them at the end of the month in southern Michigan. Wait a week or two if you are in northern Michigan.

LAWNS

Make the most out of every action. Plan to use sod removed to create new planting beds to repair bare spots in the lawn. Secure a sod cutter and tentatively schedule to perform both tasks at the same time.

PERENNIALS

Start perennials from seed indoors the same way you grow annuals. Check seed packets and garden catalogs for specific information on starting times and seed treatment requirements. See the preceding Annuals section for more information about starting seeds.

ROSES

Study catalogs and read books to learn more about the roses best suited to your landscape. Understand the different classifications of roses.

Modern roses were introduced after 1867. These include hybrid teas, polyanthas, floribundas, and grandifloras. Hybrid tea roses are often grafted onto a hardy rootstock. They grow 3 to 5 feet tall and produce single or double flowers on long stems. Polyanthas are hybrids that grow up to 2 feet tall and produce a proliferation of small flowers in clusters. They are hardier than hybrid teas but less popular than floribundas. Floribundas are the result of crossing hybrid teas with polyanthas. These 3-foot-tall plants are usually grafted and produce many small flowers in clusters. Grandifloras are often grafted and grow up to 6 feet tall. They produce flowers similar to the hybrid teas, though the blooms are smaller and clustered in groups of five to seven.

Tree roses can be formed from any type of rose, though hybrid teas and floribundas are the most popular. A straight trunk is grafted onto a hardy rootstock. The desired rose is grafted to the top of the trunk. During cold weather, both grafts need to be covered, or the plants should be moved indoors for winter.

Climbing roses can grow to more than 6 feet tall and can be trained over fences, on trellises, or up walls. These plants produce long canes that must be tied to the support structure.

Large-flowered climbers have thick stiff canes, bloom twice a season, and are climbing versions (mutations) of other roses. Some are grafted, and most benefit from winter protection. Some large hardy shrub roses like 'William Baffin' and 'John Cabot' can be grown as climbers and need no winter protection.

Ramblers are much hardier climbers. They typically flower once a year on long, thin, flexible canes.

Miniature roses are small versions of floribundas and hybrid teas that produce smaller leaves and flowers on 6- to 18-inch-tall plants.

SHRUBS

Take note of any shrubs that need to be moved. Transplanting can begin as soon as the ground thaws.

TREES

Contact nurseries for information about plant availability and planting stock. Trees can be purchased as bare-root, balled-and-burlapped, or container-grown stock.

Bare-root trees are the cheapest and lightweight, but they often have the poorest survival rate. They must be planted as soon as possible after digging. This makes them a less-than-ideal choice for most gardeners. Bare-root plants are only available from a few sources.

Balled-and-burlapped trees are dug in early spring before growth begins or in fall after leaf drop. The trees are dug with a small portion of the roots intact. They are more expensive and heavier to manage, but have a greater rate of survival than bare-root trees.

Container-grown trees are planted and grown in pots for several years. The smaller root system and pots make them easier to manage. They are moderately priced and can be planted spring through fall.

VINES & GROUNDCOVERS

Buy or build a support structure for new or existing vertical plantings. Install these structures prior to planting to avoid damaging tender roots and young stems. Select a structure that can adequately

HERE'S HOW

TO START NEW PLANTS FROM STEM AND LEAF CUTTINGS

1. Take a 4- to 6-inch cutting. Remove the lowest set of leaves and dip the stem in a rooting compound. This material contains hormones to encourage rooting and a fungicide to prevent rot.

2. Place cuttings in moist vermiculite, perlite, or a well-drained potting mix. Roots should form in one to two weeks.

3. Transplant rooted cuttings into a small container of potting mix. Water frequently to keep the soil slightly moist but not wet.

support the weight of the vine and provide a surface for the plant to cling around or attach to.

CARE

ANNUALS
Continue monitoring annuals stored in the basement. Pot any that start to grow, and move them to a sunny window. Water the soil thoroughly whenever the top few inches start to dry.

Pinch back indoor plantings to keep them compact. Remove the stem tip or a portion of the stem just above a healthy leaf. Start new plants using stem and leaf pieces that are 4 to 6 inches long.

BULBS
Remove several more pots of forced bulbs from storage. Stagger removal times by two weeks to extend the bloom period. See January, Care, Bulbs for more details.

Check on any remaining bulbs you have in cold storage. The soil should remain slightly moist and the temperatures between 35 and 45 degrees Fahrenheit. Gradually reduce the storage temperature or move bulbs to a cooler location if they begin to sprout.

February often means a winter thaw that has gardeners asking, "My bulbs have sprouted! What do I do?" The answer: "Nothing, now." Bulbs are tough. Any exposed leaves may be damaged by the cold, but the flower buds are usually still safely buried in the soil.

Early blooming tulips and daffodils may suffer in an extended thaw followed by a cold snap. The plants will survive, though the flowers may be lost for this year. Next fall, winter mulch areas prone to early sprouting or move the bulbs to a location that is less affected by fluctuating temperatures.

Remove spent blooms and drying leaves on forced bulbs.

EDIBLES
Continue harvesting indoor herbs. Try freezing fresh herbs in ice cubes for later use.

Finish using stored vegetables. During a winter thaw, you may dig carrots and parsnips still buried in the garden.

Prune back overgrown and leggy herbs.

LAWNS
Mowing is not needed now. Take your lawn mower to the repair shop to beat the spring rush.

PERENNIALS
Transplant seedlings from flats into individual containers as soon as the first set of true leaves appear.

Monitor plantings for frost heaving caused by the freezing and thawing of unmulched gardens. The fluctuating temperatures cause the soil to shift and often push shallow-rooted perennials such as coral bells (*Heuchera*) right out of the soil. Gently tamp these back into the soil as soon as they are discovered. Make a note to winter mulch these areas next fall after the ground freezes.

Wait for the worst of winter to pass before cleaning out the garden. Many borderline hardy perennials such as salvias and mums survive better when the stems are left standing.

ROSES
Continue monitoring roses under winter protection. Pick up and replace any rose cones, mulches, or protection that have blown off the plants.

Limit pruning to storm damaged stems.

SHRUBS
Monitor shrubs and other plants for winter damage. Check the November, Care, section for maintenance strategies to reduce winter injury.

Prune damaged or hazardous branches as they are found. Summer- and fall-blooming plants can be pruned starting now until growth begins in spring. Wait until after flowering to prune spring-blooming shrubs.

Prune a few branches from spring-flowering shrubs to force for indoor bloom. See January, Care for tips on forcing branches.

■ *Seedlings are fragile when they first sprout. Keep them moist but not soaking wet.*

TREES

Shovel snow before applying sand or deicing salt to reduce the need for products that can harm trees and other plants. Consider using a more plant-friendly deicer that is kinder to the plants and landscape.

Continue monitoring the landscape for animal and winter damage. Make notes of problems in your journal. Record problems with ice loads, snow damage, and poor drainage.

Trees can be pruned during the dormant season, when it is much easier to see the overall shape of the tree and what needs to be removed. Prune oaks in winter to reduce risk of oak wilt.

Remove damaged and hazardous branches as they appear. Crossing, parallel, or rubbing branches can also be removed. Consider hiring a certified arborist for large jobs. They have the tools, equipment, and training to do the job safely. Ask friends and relatives for recommendations. Visit www.treesaregood.com, the Arboriculture society of Michigan (www.asm-isa.org) for a list of certified arborists. These are tree care professionals who have voluntarily participated in an international program that certifies a standard of tree care knowledge.

Birches, walnuts, and maples can be pruned in late winter. The running sap does not hurt the tree; it just makes the job messy.

Save pruned branches from flowering trees such as crabapples, magnolias, and pussy willows for indoor bloom. See the January, Care section for details on forcing these to bloom indoors.

VINES & GROUNDCOVERS

Monitor the health of tropical vines overwintering indoors. Increase the light and humidity around failing plants. Move them in front of a south-facing window, and add artificial light if needed.

Increase the humidity around the plant by grouping it with other plants. As one plant loses moisture (transpires), the plants around it benefit. Or, place pebbles in the saucer, place the pot on the pebbles and keep water in the tray below the pot. As the water evaporates, it increases the humidity around the plant where it is needed.

Trim dead or damaged branches on outdoor plants. Wait until late March or April to do routine pruning.

Check vines growing indoors. Remove and discard dead leaves. Prune off wayward and dead branches. Cut them back above a healthy leaf or where it joins another branch.

WATER

ALL
The ground is still frozen, so there is no need to water outside plants. Whenever the soil thaws and dries, water aboveground planters that are overwintering outdoors and in the garage.

ANNUALS & EDIBLES
Check seeded flats and seedlings every day. Keep the soil moist until the seeds germinate. Once germinated, seedlings should still be checked every day. Water often enough to keep the soil moist but not wet.

Continue watering annuals that you are growing as houseplants. Water thoroughly until the excess runs out the bottom. Pour off excess water, and allow the top few inches of soil to dry before watering again.

BULBS
Keep the soil moist on potted bulbs that you are trying to force. Continue to water forced bulbs if you plan to rebloom them in the future.

PERENNIALS
Check perennial seedlings growing indoors every day. Keep the soil moist but not wet. Insufficient water can stunt and kill seedlings, while excess moisture can cause rot.

ROSES
Water indoor roses as needed. Water thoroughly and frequently enough to keep the soil slightly moist. Set them on a gravel tray to increase humidity around the plants. Check on container roses stored in the garage. Water them whenever the soil is dry and not frozen.

VINES & GROUNDCOVERS
Keep watering vines growing indoors for the winter. Water thoroughly so that the excess water runs out the drainage hole. Allow the water to collect in the gravel tray and increase the humidity around the plant.

FERTILIZE

ALL
There is no need to fertilize outdoor plants. Check your journal and any soil test information to start planning for spring fertilization. Fertilizing frozen soil doesn't help the plants, and it contributes to groundwater pollution.

ANNUALS
Fertilize seedlings once they begin to grow. Use a dilute solution of a complete water-soluble fertilizer every other week. Follow mixing directions on the label.

BULBS
Apply a dilute solution of any flowering plant fertilizer to amaryllis and other forced bulbs once they stop blooming.

EDIBLES
Fertilize indoor herbs that are pale, stunted, or showing other signs of nutrient deficiencies. Make sure it is a lack of nutrients, not light, causing these symptoms. Use a dilute solution of any houseplant fertilizer. Avoid excess fertilization that can ruin the flavor.

Let onions start growing before fertilizing the soil. Fertilizer can harm the sprouting seedlings.

PERENNIALS
Fertilize young indoor seedlings with a dilute solution of a complete fertilizer every other week.

ROSES

Only fertilize indoor roses that are actively growing or showing signs of nutrient deficiency. Nutrient deficient roses have stunted, pale, or off-colored leaves. Fertilize with a dilute solution of any flowering houseplant fertilizer.

VINES & GROUNDCOVERS

Fertilize nutrient-deficient vines growing indoors for the winter. Look for pale leaves and stunted growth. Use a dilute solution of any flowering houseplant fertilizer. Do not fertilize plants that are showing signs of stress from low light and humidity. Stressed plants lose leaves and have little, if any, new growth. Correct the problem before fertilizing. Adding nutrients to stressed plants can injure them.

PROBLEM-SOLVE

ALL

Check seedlings of annuals, edibles, and perennials for damping off, a fungal disease that causes sudden wilting and rotted stems. Infected plants suddenly collapse and rot at the soil line. Remove infected plants as soon as they are discovered. Apply a fungicide as a soil drench to infected plantings. Make sure the product is labeled to control damping off disease on your specific seedlings. Prevent this disease by using a sterile starter mix and clean containers.

Indoor Plants. Ignore fungus gnats. These are annoying insects that look like miniature fruit flies and flit around the house but don't harm plants. Reduce the problem by allowing the soil to dry slightly between watering, or employ an environmentally friendly product with the active ingredient *Bacillus thuringiensis israelensis*. This particular strain of the *B.t.* bacteria only kills the larvae of fungus gnats and mosquitoes. Check garden catalogs if you cannot find it in your local garden center.

Look under the leaves and along the stem for signs of mites, aphids, and whiteflies. These insects suck out plant juices, causing plants to yellow and brown. Get out the hand lens and inspect for evidence of speckling, a clear sticky substance, and the insects themselves. See the January, Problem-Solve section for pest control information.

Use yellow sticky traps to trap whiteflies. This won't eliminate the problem, but usually reduces the populations to a tolerable level. Purchase traps from a garden center or make your own.

Outdoor Plants. Secure fencing and other animal guards. Make sure animals are not able to crawl under or over the barriers and reach the plants. Make note of additional fencing or animal barriers to install prior to next winter.

Reapply repellents after severe weather, as indicated on the label. Scare tactics like noisemakers, human hair, and whirligigs may scare some animals. Use a variety of management strategies to help increase success. Keep in mind that urban wildlife is familiar with the smell and noise of humans, so scare tactics may not provide adequate control.

LAWNS

Our landscapes, especially those in the southern part of the state, often experience a winter thaw. Use this break to survey the lawn for signs of winter damage.

PERENNIALS

Continue to monitor for animal and rodent damage. See the January, Problem-Solve section for more information.

ROSES

Watch for signs of rabbit, deer, and vole feeding. Use a variety of tactics discussed in the January, Problem-Solve section.

SHRUBS

White flecks on the needles of mugo pines indicate pine needle scale. A lime sulfur spray can be used to kill the pest.

Other scale insects (those with hard shells attached to stems) can be treated with lime sulfur or dormant oil while the plants are dormant. Check the label before treatment to make sure it can be used on your particular plant. Beware: Lime sulfur can stain walkways and injure viburnums.

Check ornamental plums and cherries for Eastern tent caterpillar egg masses. The eggs look like a shiny glob of mud on a stem. Prune and destroy all that are found.

Look for and remove black knot cankers on plum and cherry shrubs. These appear as knots on the twigs.

Scrutinize the bases of viburnum, euonymus, and spirea stems for round, swollen growths called galls. Remove these galls, as they can eventually girdle and kill the stem.

Inspect dogwood for signs of golden canker. This fungal disease is common on dogwoods that have suffered heat and drought stress in summer. The twigs turn gold and die. Prune out infected stems. Disinfect tools between cuts.

TREES

Continue checking trees for overwintering insects. Look for egg masses of tent caterpillars and hairy masses of gypsy and tussock moth eggs found on tree trunks and branches. Remove these whenever found. Dormant oil sprays can be applied on warm days when temperatures stay 40 degrees Fahrenheit or above for at least twelve hours. Dormant oil sprays are used to control many gall-causing insects, some scales, aphids, and mites. Galls cause bumps on leaves, while scale, aphids, and mites cause discolored and brown leaves. Make sure you have a problem that needs treatment before using any chemicals.

■ *Watch for white flecks on pine needles, which indicate an infestation of scales.*

March

March marks the start of the winter-to-spring transition, though spring still seems far away. Those up north may be staring at an endless expanse of snow, while the rest of the state is being teased with a mixture of spring days and snowstorms. But everyone longs for a color other than white.

Bulbs give that first glimpse of color that signals spring is on its way. Just plant them in fall, provide basic care, and enjoy. Plus, the enjoyment of spring-flowering bulbs comes when you are busy with other projects. True bulbs include flowering onions, tulips, daffodils, and hyacinths. Gardeners often use the term *bulb* to include true bulbs, corms, rhizomes, tubers, and tuberous roots. These underground storage structures provide the bulb with everything it needs to sprout and flower. Once up and growing, the leaves manufacture the food that is stored in the bulb for the next growing period.

Get out your garden journal and record bloom times for bulbs. Your camera is another good way to record seasonal progressions in your garden. Small, early bulbs such as snowdrops (*Galanthus*) and winter aconites (*Eranthis*) start appearing as the snow recedes. Recording bloom times helps you identify slow blooming periods.

Take one last look at the winter garden and note any changes that should be made. Now check this against your planting plans for this year. Make any needed adjustments using design tips and hints from the January and February chapters.

Finalize your plans, start your planting list, and place orders for seeds and plants. Take advantage of nice days to stake out new planting beds and measure existing gardens where plants will be added.

Take advantage of the sunny, snow-free days. Cleanup of large perennial gardens can be a fair amount of work. It often occurs in late March when most of us are anxious to get busy outdoors and are not yet bored with maintenance tasks. Spring cleanup is also a great uncovering and discovery of the first signs of life in the garden.

Remove any weeds you find. An early start can keep weeds in check with a minimal investment of time. This prevents your garden from being overwhelmed by these unwanted plants.

Spring never seems to arrive early enough for gardeners. Get a jump on the growing season by using cold frames and row covers. They warm the soil to speed germination and establishment while protecting the leaves and stems from freezing temperatures.

MARCH

PLAN

ANNUALS

Measure the length and width of flowerbeds. Multiply these two dimensions to calculate the square footage of the bed. Use this information to calculate the number of plants you will need. See the following Vines & Groundcovers planting section for tips on calculating the number of plants you need for the available planting space.

March is also a good time to locate areas for new planting beds. Mark beds and begin preparation as soon as the soil can be worked. See April, Plan for more details.

BULBS

Start a wish list of bulbs you want to buy next fall. Consider adding early blooming minor bulbs. These bulbs add a welcome touch of color when you're starved for a glimpse of spring.

EDIBLES

Locate and repair or replace cold frames, row covers, and other season-extending materials if you plan an early start to the season.

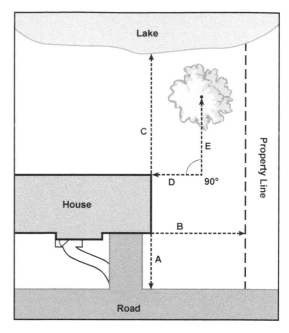

■ *If you don't know your lawn area, measure it. Don't worry about being exact; an approximate square footage will be good enough to calculate seed and fertilizer needs.*

This is a good time to decide the type of soil preparation you need. Locate sources for topsoil, compost, and other amendments. Calculate the

HERE'S HOW

TO CALCULATE THE AMOUNT OF SOIL OR AMENDMENTS NEEDED

1. A cubic yard of soil covers 300 square feet to the depth of 1 inch.

2. Multiply the length of the garden by the width. This gives you the square footage of your garden. Write this on your plan.

3. Next, multiply the area times the depth in feet of the material you want to incorporate. Convert inches into feet by dividing the number of inches you want to add by 12. Label this number as cubic feet needed.

4. Convert cubic feet to cubic yards by dividing the volume in cubic feet by 27, the number of cubic feet in a cubic yard. This is the amount of material you need to order.

    For example: Let's say your garden is 10 × 15 feet. You want to add a 2-inch layer of organic matter to the garden. Your equations would be:

    1) 10 ft. × 15 ft. = 150 sq. ft. 2) 2 in. ÷ 12 in. = 0.17 ft. 3) 150 ft. × 0.17 ft. = 25.5 cu. ft.
    4) 25.5 cu. ft. ÷ 27 cu. ft. per cu. yd. = 0.9 or about 1 cu. yd.

Lost in the math? See the Ordering Soils and Mulch Chart on page 216.

amount needed before you go shopping by using the formula on page 50.

Place your edible garden in a location that receives full sun and has moist, well-drained soil. If you have a small or shady yard or one with poor soil, carve out small areas or use containers for your garden.

Fruiting and flowering vegetables, such as broccoli, squash, tomatoes and most herbs, produce best when they receive eight to twelve hours of full sun. Plant root crops, such as radishes and beets, in full sun to part shade with at least six hours of sunlight. Leafy crops, such as spinach and lettuce, can grow in shady areas that receive as little as four hours of sun.

Use a traditional garden style if space is not an issue. Plant vegetables in rows running east and west. Place the tallest vegetables in the back (north side) to reduce the shade cast on other, shorter plants.

Try container gardening if you have limited or no space for gardening. Use a container with drainage holes that can be decorative or as simple as a 5-gallon bucket with holes punched in the bottom. Fill it with a commercial or homemade potting mix. Blend equal amounts of topsoil and peat moss, or compost and vermiculite or perlite. Incorporate a slow-release fertilizer in the mix so it releases nutrients every time you water. Plant seeds and

■ *Prepare your lawn mower for the season ahead.*

transplants just as you would in the garden. Leave enough room for the plants to reach mature size. Water thoroughly until the excess runs out the bottom of the container. Check water needs daily.

LAWNS

It's time for lawnmower maintenance. For safety's sake, if you are new at this job, ask an experienced friend or relative for help. Always disconnect the spark plug wire when working on a mower.

Clean or replace the spark plug and air filter.

Drain the oil from the crankcase of a mower with a four-cycle engine. This is not needed for two-cycle engines. Refill with the type and amount of oil recommended by the manufacturer.

Replace bent, cracked, or damaged blades. Sharpen, or have a professional sharpen, the mower's blades.

Check the tires for wear and replace them as needed. Check for loose nuts, bolts, and screws now and throughout the season.

Select the right grass for your location. Cool-season grasses are the best choices for Michigan landscapes. These grasses provide some of the first and last glimpses of green in our climate. Kentucky bluegrass is the most popular lawn grass for our region. It has a fine texture (thin leaf) and a good green color. It is best suited for sunny locations. Fine fescues are more shade- and drought-tolerant than Kentucky bluegrass. They look similar to, and are generally mixed with, bluegrass. Turf-type perennial ryegrass is quick to germinate. It is blended with other grass seeds to provide quick cover until the other grasses germinate. This, along with its pest resistance and wearability, makes it a major part of many grass seed mixes. Tall fescue is a tall, coarse-textured (wide leaf) grass used for high-use areas in full sun to part shade and in dry soils. New rhizomatous types of tall fescue make this grass more suited for lawn use.

PERENNIALS

Keep your plans simple if you are a beginning gardener or one with limited time. Gardening with fewer types of perennials but more of each is easier to maintain.

MARCH

PLANT SPACING FACTOR CHART	
SPACING (INCHES)	SPACING FACTOR
4	0.11
6	0.25
8	0.44
10	0.70
12	1.00
15	1.56
18	2.25
24	4.00
30	6.25
36	9.00
48	16.00
60	26.00

Complete a plant list including the number of each plant type you need. See the Plant Spacing Factor Chart above and Here's How sequence below for help calculating the number of plants for your space.

ROSES
Select a frost-free place to store bare-root roses that arrive prior to planting. Cover the roots with damp peat moss or newspaper and store in a cool, dark place.

TREES & SHRUBS
Complete your landscape plan and start shopping for unusual shrubs and trees. Contact specialty nurseries and garden centers to locate your desired species. You may have to make several calls to locate any new and out-of-the-ordinary varieties. Shop early to find potential sources and a better selection.

VINES & GROUNDCOVERS
Calculate the square footage of your new and existing groundcover beds. Multiply the length times the width to get the square footage of the planting beds. This information is used to calculate the number of plants and amount of fertilizer you will need.

Use the Plant Spacing Factor Chart at left to calculate the number of plants needed. Divide the square footage of the garden by the spacing factor. The answer is the number of plants you need.

PLANT

ANNUALS
Continue seeding annuals indoors. See the January and February, Plant sections for tips on starting seeds.

HERE'S HOW

TO CALCULATE THE NUMBER OF GROUNDCOVER PLANTS NEEDED

1. Calculate the square footage of the garden by multiplying the length times the width of the planting bed.
2. Check the spacing requirements of the groundcovers you plan to use. Multiply the spacing needed by that same number to get the square inches needed per plant. Divide this by 144 to convert the garden area into square feet.
3. Divide the square footage of the garden by the square footage of the mature size of the ground-cover you want to grow. The answer equals the number of plants needed to fill the planting bed.

   For example: Assume your planting bed is 10 × 12 feet. You want to grow thyme (*Thymus*) planted 15 inches apart.

   (1) Find the square footage of the garden: 10 feet × 12 feet = 120 square feet

   (2) Calculate the square footage allotted for each plant: 15 inches × 15 inches ÷ 144 = 1.56 inches

   (3) Estimate the number of plants you need: 120 ÷ 1.56 = 77 plants

Plant coleus, dusty miller, pinks, melampodium, snapdragon, and verbena in early March. Gardeners in northern portions of Michigan can wait until the middle of the month.

Seed alyssum, moss rose, and salvia in mid- to late March. Plant or repot geraniums that were stored in a cool, dark location for winter. Use a well-drained potting mix and a clean container with a drainage hole. Cut plants back to 4 to 6 inches above the container. Water the soil thoroughly, with the excess running out the bottom of the pot.

Anxious gardeners can "jump start" the season with cold frames, cloches, and floating row covers. Use them to warm the soil and protect plants from cold temperatures.

Row covers made of polypropylene spun fabrics can be used to extend the season. Row cover fabrics help trap heat around the plants while allowing air, water, and light to reach the plants. Loosely drape fabric over the plants. Anchor on the sides, leaving enough slack in the fabric to allow for plant growth.

BULBS

Start planting tender bulbs indoors in mid- to late March through early April. Cannas, dahlias, tuberous begonias, and caladiums started indoors bloom earlier in the garden. If indoor space is limited, wait and plant them outdoors in late spring.

Clean and divide bulbs if this was not done in fall. Make sure there is at least one eye (like a potato

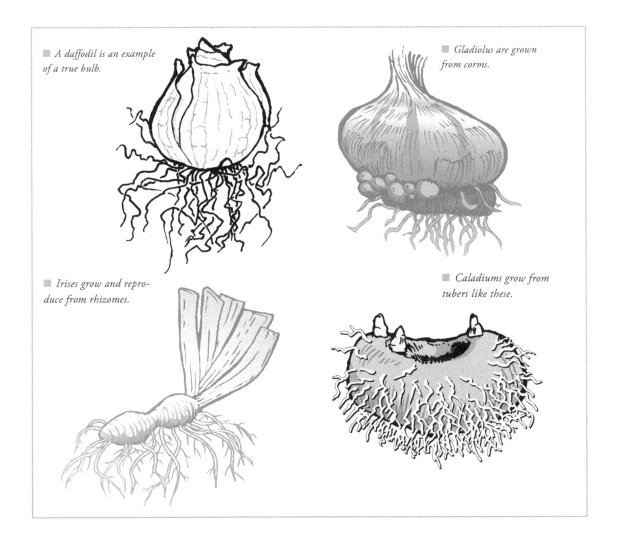

■ *A daffodil is an example of a true bulb.*

■ *Gladiolus are grown from corms.*

■ *Irises grow and reproduce from rhizomes.*

■ *Caladiums grow from tubers like these.*

"eye") for every division. Without this eye, the division will not grow and develop into a plant.

Fill flats with a mixture of one-half peat and one-half perlite or vermiculite, or use any well-drained potting mix.

Set begonia tubers hollow side up in the potting mix. Plant so that the top of the tuber is even with the soil surface.

Place canna rhizomes, eyes facing up, in the potting mix. Bury these so the upper half of the rhizome is just above the soil surface.

Plant dahlia tuberous roots in small pots so that the tuberous root is covered and the eye is 1 inch below the soil surface.

Plant caladium tubers with knobby side up in small pots. Cover tubers with 1 to 2 inches of soil.

Water and move plants to a warm location. Place planted bulbs under artificial lights or near a sunny window as soon as they sprout. Cannas and tuberous begonias can be transplanted into individual containers as soon as several leaves develop.

■ *A lettuce collection of Red Salad Bowl, Black Seeded Simpson, Bibb, Prizehead, and Dark Green Boston.*

Many florists sell hardy Oriental and Asiatic lilies as well as traditional white lilies for Easter. Keep your lilies healthy by placing them in a cool, bright location in your home.

Keep the soil moist, but not wet. Perforate or remove the decorative foil and place the pot on a saucer. Make sure that the water does not collect in decorative pots or baskets. This can lead to root rot. As soon as the soil is workable, you can move your lily into a well-drained garden location that receives at least six to eight hours of sun.

EDIBLES
Fill clean flats or small containers with sterile starting mix. Plant seeds in rows in flats or place one or two seeds in each container. Check the seed package for planting recommendations. Most seeds should be planted twice as deep as they are thick.

Plant the following indoors in March:

> March 1: Parsley
> March 15: Broccoli, early cabbage, cauliflower, celeriac, celery, eggplant, and lettuce

Adjust these planting times to fit your region. Wait a week or two weeks if you live in the northern part of the state.

LAWNS
It is still too early to plant grass seed, and sod is usually not available until April.

PERENNIALS
Make any needed adjustments to your planting plans. Keep your ideas simple if you are a beginner gardener or one with limited time. Complete a plant list and include the number of each plant species you will need. See the preceding Plant Spacing Factor Chart for help.

ROSES
Repot any indoor roses that have outgrown their pots and will remain in containers. Carefully slide the plants out of the existing containers. Move them to pots that are about 1 to 2 inches bigger in diameter and fill with a well-draining potting mix. Water, but do not fertilize for several weeks.

TO TRANSPLANT A SHRUB

1. Loosely tie the branches to prevent damage and keep them out of your way.

2. Dig a trench around the shrub slightly larger and deeper than the desired rootball.

3. Undercut the rootball with a sharp spade. Use hand pruners and loppers for larger or tougher roots.

4. Slide a piece of burlap or canvas under the rootball. Have several friends lend a hand. Extra hands and strong backs make the job easier and reduce the risk of dropping the shrub and damaging the rootball.

5. Set the shrub in the prepared site. Carefully cut away or slide the tarp away from the shrub.

6. Backfill the hole with existing soil, water, and mulch.

Store dormant bare-root roses in a cool, dark location until planting. Dormant roses can be stored in a spare refrigerator, root cellar, or other location where temperatures remain above freezing. Keep the roots moist and covered with peat moss or sawdust. Or heel in bare-root roses outdoors if they cannot be planted within several days. Dig a trench with one sloping side. Place the roots and the graft in the trench with the plant leaning on the side and cover with soil.

Check stored roses and move them to a cooler location if the buds begin to swell. Pot any plants that begin to grow. Move them to a sunny location and keep indoors until the danger of frost has passed.

Roses that started to grow in transit or storage need different care. Plant them in pots and grow indoors. Keep them near a sunny window. Water thoroughly, and allow the top few inches of soil to dry before watering again. Potted roses can be moved outdoors after danger of frost is past.

SHRUBS

Late winter through early spring is the best time to transplant shrubs. Moving large, established shrubs can be tricky, heavy work. Replacing overgrown or misplaced shrubs may be easier, cheaper, and more successful.

Start transplanting when the ground thaws and the soil is moist. Complete this garden task before growth begins. See Here's How, above, for more details.

TREES

Late winter and early spring are the best times to transplant trees. Moving trees can be tricky and heavy work. Save large, expensive, and special trees for professionals. They have the experience and equipment to move larger plants successfully. For more details, see September, Plant.

VINES & GROUNDCOVERS

Begin soil preparation as soon as the snow melts, the soil thaws, and it is dry enough to work. See the Introduction for more information on soil preparation.

ALL

Check shallow-rooted bulbs, perennials, and groundcovers for frost heaving. Unmulched gardens or those with inconsistent snow cover are subject to freezing and thawing temperatures. The fluctuating temperatures cause the soil to shift, pushing plants and bulbs right out of the soil. Gently tamp heaved plants back in place in the soil using your hands and water.

Wait until temperatures consistently hover near freezing before removing mulch. This is usually in late March in the south or early April in the north. Remove mulch if plants are starting to grow.

ANNUALS

Move any pansies started indoors in January to a cold frame to harden them off. The cold frame protects them from frost but allows them to adjust to the cooler, harsher outdoor conditions. Reduce watering and stop fertilizing until they are planted in a permanent location. Vent the cold frame on sunny days to prevent heat damage. Automatic venting systems are available from some garden centers and through garden catalogs.

A cold frame should only be used during the early, cooler days of the growing season when delicate seedlings need that extra protection, and for late-season frost protection.

Pinch the growing tips of leggy annuals to encourage branching. Pinched plants will develop stouter stems and more branches.

Take 4- to 6-inch cuttings from annuals you want to propagate. Root cuttings in moist vermiculite, perlite, or well-drained potting mix. Transplant rooted cuttings (usually ready in one to two weeks) into small containers filled with moist, well-drained potting mix.

BULBS

Remove mulch only if the bulbs have started to grow. Keep some mulch handy to cover bulbs during extreme cold snaps. Fortunately bulbs are tough and can tolerate cold temperatures and even a blanket of snow.

Remove forced bulbs from cold treatment. Any that were planted in November are ready to come out of cold storage.

Keep the foliage of amaryllis and other forced bulbs growing in a sunny window. See January, Care for more growing tips.

Leave bulb foliage intact on outdoor blooming bulbs. The green leaves produce energy needed for the plants to grow and flower next year. Deadhead flowers as needed.

EDIBLES

Keep soil warm and moist when germinating seeds. Keep the seedlings in a bright window or, better yet, under artificial lights. Adjust lights as the seedlings grow so they stay 4 to 6 inches above the top of the plants.

Start cleaning and preparing your garden for planting. Take advantage of any snow-free days to remove debris, take a soil test, and get started. The soil can be worked anytime it is not frozen and is only slightly moist. Check soil moisture by taking a handful of soil and gently squeezing it into a ball. Tap the ball with your finger. If it breaks apart, it is ready to work. Otherwise, wait a few days for the soil to dry. Working wet soil results in clods that last all season. See Soil Preparation in the Introduction for more details.

Trim onions that are long and leggy. Continue to cut and harvest windowsill herbs as needed.

LAWNS

Mowing is usually not needed. Wait until the grass greens and starts to grow.

Get out the rake and start work as soon as the snow and ice melt. Use a leaf rake to fluff and dry grass to reduce the risk of snow mold. Remove any leaves and debris that may have collected prior to

■ *Snow mold can appear as the snow starts to melt in spring.*

the snowfall. Never work on frozen or waterlogged soils. This can lead to damage and death of the grass.

Seeding and sodding require proper soil preparation for good results. Seeding a lawn takes more time but saves you money and increases your selection of grass-seed mixtures. Sodded lawns give you instant beauty at a price. See April, Plant for directions on installing sod and May, Plant for lawn seeding tips.

PERENNIALS

It's time to get busy cleaning up the garden! Remove any stems and seedpods left for winter interest. Hand pruners take care of most cleanup jobs. Use the loppers on some of the larger and harder-to-reach stems.

Prune back Russian sage to 4 to 6 inches above the soil. This plant (often classed as a sub-shrub) usually dies back in winter. Use a lopper or hand pruners to cut stems above an outward facing bud.

Cut back ornamental grasses before the new growth begins. Use hand pruners, an electric hedge shear, or weed whip with a rigid plastic blade for mass

■ *Cut back perennials while they are fully dormant—in late winter or early spring.*

planting of perennials and grasses to clip the plants back to several inches above the soil. Smaller grasses, such as blue fescue and blue oat grass, can be clipped back or left intact.

Cut back only the dead tips of candytuft, lavender, and thyme. Cut them back even further in late spring if the plants become leggy.

Remove dead foliage and stems of all perennials. Be careful not to damage the leaves of early emerging perennials during the cleanup process.

Remove only the dead leaves on evergreen perennials, such as lungwort, barrenwort (*Epimedium*), and coral bells. This makes a more attractive display as the new foliage fills in. Remove dead foliage on lamb's ear. The old leaves tend to mat down over winter and can rot if not removed.

Compost pest-free materials. See the Introduction for composting information.

Keep some mulch handy to protect the tender tips of early sprouting hostas, primroses, and other early risers that may be damaged by a sudden drop in temperature.

ROSES

Continue to monitor winter protection. Keep mulch, shelters, and rose cones in place until weather begins to consistently hover near freezing. Vent rose cones on warm or sunny days. The goal is to keep roses cool and dormant. High temperatures can cause premature growth that can be killed by cold temperatures in spring. Close vents when temperatures drop. Remove cones and the outer layer of mulch after a week of above-freezing temperatures, but keep the cones handy in case of an extreme drop in temperature. Gradually remove the remaining layers of mulch. Many gardeners let spring rains wash away the soil mounded over the crown.

Wait until the weather has warmed and the mulch is off to start pruning. Remove any damaged branches as they are found. Check, clean, and sharpen hand pruners while waiting for the pruning season to begin.

SHRUBS

Continue protecting plants from deicing salts, snow loads, and animal damage. Start the repair work by pruning broken branches and leaching salt-laden soil with thorough watering in dry springs once the soil thaws.

Wait until after flowering to prune lilacs, forsythia, bridal wreath, and vanhoutte spirea, and other spring-blooming shrubs. These shrubs have already set flower buds for this spring. Pruning now does not harm the plants but eliminates the bloom—the reason they are planted.

Prune summer- and fall-blooming shrubs now. Late winter pruning doesn't interfere with summer flowering and allows the plants to recover quickly. Start by removing damaged, broken, and diseased stems. To prevent the spread of disease, disinfect tools between cuts with rubbing alcohol or a solution of one part bleach to nine parts water. Clean your tools after pruning to minimize the adverse effects of bleach. See page 209 for more pruning tips.

Cut back butterfly bush and caryopteris to 4 to 6 inches above the soil surface. The tops may dieback. Yearly pruning removes dead growth and contains vigorous growth after a mild winter.

TREES

As the snow melts, animal damage and winter injury becomes more obvious. Prune or remove damaged branches.

Complete pruning before trees leaf out. Pruning during leaf expansion increases the risk of trunk and branch damage. See Pruning on page 209 for more details.

Complete pruning on oaks. Dormant-season pruning helps reduce the risk of oak wilt on these trees.

Birches, walnuts, and maples can be pruned in late winter. The running sap does not hurt the tree; it just makes the job messy.

Check the base of plants for girdling by rabbits and voles. Damage appears as a lighter area on the

HERE'S HOW

TO PRUNE A LARGE BRANCH

1 Larger branches (2 inches in diameter or greater) should be double-cut to prevent branch splitting and bark tearing. Make the first cut on the bottom of the branch about 12 inches from the trunk. Cut about one fourth of the way through the branch.

2 Make the second cut on top of the branch about 1 inch away and on the far side (further from the trunk) from the first cut. Cut the branch all the way through. It may break off in the process but the first cut will control the break and prevent it from ripping bark and damaging the tree trunk.

3 You can see the finished second cut. Notice the break at the lower cut edge. The first cut protected the tree from damage. This is important as the living tissue that carries water and nutrients between the leaves and roots lies just below the bark. Large wounds also provide an entryway to life-threatening insects and disease.

4 Cut off the branch stub remaining on the tree. Place the pruning saw just outside of the branch collar, which is the bark swelling between the branch and the main trunk. Saw all the way through to remove the stub. Do not cut the branch flush with the tree trunk as you'll interfere with wound closure.

5 As you can see the final cut is flush with the swollen area at the base of the branch known as the branch bark collar. Do not paint pruning cuts with wound dressings or pruning paints. These trap moisture and bacteria and can lead to rot and decay. A proper cut will speed wound closure and reduce the risk of pest problems. Oaks that had to be pruned during the growing season are the only exception. Whenever possible prune oaks during the dormant season to minimize the risk of oak wilt disease.

trunk. Vole and rabbit damage interrupts the flow of water and nutrients between the roots and leaves. Severe damage from feeding around most of the trunk can kill trees. When in doubt, wait and see if the tree will survive.

Severely damaged trees should be replaced. Some gardeners try bridge grafting in a last attempt to save special plants. Take a piece of branch from the damaged tree. Graft one end above and the other end below the damaged portion. You must line up the vascular system of the graft with the vascular system of the tree. This difficult process requires lots of skill and a little luck.

Research has shown wrapping tree trunks is not beneficial and can even be harmful. If you used tree wraps, remove them as temperatures warm.

VINES & GROUNDCOVERS
Remove debris and leaves that have collected in groundcover beds and under vine plantings. Remove winter-damaged leaves and stems.

Edge planting beds using a sharp spade or edging machine to keep the groundcovers in and the surrounding grass out of the planting beds.

It's time to start pruning vines and groundcovers. Remove dead and damaged stems and branches. Prune clematis to control growth, encourage branching near the base of the plant, and improve flowering. The type of clematis you grow determines the time and type of pruning it requires.

Spring-blooming clematis blooms on old wood. These are generally not hardy or commonly grown in the state. Prune after flowering.

Some flowering clematis, such as 'Nellie Moser', 'Henry', 'The President', and 'Bees Jubilee', bloom on both old and new growth. Prune dead and weak stems back to a healthy stem or ground level in late winter or early spring before growth begins. Prune the remaining stems back to a pair of strong buds.

The last group of clematis blooms on new growth. Prune in late winter or early spring before growth begins. Remove dead stems back to ground level. Cut the remaining stems back to 6 to 12 inches.

WATER

ALL
Usually there is no need to water outdoors. The northern parts of Michigan may still be blanketed in snow, and the rest of the state may experience spring one day and blizzards the next.

ANNUALS
Check seedlings every day. Water whenever the soil surface begins to dry. Apply enough water to thoroughly moisten the soil, but avoid overwatering, which can lead to root rot and damping-off disease.

Water potted annuals whenever the top few inches of soil start to dry. Water thoroughly until the excess runs out the bottom. Pour off excess water, and allow the top few inches of soil to dry before watering again.

Check your cold frame. Monitor soil moisture, and water as needed. Plants growing in the cold frame need less-frequent watering during their hardening-off process.

BULBS
Keep the soil moist for newly planted tender bulbs and flowering bulbs. Allow the top few inches of soil of forced bulbs that are finished blooming to dry slightly before watering again.

EDIBLES
Cover seed trays with plastic, or mist the soil to keep it moist during germination. Remove the plastic once the seeds sprout. Water flats and containers thoroughly. Pour off any excess water that collects beneath the container. Check seedlings every day.

LAWNS
If the spring is dry, water areas exposed to deicing salts, such as along sidewalks, driveways, and steps. This washes salts through the soil and reduces damage. Salt-damaged grass won't green up in spring. Water areas of the lawn that were seeded or sodded at the end of last season to reduce stress on young, developing root systems. Water only if the top 4 inches of the soil are starting to dry.

PERENNIALS

Check seedlings every day. Keep the soil moist but not wet. As the plants grow and develop larger root systems they need less frequent watering.

Water potted bare-root perennials often enough to keep the soil moist but not thoroughly wet. Continue to water thoroughly but less frequently as the plants begin to grow.

Keep the packing material around the roots of stored bare-root plants moist.

ROSES

Continue watering indoor roses as the soil dries. Check on container roses stored in the garage. Water them whenever the soil is dry and not frozen.

SHRUBS

Continue watering shrubs in aboveground planters. Water thoroughly whenever the soil thaws and dries.

TREES

Wait for the ground to thaw, and then check the soil moisture. In years with limited snowmelt and dry weather, you may need to water. Thoroughly water any trees subjected to deicing salt to wash the chemicals through the soil and away from the tree roots. Continue to water trees in aboveground planters. Water thoroughly whenever the soil is thawed and dry.

VINES & GROUNDCOVERS

Water indoor vines when the top few inches of soil are dry. Apply enough water so that the excess runs out the bottom of the pot. Avoid letting the pot sit in standing water.

FERTILIZE

ALL

For outdoor plants, as soon as the ground thaws, test the soil in lawns and around perennials, shrubs, trees, vines, and groundcovers. The results inform you about your fertilizer needs and save you time and money so you don't add unnecessary nutrients. It also helps avoid damaging the plants and environment by misapplying fertilizer. Retest the soil in established gardens every three to five years or when problems develop.

Contact your local Michigan State University Extension Service office or their website for soil test information. See page 10 or 13 in the Introduction for tips on taking a soil test.

There's no need to fertilize outdoor plants yet. Fertilizing this early doesn't help the plants and contributes to groundwater pollution.

ANNUALS

Indoors, start fertilizing overwintered annuals that were recently potted when new growth appears. Use a diluted solution of any flowering houseplant fertilizer. Apply any diluted mix of complete water-soluble fertilizer to seedlings every other week. Check the label for mixing rates.

BULBS

Hardy bulbs planted outdoors need little fertilization. Fertilize now through April if you want to increase vigor and if you did not fertilize in the fall. For best results, apply a low-nitrogen, slow-release fertilizer as they sprout.

Fertilize amaryllis and other forced indoor bulbs that you want to keep. Use a dilute solution of any flowering houseplant fertilizer. Apply it after they are done flowering.

EDIBLES

Use a dilute solution of any complete (10-10-10 or 12-12-12) fertilizer on established seedlings.

ROSES

Indoor roses can be fertilized with a dilute solution of any flowering houseplant fertilizer.

VINES & GROUNDCOVERS

Fertilize before growth begins if plants need a nutrient boost. Use the type and amount of fertilizer recommended by the soil test report or consider a low-nitrogen, slow-release fertilizer to promote slow, steady growth and reduce the risk of burn. Apply 2 pounds of a 5-percent nitrogen fertilizer such as Milorganite® or 1 pound of a 10-percent nitrogen fertilizer per 100 square feet.

See the Introduction for more information about fertilization techniques.

PROBLEM-SOLVE

ALL

For outdoor plants, continue monitoring animal

■ *Signs of rabbits include distinct round droppings around plants, gnawing on stems of older woody plants, clean-cut clipping of young stems and leaves, and, in winter, tracks.*

damage. Apply repellents as long as animals are present and food supply is limited.

ANNUALS

Continue monitoring for whiteflies, fungus gnats, aphids, and mites.

Capture whiteflies with yellow sticky traps. High populations causing plant damage can be controlled with insecticides. Use a product labeled for controlling whiteflies on indoor plants. Make three applications every five days in a well-ventilated location. You need to start the process over if you miss one application.

Control aphids and mites with insecticidal soap. Spray the upper and lower surface of the leaves and stems. Repeated applications may be needed to control large populations.

Monitor seedlings for damping-off disease. See the February, Problem-Solve section for more information.

BULBS

Many bulbs seem to disappear. Here are some possible causes and solutions. Check soil drainage. Soils that drain poorly or get covered with ice or standing water can cause bulbs to rot.

Review your maintenance practices. If you remove the bulb's leaves right after flowering, you reduce the bulb's capacity to store energy for continued growth. Bulbs without leaves then may disappear completely or struggle to grow.

Squirrels or other animals may be digging and moving bulbs. Animals are the biggest—not only in terms of size but in the amount of damage—bulb pests. You may have saved bulbs from marauding squirrels in the fall, but you now must fend off hungry rabbits and deer. Try a combination of strategies to reduce animal damage. Start applying repellents before the animals start eating. Add nosiemakers and other scare tactics to the mix; or plant animal-resistant bulbs such as allium, daffodils, hyacinths, squills, and grape hyacinths.

EDIBLES

Prepare the garden for planting as soon as the soil

thaws and can be worked. Cover the garden with clear plastic. Wait two to three weeks for the soil to warm and weed seeds to sprout. Remove the plastic and lightly cultivate. Avoid deep hoeing that can bring new weed seeds to the surface. These practices remove many weeds and warm the soil for early planting.

LAWNS

Lightly raking the lawn dries out the grass and reduces problems with snow mold. Tamp down runways formed by vole activity over winter. A light tamp is often enough to get the roots back into the soil, allowing the grass to recover. Severely damaged areas may need to be reseeded. Fill in any holes dug by animals or created by winter activities.

PERENNIALS

Continue to monitor for damping off in seedlings. Watch for collapsing seedlings and stem rot at the soil line. See February, Problem-Solve for management strategies.

ROSES

Continue to monitor and control rabbits, deer, and voles as needed. Reapply animal repellents after heavy rains. Check on vole traps and baits.

Check indoor roses for aphids and mites. Treat with a strong blast of water and insecticidal soap as needed. Repeated applications are usually required.

SHRUBS

Continue to remove and destroy Eastern tent caterpillar egg masses on flowering plums and cherries. The eggs are dark and shiny and appear to be cemented on the branch.

Before growth begins on mugo pines and deciduous shrubs, complete dormant sprays of lime sulfur or dormant oil to control overwintering scale. Check the label before spraying. Make sure the pest and plant to be treated are listed on the label.

Remove and destroy black knots from twigs of ornamental plums and cherries. Destroying the knots now can reduce infection for this growing season. Remove both the black and green knots for best results.

Continue removing any cankered (sunken and discolored) branches on dogwoods.

TREES

Dormant oil sprays can still be applied. Make sure the temperature will be 40 degrees Fahrenheit or warmer when you spray and for the following 12 hours. Dormant oils are used to control some scale insects, galls (mainly an aesthetic concern), and other overwintering insects. Look for bumps caused by galls and discolored or brown leaves caused by mites, aphids, and scale feeding during the growing season. Only spray if a problem exists that requires control and this type of treatment.

Continue to monitor and destroy egg masses of Eastern tent caterpillar, gypsy moth, and tussock moth.

Cankerworms are voracious insects that eat the leaves of oaks, elms, apples, crabapples, and many other trees. These brown or green wormlike insects can be seen munching on tree leaves. Fortunately birds and weather usually keep these pests under control. Severe infestations can be controlled. Apply sticky bands around the trunks of trees that were severely defoliated the previous season. Use a band of fabric treated with a sticky material to avoid injury to the tree. Put sticky traps in place in mid-March through mid-June and in mid-October through mid-December.

Prune out black knot cankers. The cankers start out as swollen areas on the branches of flowering almonds, plums, and cherries. They eventually release disease-causing spores and turn into black knots on the tree. Removing the cankers now reduces the risk of future infection.

VINES & GROUNDCOVERS

Check *Euonymus* now for scale. Mark your calendar so that you remember to treat the scale when the Japanese tree lilac is in bloom (mid- to late June).

April

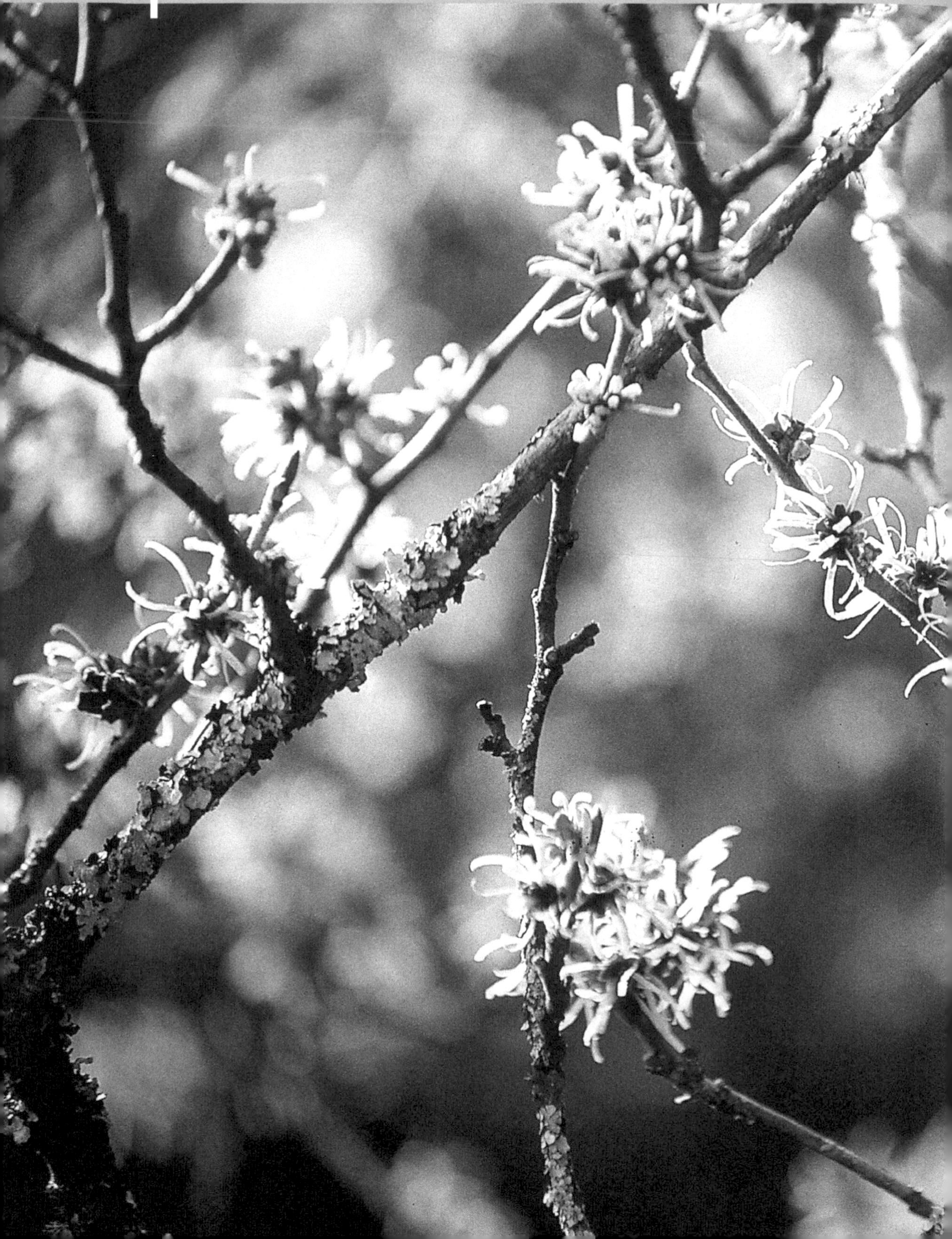

The best-laid plans can be set back by our unpredictable spring weather. Be flexible.

This month, visit local garden centers and greenhouse growers for new ideas on plants to try and combinations to employ. Find a vacant space in the landscape or add a few planters to accommodate these additions to your plan. Please don't succumb to advertisements for fantastic, no-maintenance grasses, groundcovers, and other landscape plants. If it sounds too good to be true, it probably is. Every living thing, plants included, requires some care and attention. Those that can manage on their own are often aggressive or invasive and can take over your landscape and nearby native areas.

Record weather, seed starting dates, bloom times, and other helpful garden information. Compare the current season with last year's garden records. Make needed adjustments in planting time based on current weather and past experience. Refer to these records when extreme weather patterns recur in the future. These events often affect plants later in the growing season. Experience is the best way to improve your gardening skills. Writing down your gardening experiences ensures that you remember them. Photograph or videotape your spring garden. It can make future garden planning much easier. Use your journal, this book, and past experience to help you develop a schedule and strategy for accomplishing your lawn and landscape maintenance tasks throughout the growing season.

Monitor plants for pests and gardens for weeds. Managing them as soon as they appear makes control much easier and more successful. Remove weeds as soon as they appear. Pull or lightly hoe annual weeds. Quackgrass, ground ivy, and bindweed should be pulled and destroyed to prevent rerooting. Consider treating infested gardens with a total vegetation killer prior to planting. Begin preparing the soil for your annuals four to fourteen days after treatment. Be sure to read and follow all label directions.

Those with small-space gardens should try space-saving planting strategies when planning a vegetable garden. Plant in blocks or wide rows instead of single rows. Allow just enough space for plants to reach their mature size, and make sure you can easily reach all the plants for maintenance and harvest. Grow pole beans, cucumbers, and other vine crops on fences, trellises, and other vertical structures to save space, reduce disease, and make harvesting easier.

Plant short-season crops between long-season crops. The short-season plants will be ready for harvest about the time the long-season plants need the extra space. Grow several short-season crops throughout the season in the same row. And don't be afraid to add edibles to your flower garden and mixed borders.

PLAN

ALL

Take a walk through your landscape. Note what survived the winter and what may need replacing. Adjust your landscape plans to accommodate these changes.

Take advantage of rainy days to gather and order materials you'll need this season; then create a tentative schedule for site preparation and planting. Allow time to kill or remove existing weeds and grass, work in needed soil amendments and fertilizer, and get started with early plantings. Locate an area to harden off transplants that is convenient and in plain view so that they won't be forgotten.

ANNUALS

Make sure both the air and soil are warm before planting. Only the seeds of hardy annual plants can tolerate April's cold soils.

BULBS

This is a good time to update existing plans and labels. Mark bulb locations for future plantings and transplanting. Use large, colorful golf tees to mark bulb locations. Draw the locations, and record plant names on your garden map. Color code and number the golf tees to correspond to the map.

LAWNS

Depending on the weather, mowing can begin anytime this month. Make sure your lawn mower is ready to go. See March, Plan for details on preparing your mower for the season.

ROSES

The many bare-root roses on display in local garden centers confirm that the planting season is finally here. Select Grade 1 roses for the best quality. Bare-root roses should be dormant, have firm canes, and be free of pests.

SHRUBS

Make a list of spring-blooming shrubs you have or would like to add to the landscape. Keep in mind that the flowers may only provide a few weeks of interest, while the shrubs remain all year. Consider spring-flowering shrubs that have good fruit effect, fall color, interesting shape, or other ornamental features.

■ *Bulbs planted last fall will provide fabulous color in the spring.*

TREES

Plan a special Arbor Day event for your family, friends, neighborhood, or school group. Arbor Day is the last Friday in April. Plant a tree, mulch existing plantings, or have a picnic under your favorite tree.

VINES & GROUNDCOVERS

The planting season is underway. Record the name, variety, and source for the vines and groundcovers you add to your landscape. Note pruning and trimming done on new and established plants.

PLANT

ANNUALS

Prepare annual gardens for planting using your soil test information as a guide. If this is not available, add 3 pounds per 100 square feet of a low-nitrogen, slow release fertilizer prior to planting. This will provide most, if not all, of the fertilizer your annuals need this season. See the Introduction (on page 10) for information on soil preparation.

HERE'S HOW

TO HARDEN OFF INDOOR-GROWN TRANSPLANTS

1. Move them to a cold frame or protected location two weeks prior to planting.

2. Water thoroughly, but allow the soil to go slightly dry before watering again.

3. Stop fertilizing.

4. At the same time gradually introduce plants to full sun conditions. Start by placing them in a partially shaded location. Give them direct sun for a few hours. Increase the amount of sun the plants receive each day.

5. Cover the transplants or move them into the garage when there is a danger of frost.

6. By the end of two weeks, the plants are ready to plant in the garden.

Consider creating raised beds in poorly drained soils. Use existing soil or bring in new soil to create the raised bed, which can be fancy or strictly utilitarian. See the information about soil preparation on page 10 for more details.

Start seeds for zinnia, marigold, cockscomb, blanket flower (*Gaillardia*), and calendula indoors in early April.

Plant hardened-off cool-season annuals, such as pansies, dusty miller, and snapdragons, outdoors in mid- to late April.

Let the weather and soil temperature be your guides. Keep frost protection such as row covers handy to protect transplants from unexpected drops in temperature.

Transplant seedlings as necessary. Move seedlings from flats to individual containers as soon as the first set of true leaves appear.

BULBS

Finish planting tender bulbs indoors, if you want earlier flowering outdoors this summer. See March, Plant for directions.

Purchase pre-cooled lily and other spring-flowering bulbs, and plant them outdoors as soon as the soil is workable. Hardy lilies need at least six to eight hours of sun and well-drained soils for best results. Work several inches of organic matter into the top 8 to 12 inches of soil. The organic matter improves the drainage of clay soils and the water-holding capacity of sandy soils that all bulbs prefer. Store these bulbs in a cool, dark place such as an extra refrigerator or the coolest corner of your basement until planting. Leave the bulbs packed in peat moss or sawdust in the perforated plastic bag.

EDIBLES

Make room under grow lights for more seedlings. Follow the dates below if you live in southern Michigan. Wait a week or two if you garden in northern regions of the state.

April 1: Plant pepper seeds indoors. Sprout them in a warm location to speed up germination. April 15: Seed tomatoes indoors. Starting earlier results in long, leggy plants that suffer more transplant shock.

Transplant seedlings from flats to single-plant containers. Move the seedlings after they have two sets of leaves. Fill small, clean containers with sterile, well-drained potting mix. Punch a hole large enough to accommodate the seedling's roots in the soil. Place the seedling in the hole and gently tamp the soil to ensure good root-to-soil contact. Water thoroughly until the excess runs out the drainage holes.

April 15 is the start of outdoor planting, depending on the weather and your location. Once the soil is prepared, you can start planting dormant perennial herbs and cool-season vegetable plants outdoors.

Plant asparagus roots 12 inches apart in trenches 36 inches apart. Dig the trenches 6 to 8 inches deep and 9 to 12 inches wide. Set the asparagus in the trench, spreading the roots away from the crown of the plant. Cover with 2 inches of soil. Gradually add soil throughout the season until the trench is filled.

Dig and divide existing rhubarb plants, or plant roots with the crown buds 2 inches below the soil surface. Space the plants 3 feet apart. Grow in full sun to light shade in well-drained soils.

Plant cool-season crop seeds. These include beets, carrots, chard, kohlrabi, leaf lettuce, mustard greens, onion sets, parsnips, peas, potatoes, radishes, salsify, spinach, and turnips. Dig a shallow trench using a hoe handle. Sprinkle seeds in the bottom of the trench. Cover with soil and water thoroughly. See the Planting Chart on page 52.

Get an early start on the rest of your crops by using season-extending techniques. See the planting section in the Introduction for more ideas.

HERE'S HOW

TO PLANT COOL-SEASON CROPS

1   *Root vegetables, such as carrots, parsnips, radishes, turnips, and beets, are easy to grow from seed, as long as you have relatively loose, crumbly soil. If there are lots of rocks in your soil, pick them out before planting. For heavy clay soils, mix organic matter into the top 12 inches, create raised beds and consider growing short carrots for better results.*

2   *Sow the seeds in the garden in single or wide rows according to package spacing instructions. Mix fine seeds with sand or use a seeder to help with proper spacing. Lightly cover the seeds with soil or seed starting mix. Water the seeds often enough to keep the soil slightly moist. As seedlings sprout and grow, water thoroughly whenever the top few inches of soil are crumbly and moist.*

HERE'S HOW

TO PLANT A SALAD BOWL

■ Purchase wide, shallow pots to plant salad bowls, or, if you have an old plastic salad bowl, you can drill holes in the bottom and plant it. Fill the bowl about halfway with potting soil.

■ Fill the lettuce bowl with lettuce seeds or transplants. Use onions, dill, garlic or Swiss chard as vertical accents. Add in some colorful and edible pansies. Check the soil moisture daily. Water thoroughly when needed. You'll need to water more often, possibly twice a day in hot sunny weather.

TO PREPARE A SITE FOR LAYING SOD

1. Prepare the planting site and soil as described in May, Here's How to Seed a Lawn.

2. Calculate the square footage of the area to be sodded. A roll of sod is usually 1½ feet wide by 6 feet long, covering 9 square feet.

3. Order sod to be delivered or plan on picking it up just prior to installation.

4. Select freshly cut sod with good green color. Be sure it is free of weeds and pests. Use sod that has a blend of several grass varieties and is grown on a soil similar to yours.

5. Keep sod in a cool, shady place to prevent it from overheating and drying out. Lay it as soon as possible.

6. Use a driveway, sidewalk, or curb as your starting point. Lay the first row of sod next to the longest of these straight edges. Butt sod ends together and make sure the roots contact the soil. Stagger the seams, as if you were laying bricks. Use a knife to trim the sod to fit.

7. Lay the sod perpendicular to the slope on steep hills. Use wooden stakes to hold it in place.

8. Run an empty lawn roller over the sod to remove air pockets and to ensure good root-to-soil contact. Push it perpendicular to the direction that the sod was laid.

9. Water the sod immediately, moistening it and the top 3 to 4 inches of soil. Keep the sod and soil surface moist until the sod has rooted into the soil below. Continue watering thoroughly but less frequently once this happens. Mow the sod once it is firmly rooted in place and needs cutting.

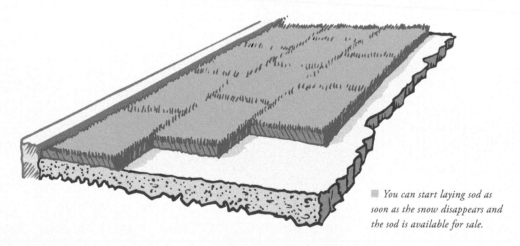

■ *You can start laying sod as soon as the snow disappears and the sod is available for sale.*

LAWNS

Repair damaged areas in the lawn. As the grass greens, it is easier to spot these problems.

You can purchase lawn repair kits or make your own. Purchased kits contain the seed and mulch needed to repair problem areas. Remove the dead turf, loosen and amend soil as needed, and then apply the patch. Make your own lawn patch by mixing a handful of a quality grass-seed mix into a bucket of topsoil. Prepare the soil and spread the seed and soil mixture. Mulch to conserve moisture. See May, Plant for tips on starting a lawn from seed.

Start laying sod as soon as the snow disappears and the sod is available for sale. Site preparation is

HERE'S HOW

TO PLANT BARE-ROOT ROSES

1. Unwrap the roots, and soak them for several hours before planting.

2. Dig a hole 12 inches deep and at least 2 feet wide. Create a cone of soil in the middle of the hole. Tamp down the cone of soil to reduce settling.

3. Remove damaged or broken roots. Drape the roots over the cone so that the graft union will end up 2 inches below the soil surface. Use your shovel or other long-handled tool to check the planting depth. Lay the handle over the hole and make sure the graft is 2 inches below or the crown (the point where it joins the roots) of non-grafted roses is even with the soil surface as indicated by the handle.

4. Fill the planting hole with soil. Water to help settle the soil; add more soil if needed.

5. Mulch the soil with woodchips, shredded bark, or other organic matter.

critical for success and the same whether seeding or sodding a lawn.

PERENNIALS

Start the planting process by properly preparing the soil. See the information about soil preparation on page 10 for details.

Begin planting after the soil is prepared and the plants are available. This is usually the middle to the end of the month in southern areas and late April to early May in the northern areas. Plant dormant bare-root plants as soon as they arrive and the weather permits. Soak the roots several hours prior to planting. Trim off any broken roots. Dig a hole large enough to accommodate the roots. Place the plant in the hole, and spread out the roots. Fill the hole with soil, keeping the crown of the plant (where stem joins the roots) just below the soil surface. Gently tamp and water.

ROSES

Plant and transplant dormant roses after severe weather has passed and before new growth begins.

Proper site preparation is important when transplanting roses. Move plants in early spring before growth begins. Plant dormant bare-root roses in spring after severe weather has passed.

Bare-root roses that began to grow during shipping or while in storage should be potted

■ Be sure to make the hole wider than the roots when planting a bare-root rose.

TO PLANT POTTED ROSES

1. Dig a hole several feet wide and deep enough to plant so the crown of a non-grafted rose is even with the soil surface or the graft union of a grafted rose is 2 inches below the soil surface. Many potted roses are grown with the graft union above the soil. Use care when transplanting potted roses. The root system may not be established.

2. Move the rose near the planting hole. Cut off the bottom of the container. Set the rose, pot and all, in the planting hole. Adjust the planting depth.

3. Slice the side of the pot, and peel it away. This reduces the risk of damaging the developing root system.

4. Backfill the planting hole with the existing soil. Water to help settle the soil.

5. Mulch the soil with a 1- to 3-inch layer of woodchips or shredded bark. The coarser the material used, the thicker the layer of mulch should be.

TO TRANSPLANT ROSES

1. Make sure the soil around the rose is moist, not wet. Water dry soil the night before transplanting roses. Moist soil holds together better during transplanting.

2. Dig out as much of the root system (2 feet or more in diameter) as possible. Make the rootball only as large as you are able to handle.

3. Use your shovel or spading fork to lift the rose out of the planting hole. You may need to cut attached roots with your pruning shears.

4. Slide a plastic or burlap tarp under the rootball. This makes transporting the plant easier and reduces the risk of damaging the rootball.

5. Slide the plant off the tarp and into the planting hole. Plant it at the same depth as it was growing before. The graft on grafted roses should be 2 inches below the soil surface.

6. Fill the hole with soil and water.

and grown in a protected (frost-free) location. These plants can be planted outdoors after the danger of frost has passed.

Potted roses growing in greenhouses need to be hardened off before moving outdoors. Many garden centers will do this for you, but you can do this too; wait until after the danger of frost has passed. See September, Plant for tips on planting shrub roses.

SHRUBS

The growing and planting season has begun. As the soil thaws and temperatures warm, nurseries are busy digging, transporting, and selling shrubs. You can get busy planting. Finish transplanting shrubs before growth begins.

A few catalogs and garden centers sell bare-root shrubs. While they are less expensive, they often have a lower survival rate and require your immediate attention for good results. Store bare-root plants in a cool, shaded location. Pack roots in peat moss and keep them moist. Soak overnight before planting. Place the shrubs in the planting hole so the crown is at or slightly above the soil surface.

Start planting balled-and-burlapped and container-grown shrubs. Plant them with the crown (the point where the roots meet the stem) even with the soil surface. Reduce root damage by cutting away containers, burlap, and twine.

HERE'S HOW

TO PLANT A SHRUB

1. Call 811 to locate underground utilities at least three days prior to digging. Adjust planting locations to avoid underground and overhead utilities.

2. Locate the crown (place where roots and stem meet) and pull away the excess soil covering it. Dig a hole that is the same as or slightly shallower than the depth of the crown to the bottom of the rootball. Make it at least two times as wide as the roots.

3. Roughen the sides of the planting hole to avoid glazing. Smooth-sided holes prevent roots from growing out of the planting hole and into the surrounding soil. Use your shovel or garden fork to nick or scratch the sides of the planting hole.

4. Remove the plant from the container. Potted plants need special care, since their root systems may not be well established in the container. Minimize root disturbance by using the technique described in the preceding Roses section.

5. Loosen the roots of potbound container-grown shrubs. Use a cultivator to loosen or sharp knife to slice through the rootball. Make several shallow slices (running top to bottom of the rootball) through the surface of the roots. This will encourage roots to grow out into the surrounding soil.

HERE'S HOW

TO PLANT BALLED-AND-BURLAPPED SHRUBS

1. Prepare the planting hole as described in Here's How to Plant a Shrub. Place the shrub in the hole. Remove the twine, and peel back the burlap. Cut away the fabric and wire basket.

2. Fill the hole with the existing soil. Use water, not your foot or a heavy tool, to settle the soil.

3. Water the planting hole and surrounding soil. Cover the soil surface with shredded bark or wood-chips to conserve moisture, insulate roots, and reduce weeds.

Check new plantings once or twice a week. Water shrubs in clay soil every seven to ten days. Those growing in sandy soils should be checked twice a week. Water when the top 3 to 4 inches of soil are crumbly and moist. Water thoroughly to moisten the top 12 inches of soil.

Container plants grown in soilless mixes need special attention. These potting mixes dry out faster than the surrounding soils. Check often and keep the root system moist; be careful not to overwater.

Wait until next year to fertilize new plantings. Fertilizer can damage the young tender roots and interfere with establishment.

Remove only branches damaged in the transport and planting process. The more branches left on the plant, the more leaves that will be formed and the more energy will be produced for the plant.

Add new plantings to your landscape plan. Enter the planting information in your journal. Include the plant name, place of purchase, and planting date.

TREES

Start planting trees as soon as they are available. Dig a wide, shallow hole two to five times wider than the rootball and the same depth as the distance from the rootflare to the bottom of the rootball. See the tree planting information on page 208.

HERE'S HOW

TO PLANT VINES & GROUNDCOVERS

1. Dig a hole at least two to three times wider but no deeper than the container.

2. Use the trowel or shovel to roughen up the sides of the planting hole. This eliminates a glazed surface that prevents roots from penetrating the surrounding soil.

3. Gently push on the container sides to loosen the roots. Slide the plant out of the pot. Do not pull it out by the stem. Place the plant in the hole so that the rootball is even with the soil surface. Cut away the pot from the delicate, poorly rooted, or pot-bound plants. Remove the bottom of the container. Place the plant in the hole with the rest of the container still attached so that the rootball is even with or slightly higher than the soil surface. Once the pot is in place, slice through the side of the pot, and peel it away from the rootball. Use special care when planting clematis. Try to protect the plants from breakage. Leave the stakes attached that came with the plants. Use the cut-away pot method to minimize stress on the clematis.

4. Loosen or slice through girdling roots.

5. Fill the hole with the existing soil. Water to settle the soil and eliminate air pockets.

6. Mulch the plants with shredded bark, woodchips, or other organic matter.

VINES & GROUNDCOVERS

Prepare the soil for planting. See page 10 in the Introduction for details on preparing soil.

Plant bare-root plants as soon as they arrive. Pack the roots in moist peat, and keep the plants in a cool, frost-free location until planted. Plant so that the crown (the point where the stem joins the roots) is even with the soil.

Thinning your new seedlings allows the strongest ones to survive and thrive.

CARE

ANNUALS

Adjust indoor grow lights so they about 6 inches above the tops of seedlings. Lower the lights if seedlings are long and leggy. Raise the lights as seedlings grow. Check seedlings and transplants growing in cold frames. Open the lid on sunny days to prevent heat buildup. Lower the lid in late afternoon to protect cold-sensitive plants from cold nights. Consider purchasing an automatic ventilation system to make your job easier.

Prune back leggy annuals as needed. Use the cuttings to start additional plants for this summer's garden.

BULBS

Remove forced bulbs from storage. Use some for indoor enjoyment. Move a few of the potted bulbs from cold storage directly outdoors to planters and window boxes. This is a great way to brighten up drab areas and create a surprise in the landscape.

Remove winter mulch as the bulbs begin to grow and the weather consistently hovers near freezing. Northern gardeners may want to keep a little mulch handy in case of sudden and extreme drops in temperature.

Replant or firm frost-heaved bulbs back into place.

Leave the leaves on tulips, daffodils, and other bulbs intact. They are manufacturing the energy needed for plants to grow and bloom next season.

Remove faded flowers. Deadheading hybrid tulips and hyacinths helps to lengthen their lifespan. Deadhead other bulbs for aesthetic reasons.

EDIBLES

Prepare the garden for planting. Work the soil as soon as the ground thaws and the soil is ready. Add needed fertilizer and amendments.

Begin hardening off transplants two weeks before planting them outdoors. See page 67.

Begin harvesting three-year and older asparagus when spears are 6 to 8 inches long. Snap or cut the spears off below the soil surface. Harvest three-year-old plantings for just one month. Four-year and older plantings can be harvested for six to eight weeks through May or June.

Harvest established rhubarb for six to eight weeks. See May, Care for details.

Examine lavender, sage, and thyme for winter damage. Healthy buds look firm and plump and branches are pliable. Wait for new growth to begin. Remove dead tips and trim as needed. Always leave some healthy buds for new growth.

LAWNS

Rake out any dead grass and be patient. Wait for grass roots to resprout and surrounding grass to fill in. Reseed bare spots in late April and early to mid-May.

Start mowing as soon as the grass greens and starts to grow. Keep the grass no shorter than 2½ inches tall but preferably 3 to 3½ inches tall. Taller grass forms a deeper root system. Stronger plants are better able to fight off insects, disease, and weeds.

Mow often enough that you remove no more than one-third of the total height. You may need to cut the grass several times a week in the spring. This practice reduces the stress on the plants. The shorter clippings can be left on the lawn to add nitrogen, moisture, and organic matter to the soil. Vary the direction and pattern of mowing to reduce the wear and tear on the lawn.

PERENNIALS

Continue removing winter mulch as temperatures consistently hover near or above freezing. Remove mulch as soon as plants begin growing, but keep some mulch handy to protect tender plants from sudden and extreme drops in temperature.

Finish cleanup early in the month. Cut dead stems back to ground level and remove dead leaves on evergreen plants. See March, Care for more details.

Use a cold frame or row covers for starting seeds outdoors and hardening off transplants.

HERE'S HOW

TO FIX BARE SPOTS IN THE LAWN

1. Start by loosening the soil surface. Use a hand rake to spread compost, topsoil, or garden soil in a ½-inch layer covering the bare spot. While you can sow seeds directly in the bare spots, the grass will sprout more quickly and won't dry out as easily if it can start growing in loose, fresh soil.

2. Use a hand spreader to spread grass seed thickly and evenly over the entire area, slightly overlapping the edges of the grass that aren't covered with soil. When you're done seeding, the ground should look like it snowed lightly.

3. Sprinkle weed-free straw, which you can get at garden centers and home-improvement stores, over the newly seeded area. The straw mulch helps keep the soil moist and will increase your success.

4. Water the newly seeded areas several times a day or as often as needed to keep the seed and top few inches of soil moist. Continue until the grass begins to grow. Then water the newly seeded areas thoroughly but less often. Water when the top few inches of soil are crumbly and moist. This encourages deep roots that are more drought tolerant and pest resistant. Wait until the grass is actively growing and has reached full size before mowing. Grass seedlings are fragile and can be damaged by mowers and foot traffic.

HERE'S HOW

TO DIVIDE PERENNIALS

1. *Tie up tall shoots or cut back mature plants by one-half to two-thirds if needed.*

2. *Use a shovel or garden fork to dig up the perennial. Dig out the clump, and place it next to the hole.*

3. *Use a knife or two shovels to divide the clump into several pieces.*

4. *Prepare the new planting location. Amend the existing area by working compost, peat moss, or other organic matter into the soil. Plant one of the divisions in the original location. Water thoroughly. Check every few days, and water whenever the top 4 inches of soil begin to dry.*

GUIDELINES FOR PRUNING VINES & GROUNDCOVERS

- *English ivy (groundcover): Prune in early spring. For established plants, use a mower or hedge shears to control growth.

- *Wintercreeper (groundcover): Prune in early spring. Cut established plants back to 4 to 8 inches to encourage vigorous, dense growth. Use a hedge clipper or a mower adjusted to its highest setting.

- Juniper: (groundcover): Prune in early spring or early to mid-July. Remove dead branches and shape.

- American Bittersweet (vine): Prune in winter or early spring. Prune to train young stems to climb the plant support. For established plants, trim to control size. Cut overly long shoots back to three to four buds from the main stem. Prune back large shoots to 12 to 16 inches above ground level.

- Boston ivy and Virginia creeper (vines): Prune during the dormant season. After planting, train young stems to their supports. For established plants, prune to control growth and keep them inbounds. Remove or shorten any stems that are growing away from their support. Renovate overgrown plants by pruning them back to 3 feet of the base.

- *English ivy (vine): Prune in late winter or early spring. After planting, pinch back weak stems to encourage new growth. For established plants, remove dead tips and stems killed over winter. Remove any wayward growth back to a healthy bud.

- *Euonymus (vine): Prune in mid- to late spring. For young plants, tip prune to encourage fuller growth. For established plants, remove old and dead wood.

- Five-leaf akebia: Prune after flowering. After planting, cut back to strong buds about 12 to 16 inches above the ground. Train five to seven strong shoots on the support. Next spring, prune laterals by one-third and weak laterals back to one or two buds. For established plants, shorten growth by one-third to one-half to control its size. Occasionally remove an old stem to ground level.

- Grapes: Prune in late March or early April. See Pruning Tips on page 213 for more information.

- Hardy kiwi: Prune in late winter or early spring. Follow the pruning guidelines for five-leaf akebia.

- Honeysuckle (vine): Prune in early spring. After planting, cut back young plants by two-thirds. Next year, select strong shoots to form a framework. Remove other shoots. For established plants, prune the tips of shoots that have reached the desired height. Cut off overly long shoots to healthy buds. Renovate overgrown plants by pruning stems back to 2 feet above the ground.

- Trumpet vine: Prune in late winter or early spring. After planting, prune all stems back to 6 inches above ground level. Remove all but two or three of the strongest shoots. Train these stems to the support. For established plants, prune yearly to control growth. Remove weak and damaged stems to the main framework. Cut the side shoots back to two or three buds from the main stems forming the framework. Prune out dead main branches to the base. Train the strongest shoot to replace it. Renovate by cutting all growth back to 12 inches above the ground.

- Wisteria: At planting, cut back the main stem (leader) to a strong bud about 30 to 36 inches above ground level. Train two strong side shoots (laterals) over the fence, trellis, or arbor. Next spring, prune the leader back to 30 inches above the topmost lateral branch. Shorten the laterals by one-third of their total lengths. Select another pair of laterals to grow and help cover the trellis. Next winter, cut the leader back to 30 inches above the uppermost lateral. Then prune all the laterals back by one-third. Repeat each winter until the plant reaches full size. Prune established plants in early summer right after flowering. Cut offshoots (small branches) back to within five or six buds of a main branch.

*Consider replacing these invasive plants.

Watch for late-emerging perennials, such as butterfly weed and hardy hibiscus. Use a plant label or consider adding spring-flowering bulbs next fall to mark their locations. This helps you avoid damaging them in the spring.

Overgrown perennials fail to bloom, open in the center, and tend to flop. Dig and divide overgrown perennials in early spring as new growth is emerging or in early September. The old saying "divide fall bloomers in spring and spring bloomers in fall and summer bloomers at either time" applies. But with experience you will find most perennials are tough and can be divided at other times during the season as long as proper post-transplant care is provided.

ROSES

Start or continue removing winter protection as the temperatures consistently hover near freezing. Remove protection gradually. Continue to vent rose cones on warm sunny days until all protection is removed.

Tip climbers and tree roses back into an upright position if they're buried for winter using the Minnesota Tip Method. See Rose Protection on page 179. Firm the soil around the roots and water. Attach climbing roses to trellises and tree roses to stakes as needed.

Move stored roses out of storage after severe weather has passed.

Indoor roses need to remain indoors. Their tender leaves are not ready for the unpredictable and often cold days of April.

Assess animal and winter damage. Remove only dead and damaged canes on climbers and old roses. These roses bloom on the previous season's growth. Major pruning is done after flowering.

Prune hybrid tea and other modern roses just before growth begins. Remove old, dead and winter damaged canes and tips on repeat-blooming shrub roses. Living canes are green with white pith in the center. Prune at least 1 inch below the darkened dead tissue. Cut each cane at a 45-degree angle above a healthy,

outward-facing bud. Remove all spindly weak growth, crossing stems, and canes growing toward the center of the plant. Prune out any suckers that grow from beneath the graft. Cut them off below the ground near the rootstock. Shape the plant to 16 to 18 inches tall.

After severe winters, there may be nothing left to shape after you remove all the winter damage. Wait to see what survives on plants that die back to ground level.

SHRUBS

Move aboveground planters out of winter storage. Wait until temperatures hover around freezing if the leaves have begun to grow.

Remove and store winter protection. Make notes of any changes in winter protection that need to be made for next season.

Finish dormant pruning of summer- and fall-blooming shrubs before growth begins. See Pruning Shrubs on page 211 for more details. Wait until after flowering to prune spring bloomers.

TREES

Remove screening, cloth strapping, and other winter protection. Hardware cloth fencing can stay in place. Make sure the material is not rubbing or girdling the plant.

Remove winter insulation such as bales of straw or move trees growing in aboveground planters out of winter storage.

Renew the mulch around trees in lawn areas and planting beds. Maintain no more than a 2- to 3-inch layer of shredded bark or woodchip mulch to conserve moisture, reduce weeds, and add organic matter. Keep the mulch away from the trunk of the tree. Freshen existing mulch by turning with a garden fork.

Keep lawn mowers and weed whips away from tree trunks. Mower blight (tree decline due to equipment damage) is the biggest killer of trees. Mulch, groundcovers, or planting beds reduce the need to hand trim and protect trees from mowing equipment.

Do not prune after the buds open and the leaves begin to grow. The tree is very susceptible to damage during this phase of growth. Resume pruning once the leaves are fully expanded.

Do not prune oaks once growth begins to reduce the risk of oak wilt disease.

WATER

ANNUALS

Keep potted annuals, seedlings, and transplants growing and thriving with proper watering. Check seedlings and young transplants daily. Water potted annuals thoroughly every time the top few inches of soil start to dry.

Check plants growing outdoors in a cold frame or garden. Water only when the soil is slightly dry. Overwatering can lead to root rot.

Thoroughly water any trees, shrubs, perennials, and lawn areas exposed to deicing materials. Heavy spring showers or a thorough watering will help wash these materials through the soil and away from the roots.

BULBS

Water indoor plants as needed. Keep the soil of newly planted tender bulbs and blooming plants moist. Continue to water forced bulbs thoroughly as the soil just starts to dry.

Outdoor bulb plantings may need to be watered in a dry spring. Water when the bulbs show signs of wilting. Water thoroughly with 1 inch or enough water to moisten the top 6 to 8 inches of soil.

EDIBLES

Keep the soil moist for seedlings growing indoors and out. Water thoroughly enough to moisten all the soil in the container or the top 2 to 3 inches outdoors.

Check new plantings of rhubarb and asparagus several times a week. Wet the top 4 to 6 inches of soil for rhubarb and 8 inches for asparagus (the root zone). Water whenever this area begins to dry.

LAWNS

Water newly sodded or recently seeded areas of the lawn. Keep the soil surface moist in these areas.

PERENNIALS

Thoroughly water transplants and divisions at the time of planting. Water when the top few inches of soil begin to dry. Always water thoroughly enough to wet the top 4 to 6 inches of soil. Reduce watering frequency as the plants become established.

ROSES

Begin watering when winter protection is off and the ground begins to dry. Established roses need about 1 inch of water each week. Cool, wet spring weather often eliminates or reduces the need to water. Apply water in one application each week in clay soils and in two applications in sandy soils.

As roses are moved out of storage, they need more frequent watering. Check plants daily and water as the soil dries. Keep the soil moist around newly planted roses. Once the plants are established, water deeply and less frequently.

With the increase in light, indoor roses may need more frequent watering. Adjust your watering schedule so the soil stays slightly moist.

SHRUBS

New plantings should be watered often enough to keep the top 6 to 8 inches of the soil moist. Water thoroughly, then wait until the soil is crumbly but moist before watering again. Check clay soils weekly and sandy soils twice a week.

Established shrubs only need supplemental water in dry weather. Water thoroughly when the top 4 to 6 inches begin to dry.

TREES

Water trees when the ground thaws and the soil is dry. Established trees need watering only during dry periods. Thoroughly soak the area under the drip line when the top 6 to 8 inches of soil are moist and crumbly. Apply 1 to 2 inches of water (about 10 gallons per inch diameter of trunk). Water more often with sandy soils and during high temperatures.

Water new plantings often enough to keep the rootball and surrounding soil slightly moist. Provide 1 inch of water when the top 6 to 10 inches are moist and crumbly. This may be several times each week in sandy and gravelly soil and as little as every two weeks in clay soils. Check container-grown plants several times a week. Water the rootball often enough to keep it moist. Water surrounding soil as needed.

Continue to water trees in aboveground planters. Water until the excess drains out of the bottom of the pot. Check containers at least twice a week.

VINES & GROUNDCOVERS

Continue to water as described in March and May, depending on the weather. Keep the soil moist around new plants.

FERTILIZE

ANNUALS

Incorporate fertilizer into the soil before planting. Follow soil test recommendations. If these are not available, apply 3 pounds of a slow-release, low-nitrogen fertilizer per 100 square feet. You'll provide most if not all the nutrients your plants need for the season without the risk of burn.

Continue fertilizing indoor plants and transplants every two weeks. Use a dilute solution of any complete water-soluble fertilizer.

BULBS

Most bulbs get sufficient nutrients from the garden soil. Fertilization can help increase flowering and vigor. Use a low-nitrogen fertilizer once in spring as they begin to sprout. Do not fertilize if it was done last fall.

■ *When using a slow-release fertilizer, you'll only need to apply once at the start of the season. A second application may be needed for containers and annual plantings.*

EDIBLES

Apply fertilizer during the soil preparation just prior to planting. Make one application of a low-nitrogen, slow-release fertilizer in spring for season-long benefits. Additional applications can be made as needed for individual crops.

Apply a slow-release, low-nitrogen fertilizer or spread well-rotted manure around rhubarb in the spring before growth begins; or wait until after harvest (June) to apply fertilizer.

Fertilize young (one to three years old) asparagus plantings with the rest of the garden. Add 1 pound of a low-nitrogen fertilizer per 100 square feet of garden. Wait until after the final harvest to fertilize four-year and older plantings.

LAWNS

Wait until late May to fertilize lawns. Fertilizing now means more grass to cut, and the lush, succulent spring growth is more susceptible to disease.

PERENNIALS

Perennials grown in properly amended soil need very little fertilizer. Topdressing with an inch or two of compost every other year is often enough to keep most perennials healthy and well fed.

Always follow soil test recommendations before fertilizing. Use a low-nitrogen, slow-release fertilizer if you feel a nutrient boost is needed.

ROSES

Fertilize old garden, shrub, species, and climbing roses as the buds begin to swell. Start with a soil test to determine how much and what type of fertilizer your roses need. Our soils are generally high to excessive in phosphorus and potassium. Adding more of these elements can interfere with the uptake of other nutrients.

Apply a low-nitrogen (5 to 6 percent), slow-release fertilizer at a rate of 2 pounds per 100 square feet or 2 heaping tablespoons per plant.

Use a complete fertilizer—one that contains nitrogen, phosphorus, and potassium—such as

5-10-10 or 6-12-12 only if a soil test indicates all three elements are needed.

Fertilize repeat-blooming old roses in early spring and again after their first bloom period.

Wait to fertilize hybrid tea roses until after the new spring growth has developed. Reapply every five to six weeks. Stop fertilizing August 1. Late-season fertilization leads to late-season growth that is more likely to be killed over the winter.

Apply the recommended amount of fertilizer twice as often to container roses. Stop fertilizing by August.

SHRUBS

Wait a year or two before fertilizing new shrub plantings. Use your soil test as a guide to fertilizing existing plantings.

Apply fertilizer if needed once in spring or early summer. Additional applications are not needed, because most shrubs put out one flush of growth a year. Fertilize young shrubs every couple of years to promote rapid growth. Established shrubs need infrequent or no fertilizer. They receive nutrients from grass clippings left on lawn, organic mulches as they decompose, and fertilizer applied to nearby plants.

Apply 1 to 2 pounds per 100 square feet of a low-nitrogen fertilizer if soil test results are not available. Try a slow-release formulation to reduce risk of overfertilizing, burn, and to improve results.

TREES

Spring—before growth begins—is a good time to fertilize established trees in need of a nutrient boost. Let the plant and a soil test be your guides. Trees often get nutrients from decomposing mulch, lawn fertilizers, and grass clippings left on the lawn.

Check trees for signs of nutrient deficiencies. Poor growth and off-color leaves may indicate the need to fertilize. Wait a year to fertilize new tree plantings. They have been well tended in the nursery, and fertilizer may harm the newly developing roots.

If soil tests are not available, use a slow-release fertilizer with little or no phosphorous and potassium, as our soils tend to be high or excessive in these nutrients. Follow label directions or apply 2 to 3 pounds of actual nitrogen per 1,000 square feet. This is equal to 20 to 30 pounds of a 10-percent-nitrogen fertilizer.

Fertilizer can be sprinkled over and raked through mulch. Place fertilizer in the soil for trees growing in lawn areas. Punch a hole in the ground with a long screwdriver or remove small cores of soil 6 inches deep and 2 to 3 feet apart throughout the area around the tree. Holes should start several feet away from the trunk and continue several feet beyond the drip line of the tree. Divide needed fertilizer evenly between the holes. Water until the top 12 inches of soil are moist.

VINES & GROUNDCOVERS

Incorporate fertilizer into the soil as indicated by a soil test, prior to planting. Fertilize existing plants in spring before growth begins. See March, Fertilize for details.

PROBLEM-SOLVE

ANNUALS

Continue monitoring and controlling mites, aphids, and whiteflies on indoor plants. Spray the upper and lower surfaces of leaves and stems with insecticidal soap to control high populations of aphids and mites. Repeat as needed. Try trapping whiteflies with commercial or homemade yellow sticky traps. See December, Problem-Solve for additional details.

Avoid damping-off disease by starting with clean containers, sterile starting mix, and providing watering, proper germination conditions, and care of seedlings. Use a fungicide soil drench to treat infected flats.

BULBS

Continue to monitor and manage animal damage and disappearing bulbs. Try a mixture of repellents and scare tactics or replace with animal-resistant bulbs listed in March, Problem-Solve.

Bud blast causes brown, dry, and failed daffodil flower buds. It appears to be more common on late-blooming and double-flowering cultivars. Extreme temperature fluctuations, inadequate water, and wet fall seasons have been blamed for this disorder. Adjust care and replace varieties that continually suffer from this disorder.

Frost can damage daffodil buds and prevent them from fully developing. The emerging flower stalks of daffodils are often overlooked in spring. A cold snap can damage the tender buds. Plant later-blooming daffodil varieties or mulch the bulbs next fall to prevent early sprouting.

Proper sanitation in the fall prevents iris borers. If this wasn't done, and borers have been a problem, you may want to use an insecticide. Read and follow label directions; these pesticides should be handled carefully. Apply an insecticide labeled for use on iris borers when the leaves are 4 to 6 inches tall. Later applications are not effective, as the borers are safely inside and eating. Or, go online and order beneficial nematodes. Purchase those known to control iris borer, and follow label directions. Not sure you have borers? Make a note in your journal to dig and divide declining iris 6 to 8 weeks after flowering. Check the rhizomes, cut out the borers, if found, and the surrounding tissue before replanting. Monitor these for future problems.

EDIBLES

Protect new plantings from birds and animals. Spread bird netting or season-extending fabric over the garden. Anchor the sides securely. This keeps birds out and may discourage other animals.

Install a chickenwire or hardware cloth fence around the garden. Make the fence at least 4 feet high and tight to the ground to keep out rabbits. Bury at least 12, but preferably 18, inches of the fence into the ground to discourage woodchucks.

Repellents labeled for use in food gardens may be used, or try placing slivers of deodorant soap or handfuls of hair in old nylon stockings throughout the garden. The smell may discourage animals.

■ *Fine netting can be used to protect vegetables from birds and animals.*

LAWNS

Prevent crabgrass problems with proper care. Keep the lawn grass tall and water during droughts. If this has not worked, you may choose to use a crabgrass pre-emergent. Iowa State University discovered that corn gluten meal makes a good organic pre-emergent for preventing crabgrass and other plants from germinating. You can reduce lawn weeds by as much as 80 percent after three years of spring and fall applications of corn gluten meal.

Apply crabgrass pre-emergents to problem areas, about the time that the Vanhoutte (bridal wreath) spirea start to bloom or lilac buds swell, usually in late April or early May when soil temperature is 50 degrees Fahrenheit. Do not use these products if you plan to seed or overseed the lawn this spring. Pre-emergents will kill the desirable grass seeds as well as the weed seeds.

Michigan lawns are not prone to many damaging insects. Be sure that insects are causing damage before you use an insecticide. Unnecessary use of pesticides kills the beneficial insects that create a good growing environment for the lawn.

This is the time to watch for adult billbugs. These small insects can be seen on the sidewalks. Treat them only if your lawn has suffered from browning or dieback that you know was caused by this insect.

PERENNIALS

Complete garden cleanup. Sanitation is the best defense against pest problems. Inspect new growth for signs of pests. Remove insects and disease-infested leaves as soon as they are found. Make this a regular part of your gardening routine.

Use netting and repellents to protect emerging plants from animal damage. Start early to encourage animals to go elsewhere to feed. Reapply repellents after severe weather or as recommended on label directions.

ROSES

Seal fresh pruning cuts to prevent cane borer. This is particularly important for roses with a history of this pest. Dab cut ends with pruning paint, yellow shellac, or white glue to prevent the borer from entering through openings.

The bud graft (the swollen portion of the stem of a rose grafted onto hardier rootstock) may die due to extremely harsh weather, improper winter protection, or shallow planting. If the bud graft dies, the rootstock, a different rose entirely, takes over. Look for these signs if you suspect the bud graft has died: Canes are thicker, with more thorns and fewer leaves; the plant fails to bloom or produces flowers that are different. If this happens, replace the rose with a hardier shrub rose, hybrid tea rose on its own rootstock, or a rose with the graft 2 inches below the soil surface.

SHRUBS

Continue to locate and destroy egg masses of Eastern tent caterpillars. The eggs hatch and the caterpillars start building their webbed tents when the saucer magnolias (*Magnolia soulangeana*) are in the pink bud stage. Prune out and destroy tents as they are found.

Do not apply dormant sprays once growth begins. These products can cause more damage to the expanding growth than the insects you are trying to control.

Watch for European pine sawflies on mugo and some of the other pines when saucer magnolias (*Magnolia soulangeana*) begin dropping their petals. These wormlike insects feed in large groups, devouring pine needles one branch at a time. Smash them with a leather glove–clad hand or prune out and destroy the infested branch.

Finish pruning off any green and black knots on flowering cherries, almonds, and plums.

TREES

Reduce the spread of spruce gall on small trees. Prune out any small swollen sections that resemble miniature cones or pineapples on the stem while they are green and the insects are still nesting inside.

Start checking crabapples, birches, and other ornamental trees in late April for signs of Eastern tent caterpillars. These wormlike insects build webbed nests in the crotches of tree branches. Remove or destroy the tent to control this pest.

Birch leaf miners are insects that feed between the upper and lower surface of the leaves. Their feeding causes the leaves to turn brown. They do not kill the tree but add to its stress, making the white-barked birches more susceptible to borers. A soil systemic labeled for use on birches to control leaf miner can be applied in fall to prevent infestations. This also controls Japanese beetles that attack these trees. Make a note to apply it later if you see problems now.

Dead branch tips on your Austrian pine may mean it has Zimmerman moth. Consult a certified arborist for advice and treatment. Spray applications should be made when the saucer magnolia (*Magnolia soulangiana*) is in the pink bud stage.

Apple scab is a common problem on crabapples and apples. This fungal disease causes black spots and eventual leaf drop. Raking and destroying infected leaves reduces the source of disease. Fungicides labeled to control apple scab on crabapples reduce infection on susceptible trees. You need four to five applications, 10 to 15 days apart, starting at pink bud stage. Consider hiring an arborist with the training and equipment to do the job safely. Better yet, replace susceptible trees with more disease-resistant cultivars.

Dead branches on spruce are often caused by *Cytospora* canker. You'll also notice a white substance on the trunk and branches. Remove branches that are infected and disinfect tools between cuts with rubbing alcohol or a solution of one part bleach to nine parts water. Mulch the soil under the tree and water during dry periods. *Rhizosphaera* needle cast is a major problem on Colorado spruce. Get out the hand lens and look for rows of small black spots on infected needles. Fungicides applied every three to four weeks during wet weather can prevent spread of the disease. Keep in mind that timing and complete coverage are critical for successful control. Consult a tree care professional if you plan to treat.

VINES & GROUNDCOVERS

Pull weeds as soon as they appear.

May

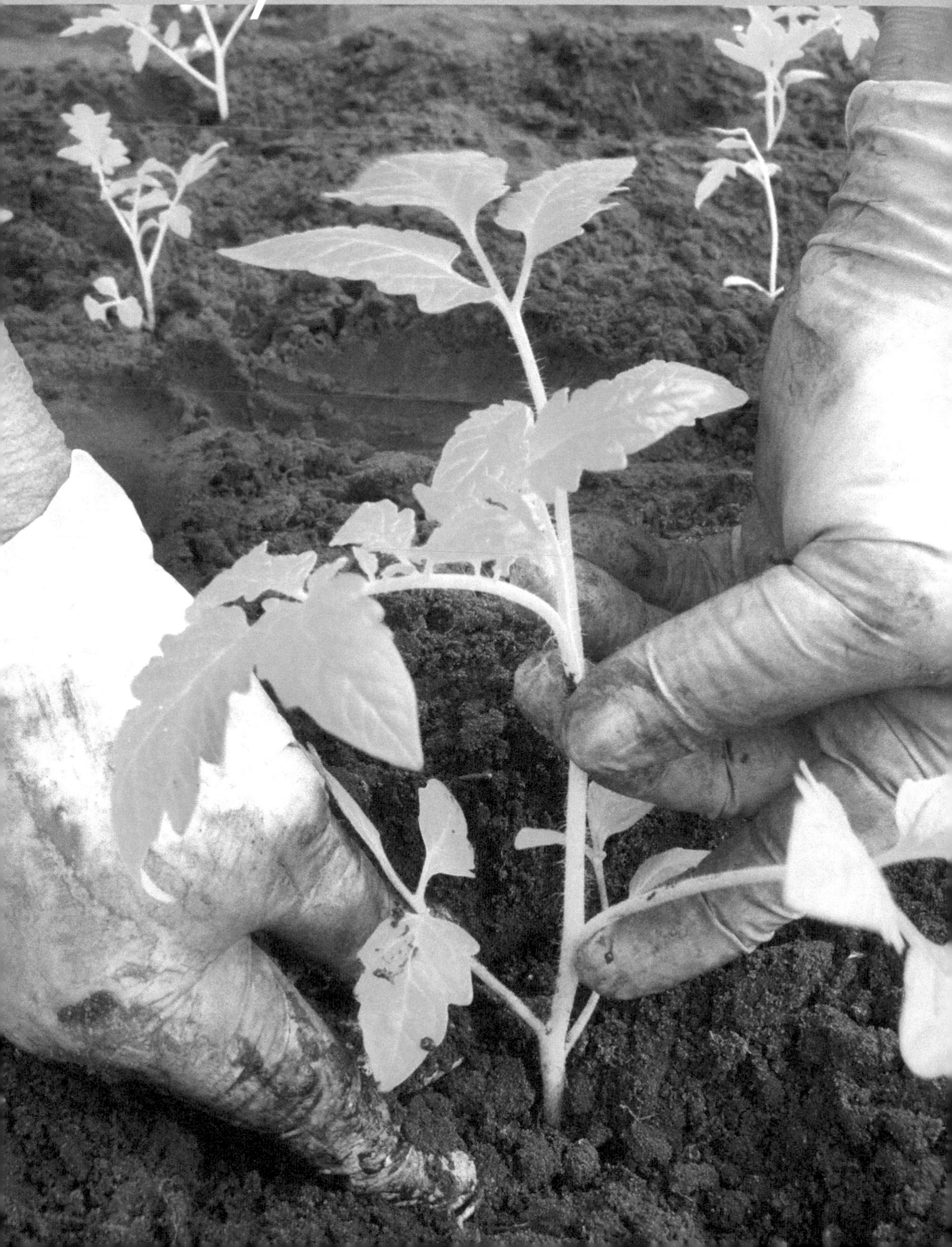

The growing season is finally becoming a reality and that means more opportunity to garden. Be sure to wear sunscreen, a hat, sunglasses, and gloves. You'll protect your skin and eyes from harmful UV rays and hands from cuts and scratches.

Further increase your enjoyment, extend your energy, and avoid muscle strain by gardening wisely. Do some gentle back and body stretches before working in the garden. Take frequent breaks throughout the day, and drink plenty of water. Then ask for help or use equipment to move heavy loads. Invest in a garden cart, wheelbarrow, or a "pot lifter." Or, convert a child's wagon, old snow saucer, or golf cart into a tool caddy or cart.

Keep tools handy with the help of a tool caddy, bucket, or wheeled trashcan. Convert an old mailbox into a storage space for hand tools, and install it in distant garden beds. And use the right tool for the task. You'll conserve energy and avoid injury while ensuring the health and beauty of your landscape by using the proper tools.

Hopefully you made a plan before you started plant shopping and planting. Visiting a garden center in spring is like grocery shopping when you're hungry. A list helps curb your plant-buying appetite. If you had a plan but the labels and pictures of other plants, new varieties, and sale plants were too tempting to resist, join the club! With some creativity you can find a space or container for those extra plants.

Just be sure to inventory and reevaluate planting space and garden locations after each trip. And check the growing conditions and your planting plans before your next trip to the garden center or nursery.

Keep your landscape plan and garden journal handy. Record purchases and new additions to the garden. Use a rainy spring day to catch up on your garden records and update landscape plans to include all those new additions. Record the name, variety, source, and planting information for each added plant.

Enjoy the spring blooms, and use your camera to record your spring garden's beauty and make plans for new additions.

And though spring often means plenty of rain, you may still need to lend a hand in dry years or with new plantings. Consider installing rain barrels to capture rainfall and soaker hoses or drip irrigation to help you conserve water and make watering now and throughout the hot, dry months more convenient.

MAY

PLAN

ALL

Use your landscape and garden design as a working document. We all make changes to our plans. Sometimes the plants we wanted are not available—and then there are those few unplanned additions that we just could not resist at the garden center. It is all too easy to succumb to temptation and end up with too many or the wrong type of plants for the available space.

If you do end up with extra plants but no space, tuck them into containers, or share with a friend. My daughter often "shops" for her plants in the overflow on my patio. And I often justify my extra plants by sharing them with her and others.

ANNUALS

Take a walk around your landscape and reevaluate the sun and shade patterns in the yard. These conditions change with each season and over time. Make any needed adjustments in your plans.

And if you did not already calculate the number of plants needed for this year's garden, do so before heading out on your plant shopping expeditions. See page 52 for tips on calculating the number of plants needed.

BULBS

Identify possible planting locations for fall additions of spring-flowering bulbs. This will reduce stress and improve results during the fall scramble to get bulbs into the ground.

Finalize summer bulb garden plans. Consider using tender bulbs such as dahlias and cannas to fill voids left by early bloomers or winter-killed plants. Use them in containers to dress up the steps, patio, or other areas that lack planting space.

As bulbs fade, plan how to deal with the fading foliage. Do not remove the leaves until they naturally decline. Try these ways to mask their untidy appearance:

Plant annuals between bulbs. Pansies are a nice choice for an early season display. Plant cold-hardy pansies in fall and watch for their spring return, or select a heat-tolerant pansy or other annuals. You'll cover the fading foliage and add more variety.

Mix bulbs with perennials. As the bulb foliage declines, perennials start growing and hide the leaves. You also avoid digging and disturbing bulbs with yearly planting.

Your local garden center will have a wide variety of herbs for you to choose from in May.

Tie foliage with string or rubber bands. This is not the best for the plant but may be an acceptable compromise between aesthetics and plant health.

Treat them like annuals. Remove the foliage and flowers right after bloom. Plant new bulbs each fall, or leave the foliage intact, dig, and share with a friend. You won't have to look too far to find gardeners willing to add them to their landscape.

EDIBLES
Look for ways to add edibles to your landscape. Use strawberries as an edible groundcover in sunny locations and Swiss chard as an annual option for shady areas. Include a tomato, pepper, or eggplant with colorful fruit in containers and flowerbeds.

LAWNS
Monitor the health and vigor of your grass as you work your way through the landscape. Watch for changes in color, density, and overall vigor. Problems caught early are easier to control. Contact a lawncare professional or your local Michigan State University Extension Service or website for help diagnosing problems.

ROSES
Evaluate the health and survival rate of existing roses. You may need to purchase some replacement plants for those that were killed over the winter. Wait for signs of new growth. The aboveground growth may be dead, but the graft (on grafted plants) and roots may still be alive. Watch for signs of new growth emerging from roots or above the graft union on grafted roses.

PLANT

ANNUALS
Continue planting cool-season annuals. Plant half-hardy annuals in the garden after the danger of a hard frost has passed. See the frost charts on pages 218 to 221. Wait until both the air and the soil are warm to plant tender annuals like coleus, usually in late May in southern regions and early June in northern areas.

Proper soil preparation is critical to planting success. Add organic matter and fertilizer to the top 6 to

■ May is the time to really start "digging in" to your garden.

12 inches of garden soil. Rake it smooth and allow the soil to settle.

Harden off indoor-grown transplants prior to placing in the garden. Two weeks prior to planting, allow soil to dry slightly before watering again, and stop fertilizing. Move transplants outdoors to a protected location. Cold frames and row covers can help in this process. Give plants several hours of direct sun. Increase the amount of sun each day. Cover or move transplants into the garage in case of frost.

Carefully remove transplants from their containers. Squeeze the container and slide the plant out of it. Do not pull it out by the stem. Gently and ever so slightly loosen the roots of rootbound transplants. Place annuals in the soil at the same depth they were growing in the pot. Cover with soil, and gently tamp to remove air pockets.

HERE'S HOW

TO SOW SEEDS OUTSIDE

1. Use a trowel or tool handle to dig a 1- to 2-inch deep furrow in properly prepared soil.

2. Plant seeds according to label directions. Most seed packets recommend planting the seeds closer than their final spacing. If all the seeds successfully sprout and grow, thin out excess plants by transplanting or clipping off excess seedlings. The remaining seedlings will then have room to reach full size. Check the packet for thinning and final spacing recommendations.

3. Cover with soil and gently tamp to ensure good seed-to-soil contact. You can use a seed starting mix to cover fine seeds like carrots. Gently water. Keep soil moist until the seeds sprout.

4. Label the rows to make identification of seedlings for thinning and weeding easier.

Space plants according to the directions on the plant tag. Do not crowd annuals. Overplanting reduces air circulation and increases the risk of disease problems. Use excess plants for container gardens, herb gardens, shrub beds, or to fill bare spots in perennial gardens; or share them with a friend or neighbor so you both get to enjoy them.

Remove flowers and cut back leggy annuals at the time of planting. This encourages root development, branching, and better looking, healthier plants in the long run. Can't stand to remove those beautiful flowers? Remove the flowers on every other plant or every other row at planting. Remove the remaining flowers the following week so it won't seem so long before the new flowers appear.

BULBS

Prepare the soil before planting tender bulbs outdoors. Add organic matter to the top 8 to 12 inches of soil. Once the soil warms, you can begin planting.

Plant gladiolus corms every two weeks from mid-May through June. This will extend the bloom time throughout the summer. Plant full-sized, healthy corms 4 inches deep and 9 inches apart.

Cut canna rhizomes into smaller sections with at least one or two eyes per division. Plant them 4 to 6 inches deep and 12 to 20 inches apart.

Divide dahlias so that each tuberous root has a portion of the stem containing at least one eye. Plant each 4 inches deep with the tuber on its side and the eye facing upward. Install the stakes for tall dahlias at this time so you won't spear the buried tuber later.

Plant tuberous begonias and caladiums outdoors in late May or early June when the soil is warmer. Plant tuberous begonias, hollow side up, and caladiums 1 inch deep and 12 inches apart. Both are good shade-tolerant plants.

In late May (early June for those in the north), plant forced bulbs outdoors. Move amaryllis plants outside for the summer.

EDIBLES

Adjust indoor and outdoor planting dates based on your location. Add a week or two if you live in the northern part of the state.

Beginning May 1, plant muskmelons, pumpkins, and winter squash indoors. Use peat pots to reduce transplant shock. Fill the peat pots with sterile planting mix. Plant two seeds per pot at a depth twice the diameter of the seed. Cover with soil and water. Moisten the soil until the pot is wet. Transplant the seedlings from flats into small containers filled with a sterile potting mix. Check seedlings that have been directly planted in small containers. Remove all but one seedling per container. Cut off, at ground level, the smaller and weaker seedlings.

Beginning in early May, plant parsley, head lettuce, cauliflower, broccoli, Brussels sprouts, early cabbage, collards, kale, and onion plants in the garden. Use a trowel to dig a hole large enough for the roots. Loosen roots of potbound transplants. Place the roots in the hole, and backfill with soil. Gently tamp to remove the air pockets and to ensure good soil-to-root contact. Water thoroughly until the top 4 to 6 inches are moist.

Beginning in mid-May, plant seeds of snap beans, late cabbage, Brussels sprouts, and sweet corn.

Beginning in late May, place transplants of winter squash, pumpkins, celeriac, muskmelons, celery, tomatoes, and herbs in the garden. Remove the upper lip and the bottom of peat pots before planting. You may want to slice through the side to encourage quick rooting. Sow seeds of lima beans, cucumber, melons, and summer squash. Select short-season varieties of squash and melons that will reach maturity and be ready for harvest before the first frost.

LAWNS

This is the second-best time to seed or overseed lawns (mid-August through mid-September is the best time). Proper soil preparation is the key to creating a healthy lawn that can withstand pests and the rigors of our weather.

■ *Use a spreader to overseed thin and sparse lawns.*

Use a grass mix suitable for your light conditions and one that contains mostly bluegrass, some fescue and the rest turf-type perennial ryegrass for sunny areas. Use a mix with mostly fine fescue, some bluegrass and the rest turf-type perennial ryegrass for shady areas.

This is still a good time to install sod. See April, Plant for details.

PERENNIALS
Complete soil preparation. Invest time now to ensure many years of success with your perennial garden. See the Introduction for tips on soil preparation and April, Plant, the section on bare-root planting.

Move field-grown container plants right into the garden. Harden off plants that were started indoors or in the greenhouse before planting outdoors. See page 67 for hardening off details.

Cut back any overgrown and leggy transplants. Prune the stems back by one-third to one-half at planting. This encourages new growth and results in a fuller, sturdier plant.

Label plants and record the planting information on your landscape plan and in your journal. Make a note of the cultivar (cultivated variety), planting date, and plant source.

Dig and divide overgrown perennials or those you want to propagate. Spring is the best time to divide summer- and fall-blooming perennials. See April for tips on dividing perennials.

Dig and divide your woodland wildflowers after blooming. Do this only if you must move existing plants or to start new plantings; otherwise leave your wildflowers alone.

HERE'S HOW

TO SEED A LAWN

1. Take a soil test to determine what nutrients and soil amendments should be added to the soil prior to planting. See the book introduction or contact your local county office of the Michigan State Extension Service or their website for soil testing information.

2. Kill the existing grass and weeds with a total vegetation killer. Old, neglected, or extremely weedy areas may benefit from two applications made two weeks apart. *Read and follow label directions exactly.* Increasing the concentration burns off the tops of plants but does not kill their roots. Lower rates will not kill the weeds and will make additional applications (more product in the long run) necessary. Check the label and wait (usually four to fourteen days after treatment) before tilling the soil.

3. Cultivate the top 6 inches to loosen compacted soil and turn under dead weeds and grass. This is your rough grade. Only work the soil when it is moist (not wet). Grab a handful of soil and gently squeeze. Tap it with your finger. If it breaks into smaller pieces it is dry enough to till. Working wet soil results in compaction and clods, while working dry soil breaks down the soil structure.

4. Rake the area smooth, removing any rocks and debris. Allow the soil to settle. Time, rainfall, or a light sprinkling with water helps the soil to settle.

5. Fill in any low spots. Slope the soil away from the house and make the final grade 1 inch lower than adjacent sidewalks and drives.

6. Till the recommended amount of fertilizer, organic matter, and any other needed amendments into the top 6 inches of the soil. In general, new lawns need 1 pound of actual nitrogen per 1,000 square feet and several inches of organic matter such as peat moss or compost.

7. Rake the soil smooth and make any final adjustments to the final grade.

8. Spread grass seed at a rate of 3 to 4 pounds per 1,000 square feet for sunny mixes and 4 to 5 pounds per 1,000 square feet for shade mixes. Using a drop-type or rotary spreader, sow half the seed in one direction and the remainder at right angles to the first.

9. Lightly rake seeds into the top ¼ inch of soil. This is usually sufficient to ensure seed-soil contact. You can also use an empty lawn roller just to be sure. Borrow one from a friend or rent it from a local tool center. Always use rollers empty to avoid soil compaction.

10. Mulch the area to conserve moisture and reduce erosion. Use weed-free straw, cellulose-based mulches, or floating row covers for mulch. Cover the area with the row cover and anchor the edges with stones, boards, or wire anchors; or spread the straw and hay over the soil surface. Apply a thin layer so some of the soil is still visible through the mulch. Thin layers of these materials can be left on the lawn to decompose naturally.

11. Water after seeding and frequently enough to keep the soil surface moist but not soggy. You may need to water once or twice a day for several weeks. Once the grass begins to grow, you can reduce the watering frequency. Established seedlings should be watered thoroughly but less frequently.

12. Mow the grass when it is one-third higher than your normal mowing height of 2½ to 3½ inches tall. Cut 4-inch-tall seedlings back to 3 or 3½ inches, and continue mowing as needed.

MAY

ROSES

Finish planting your bare-root roses. See April, Plant, Roses for details. Bare-root roses that began to grow during shipping or while in storage should be potted and grown in a protected (frost-free) location. These plants can be planted outdoors after the danger of frost.

Potted roses are now available and can also be planted.

Dormant roses can be planted right away. Those grown in greenhouses need to be hardened off as described under Annuals.

SHRUBS

Balled-and-burlapped and container-grown shrubs can be planted all season long.

Amend planting beds in difficult planting locations. Create raised beds with existing or blended topsoil, or add organic matter to the top 6 to 12 inches of the planting bed soil. Add organic matter to the whole planting bed, not just the planting hole, where shrub roots will grow.

See April, Plant for instructions on planting balled-and-burlapped and container shrubs.

TREES

Continue planting trees in the landscape. See September and the tree planting section on page 208 for details. Remove plant tags from the trunk and branches. If left in place, these can eventually girdle the stem.

VINES & GROUNDCOVERS

Kill or remove the grass and prepare the site for planting. Leave the dead grass intact to serve as mulch to control erosion on slopes and to minimize root disturbance under trees.

Prepare the soil prior to planting according to the directions in the Introduction.

Harden off annual vines started indoors or in a greenhouse as described on page 67. The plants will be ready to plant in two weeks.

CARE

ANNUALS

Thin or transplant annuals directly seeded into the garden. Leave the healthiest seedlings properly spaced in their permanent garden location. Move extra transplants to other planting beds and gardens with extra planting space.

Pinch back spindly transplants above a set of healthy leaves. Pruning encourages branching and ultimately results in more flowers.

Place stakes next to tall annuals that need staking. Early stake placement prevents root and plant damage caused by staking established annuals that are already flopping over.

BULBS

Harden off tender bulb transplants that have been growing indoors as described on page 67.

Deadhead faded flowers of tulips and hyacinths to promote more vigorous growth. Deadhead other bulbs for aesthetic reasons. You may want to remove the whole flower stem for a cleaner look.

Remove only diseased, yellow, or dried foliage. Leave the remaining leaves intact. These are producing the needed energy for next year's flower display. The same goes for bulbs naturalized in lawn areas. Keep the lawn as tall as possible to maintain bulb leaves. Mow around taller bulbs that have been grown in the lawn. Consider replacing tall bulbs with squills or grape hyacinths. These smaller bulbs are more tolerant of mowing. Keep in mind these bulbs will be a part of your lawn until you kill them and the surrounding grass.

EDIBLES

Harden off transplants before moving them from indoors or a greenhouse to the outdoors. Allow two weeks to complete this process.

Prune off damaged, dried, or discolored leaves at planting.

Harvest asparagus when the spears are 6 to 8 inches long. See April, Care for details.

■ *Remove flower stalks from rhubarb as soon as you see them.*

PLAN

ALL

Use your landscape and garden design as a
working document. We all make changes to our
plans. Sometimes the plants we wanted are not
available—and then there are those few unplanned
additions that we just could not resist at the garden
center. It is all too easy to succumb to temptation
and end up with too many or the wrong type of
plants for the available space.

If you do end up with extra plants but no space,
tuck them into containers, or share with a friend.
My daughter often "shops" for her plants in the
overflow on my patio. And I often justify my extra
plants by sharing them with her and others.

■ *Set your mower to cut the grass at 3 to 3½ inches.*

water and nutrients from reaching the grass roots. Dethatching physically removes this layer of organic matter (which is stressful on a lawn). Rake and compost the debris before overseeding. Core aeration removes plugs of soil, allowing the thatch to break down. The openings also help reduce soil compactions.

Continue to mow high and often, keeping the grass at 2½ to 3½ inches tall, and removing no more than one-third the total height.

PERENNIALS

Move or remove unwanted perennial seedlings. Coneflowers, black-eyed Susans, bee balm, and other prolific seeders may provide more offspring than needed. Dig and share with friends or donate surplus plants to nearby schools, community beautification groups, and Master Gardeners.

Put stakes, peony cages, and trellises in place. It is always easier to train young plants through the cages or onto the stakes than to manipulate mature plants into submission.

Wait for the soil to warm before adding mulch. Apply a thin layer of evergreen needles, twice-shredded bark, or chopped leaves to the soil surface. Do not bury the crowns of a plant. This can lead to rot.

Deadhead early blooming perennials. Shear phlox, pinks, and candytuft to encourage a new flush of foliage. Use hand pruners or pruning shears. Pinch back mums and asters. Keep them 4 to 6 inches tall throughout the months of May and June. Pinch back Shasta daisy, beebalm, garden phlox, and obedient plants to control height and stagger bloom times.

■ *Place several stakes in and around the plant clump to serve as a framework and as individual supports. If one branch is particularly large and floppy, put one of the stakes next to it, about an inch away from the plant stem.*

■ *Start creating a web of string between the stakes. Try to pull the string as taut as possible between stakes, without bending the stakes. You can create as many crisscrossing strings as you'd like. The more string, the more support for the plants growing through the web.*

■ *Prune lilacs as soon as they are done blooming.*

Disbud peonies (remove the side flower buds) if you want fewer but larger flowers.

Thin garden phlox, bee balm, and other powdery mildew-susceptible plants when the stems are 8 inches tall. Remove one-fourth to one-third (leaving at least four to five) of the stems. Thinning increases light and air to the plant thus decreasing the risk of powdery mildew.

Trim any unsightly frost-damaged leaves.

ROSES
Begin hardening off indoor roses and greenhouse roses in the middle of the month.

Stake or trellis climbing and tree roses as needed. Use fabric, twine, or flexible ties to avoid damaging the trunk and stems.

Remove only dead and damaged canes on old roses and climbers. Major pruning should be done after flowering. Finish pruning hybrid tea roses. See April, Care for more detailed information.

SHRUBS
Shrubs wintered indoors in heated garages, the basement, or other warm locations should be allowed to gradually adapt to cooler, harsher outdoor conditions.

Shrubs overwintered in an unheated porch or garage should be moved outdoors before growth begins.

Prune spring-flowering shrubs as soon as they are done blooming. Finish pruning by early June so that the plants have enough time to set flower buds for next spring.

Renewal prune suckering shrubs, such as forsythia, bridal wreath spirea, and lilac, by removing one-third of the older stems to ground level. See the pruning pointers starting on page 209 for details.

Remove faded flowers on lilacs and rhododendrons to encourage better flowering next year.

TREES

A wide mulch ring that covers most of the area under the tree canopy creates a good environment for tree roots. Shredded bark and woodchips help conserve water, reduce weed growth, and add nutrients to the soil beneath. Avoid using weed barriers under bark, woodchips, and other organic mulches. They are a temporary solution for weed growth and can create a maintenance headache in the long run. As the mulch on top of the weed barrier decomposes, it creates a perfect place for weeds and grass to grow. It also prevents the organic matter from improving the soil beneath the barrier.

Get the greatest benefits by mulching both new and established trees. Maintain no more than a 3-inch layer of mulch around trees. Keep the mulch away from the tree's trunk. Piling mulch around the trunk can lead to decay.

Give your saw a temporary break. Limit pruning to disease control and repair. Save major pruning for after the leaves have fully developed. This reduces the risk of damaging the bark.

Do not prune oaks. Pruning cuts increase the risk of oak wilt. Save oak pruning for the dormant season whenever possible.

VINES & GROUNDCOVERS

Move tropical vines outdoors at the end of May or in early June, once the danger of frost has passed. Gradually introduce them to the outdoors. Follow the same procedures used for hardening off annuals.

Dig and divide overcrowded, declining, and poorly flowering groundcovers. Use a shovel to lift plants. Remove and compost the dead centers and declining plants. Cut the remaining clump into several smaller pieces. Add organic matter and a low-nitrogen, slow-release fertilizer to the top 6 to 12 inches of the soil. Plant the divisions at the recommended spacing for that species.

WATER

ALL

Water transplants and potted plants growing indoors as needed. Keep the soil moist but not wet.

Cut back on watering as you prepare the plants to move outdoors.

Check new transplants daily. Water deeply enough to moisten the rootball and surrounding soil. Apply water when the top few inches of soil start to dry. Reduce watering frequency as the transplants become established.

Keep the soil around new transplants moist. Water thoroughly and less frequently as the plants become established.

EDIBLES

Keep the soil surface moist while germinating seeds both indoors and out. Once the seedlings sprout, water thoroughly to encourage deep rooting. Keep the soil around the roots of recent transplants slightly moist. Water enough to moisten the top 4 inches of soil. Water again as the top 1 to 2 inches begin to dry. Reduce watering frequency as the root system develops in several weeks.

Check containers daily. Water any time the top 2 to 3 inches begin to dry. Apply enough water so that the excess runs out the bottom.

LAWNS

Newly planted lawns need extra attention. Keep the soil surface moist until the sod is well rooted or the grass seed has sprouted. Established lawns need an average of 1 inch of water each week. Spring rains usually provide the needed moisture. You can step in with the sprinkler as needed.

ROSES

Water container roses as soon as the soil becomes dry. Check soil moisture daily and water as needed. Keep the soil around newly planted roses moist. The new plants will begin to root into the surrounding soil in several weeks. At that time, water thoroughly but less frequently.

SHRUBS

Give new plantings special attention. Water thoroughly whenever the top 4 to 6 inches of soil start to dry. Check clay soils once a week and sandy soils twice a week. Check often and water roots of shrubs grown in soilless mixes several times a week.

Established plantings only need to be watered during dry weather. Water thoroughly and wait for the top 6 to 8 inches to dry before watering again.

Water aboveground planters whenever the top few inches of soil begin to dry. Water thoroughly so that the excess drains out the bottom. Check planters every few days, daily during hot weather.

TREES
Keep the rootball and surrounding soil of newly planted trees slightly moist but not wet. Water the area thoroughly so that the top 10 to 12 inches of soil are moist. Water when this area begins to dry. New plantings usually need to be watered once every seven to ten days in clay soil and twice a week in sandy soil. Adjust watering to accommodate container plants grown in soilless mixes. Keep the rootball and surrounding soil moist, not wet.

Established trees have a larger root system to retrieve water. Spring rains usually provide the needed moisture. Give established trees a thorough watering every two weeks during extended dry periods. Paper birches and other moisture-loving trees should be watered regularly during dry weather. Check these plants once a week, and water when the top 6 inches of soil are crumbly but slightly moist.

Water aboveground planters thoroughly so that the excess water drains out of the bottom. Check regularly, and water as the top few inches of soil begin to dry.

FERTILIZE

ANNUALS
Stop fertilizing indoor- and greenhouse-grown transplants two weeks prior to planting outdoors as part of the hardening off process.

BULBS
Incorporate a low-nitrogen, slow-release fertilizer into the soil prior to planting tender bulbs. Follow the soil test recommendation or use 1 pound of low-nitrogen fertilizer per 100 square feet of garden space.

EDIBLES
See April, Fertilize for tips.

LAWNS
Late May or early June is the first time to fertilize your lawn. Use a phosphorous-free fertilizer unless the soil test recommends the addition of phosphorous. Apply ½ pound of nitrogen per 1,000 square feet. This is equal to 10 pounds of a 5-percent-nitrogen fertilizer or 3 pounds of a 16-percent-nitrogen fertilizer. Consider using a low-nitrogen, slow-release fertilizer to reduce the risk of burn on non-irrigated lawns.

Most Michigan lawns are a blend of Kentucky bluegrass, fine fescues, and perennial ryegrass. These lawn areas need 1 to 3 pounds of actual nitrogen per season. Select the fertilizer recommended by your soil test or use a low-nitrogen, slow-release, phosphorous-free fertilizer. Avoid midsummer fertilization on non-irrigated lawns, as it can damage turf and encourage weed growth.

PERENNIALS
Perennials need very little fertilizer. Incorporate organic matter at the time of planting. Top-dress established plantings by spreading an inch or two of compost every other year to provide the majority of the plants' nutrient needs.

ROSES
Fertilize old garden, shrub, species, and climbers if you have not already done so. Follow soil test recommendations, or apply 2 heaping tablespoons per plant or 2 pounds per 100 square feet of a low-nitrogen, slow-release fertilizer. Use the same rate to fertilize modern roses once their new spring leaf growth is full-sized.

Fertilize new roses three to four weeks after planting. Fertilize roses growing in planters once or twice a month with any flowering plant fertilizer.

SHRUBS
Finish shrub fertilization. Only fertilize plants that are young or are showing signs of deficiencies for which the soil test report indicates a need.

Granular fertilizer is easy to spread evenly with a spreader.

TO CALCULATE THE AMOUNT OF LAWN FERTILIZER NEEDED

- Calculate your lawn area by measuring the length and width of each section. Multiply the length times width to find the square footage of that portion of lawn. Approximate the area of irregularly shaped parcels.

- Highly managed and frequently used lawn areas should receive several applications of fertilizer. Consider fertilizing Memorial Day, Labor Day, and sometime between Halloween and Thanksgiving before the ground freezes. Low maintenance lawns with less activity can get by with just one or both of the fall applications.

- Calculate the amount of fertilizer needed. Most fertilizer spreader settings are based on applying 1 pound of actual nitrogen per 1,000 square feet; or you can calculate the amount of fertilizer needed with this formula:

  - Divide 100 by the percentage of nitrogen in the fertilizer that you are using. Multiply that number by the amount of actual nitrogen recommended by the results of your soil test or fertilization schedule noted above. This will give you the amount of fertilizer needed per 1,000 square feet.

  - Apply half the needed fertilizer in one direction and the remaining half in the other direction. This will reduce the risk of striping and fertilizer burn. Be careful not to overlap or leave the spreader open when turning.

Apply 1 to 2 pounds of a low-nitrogen fertilizer per 100 square feet if the soil test results are not available. Try a slow-release formulation to reduce risk and improve results.

Wait a year or two before fertilizing new plantings.

TREES

We often kill our plants with kindness. Trees receive many nutrients from grass clippings left on the lawn, decomposing mulch, and lawn fertilizers. Fertilize only when needed. Start with a soil test or consult a tree care professional if your trees aren't healthy.

Fertilize aboveground planters with any complete or organic plant fertilizer. Follow label directions for frequency and concentration.

VINES & GROUNDCOVERS

Fertilize existing plantings in need of a nutrient boost if this has not yet been done. Use the type and amount of fertilizer recommended by the soil test report or consider a low-nitrogen, slow-release fertilizer to promote slow, steady growth and reduce the risk of burn. Apply 2 pounds of a 5-percent-nitrogen fertilizer such as Milorganite® or 1 pound of a 10-percent-nitrogen fertilizer per 100 square feet.

PROBLEM-SOLVE

ALL

Continue to monitor and control animal damage. Deer, rabbits, and woodchucks appreciate fresh food—your new plants—in their diets. Repellents applied before they start feeding may give you control. Five-foot-tall fencing around small garden areas may help keep out deer, as they do not seem to like to enter small, fenced-in areas. Use decorative posts and a black or green mesh fence. It keeps animals away without being too obtrusive. A 4-foot-high fence anchored in the ground helps keep rabbits out. Fencing may not be the most attractive remedy, but it beats having no flowers at all.

Continue to pull weeds as they appear. Early control reduces future problems and results in a more attractive display.

ANNUALS

Protect new plantings from cutworm damage. These insects chew through the stems of young transplants. They are most common in planting beds recently converted from lawn. Make cutworm collars from paper towel and toilet paper cardboard tubes, plastic margarine tubs, soup cans, or yogurt containers. Remove the bottom of the plastic containers, and cut the paper rolls into 3- to 4-inch lengths. Slice the containers down the sides. Place collars around the new transplants, and sink the bottoms several inches into the soil.

Start watching for aphid, mite, spittlebug, slug, plantbug, and earwig damage. Pull or cultivate weeds as soon as they appear. Be careful not to damage the tender roots of transplants while weeding.

Protect hanging baskets from birds and chipmunks. Cover baskets with bird netting. Secure the netting above and below the container. Do this at the first signs of a problem. Quick action will encourage the birds and animals to go elsewhere. Remove netting once wildlife is no longer a threat.

BULBS

Continue to monitor for bulb rot. Remove infected plants, and plan on improving soil drainage at the end of spring or next fall. Remove any spotted or disease-infested leaves.

See April, Problem-Solve for tips on dealing with iris borer.

Monitor lilies for stalk borer. Infested stems start to wilt, leaves turn yellow, and the stem can eventually die. Fall cleanup and a weed-free garden are the best defenses against this pest. Remove and destroy borer-infested stems as found.

EDIBLES

Avoid seed corn maggot damage on corn and beans by waiting to plant until the soil warms. Quick-germinating seeds are less susceptible to this damage. Seed corn maggots feed on germinating seeds, preventing germination or causing deformed seedlings that never develop.

Cover broccoli, cabbage, turnips, and radishes with floating row cover fabric, which prevents harmful insects from reaching the plants while allowing air, light, and water through.

Rotate onions with other unrelated crops to prevent problems with onion maggots. The immature stage of this insect feeds inside the onion bulb.

A thorough spring cleanup reduces asparagus beetle problems. These orange-and-black beetles feed on emerging spears. Handpick and destroy or use an insecticide labeled for use on beetles in asparagus.

Handpicking is the best control for the Colorado potato beetle. Many insecticides do not provide adequate control. Watch for yellow-and-black striped beetles or the red humped larvae feeding on the leaves.

Place white sticky traps in the garden if flea beetles have been a problem in the past. Otherwise, handpick or just allow healthy transplants to outgrow the damage.

Remove and destroy the yellow-and-green striped or spotted cucumber beetles found on vine crops in spring or late summer. The beetles not only feed on leaves and fruit, but also transmit a deadly bacterial disease to a plant.

Use scare tactics such as clanging pans or cover susceptible plantings with netting to prevent bird damage.

LAWNS

A healthy lawn is the best defense against weeds. See April, Problem-Solve for crabgrass control. Broadleaf weed killers can help get problem areas under control. Creeping Charlie, also known as ground ivy, is one of the more common weeds. It has round scalloped leaves that smell somewhat minty when crushed. The purple flowers appear in mid- to late May. There is good news for those who are losing the battle and don't want to keep it as a groundcover. Broadleaf weed killers containing 2-4D and MCPP will work. Timing is the key. Treat creeping Charlie when it is in full bloom. Spot treat problem areas only. It may take several years to eliminate the offspring of these weeds. An iron-based natural product with the active ingredient of Fehedta or Hedta controls this and other broadleaf weeds. As always, read and follow label directions.

Insects are not usually a major threat to Michigan lawns. See June, Problem-Solve for more information on lawn insects.

Our cool, wet springs often increase the risk of lawn disease. Be on guard for these common lawn diseases:

Helminthosporium leafspot and melting-out diseases cause irregular patches of brown and dying grass. A close look at nearby blades reveals brown to black spots on leaves. As the disease progresses, the patch gets larger and the grass

■ *Fairy ring is a fungus growing in the lawn.*

begins to disintegrate and disappear (melt away). Overseed areas with resistant grass varieties.

Snow mold is most evident in the spring as the snow and ice melt. Infected lawns have small to large patches of white or gray matted turf. The grass thins and is slow to recover in spring. Rake the lawn in early spring, and avoid overuse of nitrogen in the spring.

Powdery mildew looks as though someone has sprinkled baby powder on the leaves. It is most common on shady lawns in the fall, but it can appear anytime during the growing season. Overseed shady areas with fine fescue, or increase the sunlight by having a tree care professional thin the crowns of trees.

Rust-infected lawns have brown, orange, or yellow spots on the grass blades. This is a common problem on drought-stressed and newly seeded lawns with a high percentage of ryegrass. As the percentage of bluegrass and fescue increases, the rust usually becomes less of a problem. Proper care increases turf health and allows it to tolerate damage. Treatment is usually unneeded.

Necrotic ring spot (formerly known as fusarium blight) appears as circles or irregular patches of dead grass with tufts of green grass in the center. All bluegrass and fescue varieties appear to be susceptible. Overseeding with perennial ryegrass may help mask symptoms. Proper care combined with allowing time for the disease to run its course is usually the most successful treatment.

Fairy ring is not life threatening for grass, but it can cause aesthetic concerns. Infected lawns have rings of dark green, yellow, or dying turf. The rings appear for a short time, disappear, and then return—slightly larger in diameter—later or the next season. During wet periods, mushrooms appear within the ring. No control is needed—or practical. Water fairy rings during drought to minimize the symptoms.

PERENNIALS
Monitor the garden for pests. Remove infected leaves when discovered. Watch for four-lined plantbugs, slugs, and aphids.

Check columbine plants for leaf miners. The leaf miner causes white, snake-like lines in the leaves. Prune back badly infested plants after flowering. The new growth will be fresh and pest free. Columbine sawfly is a wormlike insect that eats holes in the leaves so quickly that it seems to devour the plants overnight. Remove and destroy any that are found. You can use insecticides labeled for controlling sawflies on perennials. Check wilted columbine plants for stalk borers. Look for holes and sawdust-like droppings at the base of the plant. Remove infested stems and destroy the borer.

Pull weeds as soon as they are discovered. Thistle, dandelions, and quackgrass are among the first to appear. Removing weeds before they set seed saves pulling hundreds more next year.

ROSES
Check for pests at least once a week. Small populations of aphids can easily be removed by hand or with a strong blast of water.

Seal recent pruning cuts on roses that have suffered from cane borer in the past. Dab cut ends with pruning paint, yellow shellac, or white glue to prevent borers from entering through the opening.

Clean up any dead leaves and debris near roses. This helps reduce the source of infection for this growing season.

SHRUBS
Remove Eastern tent caterpillars as soon as they are found. Knock or prune out tents and destroy caterpillars.

Continue checking mugo pines for European pine sawflies. Prune off infected branches or smash sawflies with a leather glove-clad hand. Treat mugo and other pines infested with pine needle scale. Apply insecticidal soap when the Vanhoutte (bridal wreath) spirea is in bloom and again seven to ten days later.

Check and treat lilacs, dogwood, and other deciduous shrubs infested with oyster shell scale. These hard-shelled insects look like miniature oyster shells. Spray the stems and leaves with an ultrafine oil or insecticide labeled for use on shrubs

Honeylocust plantbugs and leafhoppers begin feeding soon after buds break, causing new growth to be distorted and sparse. Once the insects are done feeding, healthy trees will leaf out and be fine. Patience and proper care is the best control.

Remove tent caterpillar nests from infested trees. Do not burn the nest while it is in the tree. This is more harmful to the plant than the insects.

Watch for signs of gypsy moth larvae. These wormlike insects eventually grow to 2 inches long and have two rows of red and blue warts on their backs. Catch caterpillars as they crawl down the tree trunk looking for shade during the day. Wrap a 12- to 18-inch-wide strip of burlap around the tree trunk at chest height. Tie a string around the burlap 6 inches from the top. Let the top 6 inches of burlap flop over the string. Check under the burlap every day between 2 and 6 p.m. Use gloves to remove caterpillars; drop them in soapy water to kill the insects.

European pine sawflies are wormlike insects that feed in colonies. They will do a little dance for you when you get too close. Check mugo and other common landscape pines for feeding colonies of this insect. Even in large numbers, they are easy to control. Slide on a leather glove and smash the insects; or prune out the infested branch and destroy the insects.

Aphids and mites are common landscape pests. They suck out plant juices, causing leaf discoloration and distorted growth. Nature usually keeps them in check with rains and natural predators like lady beetles. In dry seasons, use a strong blast of water from a garden hose to dislodge the insects and reduce the damage.

Phomopsis blight is a fungal disease that attacks junipers and Russian olives. It is most prevalent in cool, wet springs. The infected branches turn brown and die. Remove infected branches below the canker and disinfect tools between each cut.

Fireblight is a bacterial disease that infects susceptible crabapples. It causes the leaves to turn black and branch tips to curl. This disease spreads by splashing water, pollinating bees, and infected

Mulching around your garden beds will help keep the weeds down as the heat starts to build.

with scale. Spray when Vanhoutte (bridal wreath) spirea is in bloom and again when the hills-of-snow hydrangea blossoms change from white to green.

Watch for phomopsis blight on junipers. Infected plants have cankered branches (sunken discolored areas) with brown and dead needles. Prune out infected branches 9 inches below the canker. Disinfect your tools between cuts.

TREES

Continue monitoring for the pests described in April.

tools. Avoid pruning crabapple trees during wet periods. Prune out infected branches 12 inches below the canker (sunken, discolored area) on the stem. Disinfect tools between cuts with rubbing alcohol or a solution of one part bleach to nine parts water.

VINES & GROUNDCOVERS

Monitor euonymus and wintercreeper vines for euonymus caterpillar. These wormlike insects spin a webbed nest in the plants. Remove and destroy, or treat with *Bacillus thuringiensis*. Spray the webbed nests and surrounding foliage. This bacterial insecticide kills the caterpillars but will not harm people, pets, wildlife, or other types of insects.

Check junipers for phomopsis blight. This fungal disease causes individual stems to turn brown and die. Prune dead branches back to a healthy stem or the main trunk. Disinfect tools between cuts with rubbing alcohol or a solution of one part bleach to nine parts water.

Cut back creeping phlox after the flowers fade. Prune plants back halfway to encourage fresh, new growth.

To prevent fireblight on your crabapple tree, avoid pruning the trees during wet periods.

This month is filled with variety! Planting and pest management continue, but harvesting begins.

You will be picking greens, digging radishes, and picking peas to add some homegrown freshness to your meals. Proper and regular harvesting ensures the best flavor and maximum productivity.

Pluck a few fresh herb leaves or clip a leafy stem just above a set of healthy leaves. Regular harvests will encourage more compact growth for future harvest and better-looking plants.

And then there are the beautiful bouquets of flowering bulbs and perennials. Increase the vase life of cut flowers by using a sharp knife or cutting scissors to cut the base of the stem on an angle. Place flowers in water right after cutting. Take a bucket of water along with you to the garden. This is better for the flowers and makes it easier for you to manage the blooms.

Further extend the life of cut flowers by curing them before placing them in an arrangement. Cut the flowers and place them in a container of warm water in a cool location. After they have had a few hours or overnight to adjust to the indoors, cut the stems on an angle again and arrange in a vase filled with fresh water and floral preservative.

Always remove the lower leaves to reduce bacteria and fungi that can develop on leaves submerged in the water. And freshen things up by changing the water every few days to lengthen the life of your cut flowers.

Cut rose flowers early in the morning just as the top of the bud is starting to open. Make the cut on a slight angle above an outward-facing, five-leaflet leaf. Cut flowers back to a three-leaflet leaf on young plants that may not tolerate this amount of pruning. Remove the lower leaves on the stem.

Add a few containers of annuals on the steps or in the garden for added color or a needed focal point. Then pot up a few individual plants or combinations in recycled containers to use as centerpieces for your summer parties. Give them to your guests as party favors or keep them growing and use them throughout the summer.

Attend one of the many garden walks offered throughout the state. It is a great way to meet new gardeners, gather ideas, be inspired, and get a close look at the backyards of some amazing landscapers. And most walk fees support community gardening efforts or other charitable causes.

PLAN

ALL

Keep adjusting your garden plans and making notes on the changes as they occur. You may find these changes actually improve the original plan. Draw a sketch of your lawn and garden areas, and record any problems that may require further evaluation or treatment.

Record visitors to your garden. Note in your journal the birds, butterflies, and beneficial insects stopping by to nest or feed. You may want to add water, birdhouses, and butterfly houses to encourage your winged guests to stay.

Start a wish list for new plants for future gardens. Record the name, bloom time, size, hardiness, and other features of the plant.

■ *You can combine annuals and edibles into one pot that's both decorative and useful.*

Record problems encountered throughout the season. List the plant affected, the pest problem, and the control methods used. Evaluate and record the results to help you avoid and control future problems.

ANNUALS

Look for bare or drab areas in your yard that would benefit from some annual color. Use annuals to mask declining spring bulbs and early blooming perennials. Consider adding a pot of annuals to the patio, deck, or entranceway.

BULBS

Make sure all your bulbs are marked and mapped on your garden plan. This will be the last sign of many of them until next spring.

EDIBLES

Locate an area for your compost pile. It can be either in sun, where it dries out quickly, or in the shade, where it decomposes slower, but it should be in a well-drained location.

LAWNS

As the temperatures rise, grass growth slows. Monitor the lawn for weeds, insects, and disease.

PERENNIALS

Harvest flowers for arrangements and drying. Experiment with different flower combinations. If they look good in a vase, they will probably look good as planting partners in the garden, as long as they require the same growing conditions.

ROSES

By early June there should be no doubt about winter survival. Remove dead and struggling plants. Select an appropriate replacement that may or may not be another rose. If roses keep dying in this location, it may be time to find another place for your roses.

Visit local botanical gardens to learn which roses perform best. Find rose gardens at Matthaei Botanical Gardens in Ann Arbor, MSU Horticultural Demonstration Gardens in East Lansing, and Dow Gardens in Niles.

TREES

Summer storms can leave you with broken branches and uprooted trees. Proper care and preventative pruning can help reduce storm damage to trees. Consider contacting a certified arborist (tree care professional) to evaluate the health and soundness of your trees. Together you can develop a long-term plan to maintain or improve your tree's storm resistance. See November, Plan for tips on hiring an arborist.

PLANT

ANNUALS

Get busy. Early June is peak planting time for gardeners in the northern areas of the state. The air and soil have finally warmed. Even gardeners in southern locations benefit from the delay. The transplants quickly adjust to these warmer outdoor conditions.

Finish planting tender annuals early in the month for the best and longest possible flower display. Check out your local garden center for larger transplants. Use these for a quicker show or for later plantings.

Reduce transplant shock by planting in early morning or late afternoon. Proper planting and post-planting care help the transplants adjust to

Test out your design and speed the planting process by setting plants in their intended location.

Annuals will double or triple in size, so be sure to leave enough room for them to grow.

their new locations. See May, Plant for tips on hardening off, planting, and care.

BULBS

Always prepare the soil before planting hardy or tender bulbs and transplants. See the information about soil preparation on page 10.

Plant tender bulb plants outside after the danger of frost. Gardeners in the north may just be starting, while those in the south are finishing up. Finish planting tender caladium corms, canna rhizomes, and begonia tubers directly in the garden by early June. This will give them time to grow and flower before the snow flies.

Keep planting gladiolus corms every two weeks through June. Continual planting gives you a long period of bloom to enjoy in the garden or as cut flowers.

Dig and divide spring-flowering bulbs after the leaves fade. The plants have already stored their energy for the next season, and the faded leaves make them easy to locate. Otherwise, mark the spot and move them in fall while you are planting your other bulbs.

Plant pre-cooled lily bulbs or potted plants. They need well-drained soil and plenty of sun. Try using a few in containers. They make a nice vertical accent for planters. Bulbs grown in containers will need to be planted in the garden in the fall to survive our cold winters.

Plant annuals, perennials, or tender bulbs among spring-flowering bulbs. The new plants help mask the declining foliage of the spring bloomers.

EDIBLES

Finish planting your garden. It's fine to wait until early June when the soil is warm to plant tomatoes, peppers, eggplants, melons, and squash. They suffer less transplant shock and grow much faster.

Plant annual and perennial herbs. Most prefer full sun and well-drained soils. Follow the same steps used for vegetables.

Sow seeds of Chinese cabbage, collards, endive, kale, and rutabaga at the end of the month for a fall harvest. These seeds sprout quickly, and the flavor will be at its peak with the cooler fall temperatures.

HERE'S HOW

TO PLANT A CONTAINER-GROWN TREE OR SHRUB

1. Call 811 to mark underground utilities at least 3 days prior to digging in. Dig a shallow hole at least 2 to 5 times the diameter of the rootball.

2. Find the rootflare (where roots slope away from the tree trunk) or crown (where the stems of shrubs meet the roots). Dig the planting hole the same depth as the distance from the rootflare or crown to the bottom of the rootball.

3. Remove the container. Set the plant in the hole, moving it by the rootball, not the trunk or stems. The rootflare or crown should be even with the soil surface. Loosen or remove any girdling roots.

4. Fill in around the tree with the same soil that you removed from the planting hole. Do not add fertilizer or new topsoil. Water will move more easily, and the tree will root properly if the soil in and around the planting hole are the same.

LAWNS

You can still lay sod. Lawns installed now need a little extra water as the weather turns hot and dry.

PERENNIALS

Keep planting perennials, as the soil is warm and there are still lots of perennials available at local garden centers and perennial nurseries. Label new plantings, write their locations on your garden design, and record critical information. Read the plant label for specific planting and care information.

Dig and divide overgrown Siberian iris after they finish blooming. Keep the soil around the transplants moist but not wet. It may take divisions more than a year to recover and bloom. You can also dig and divide other overgrown perennials. See April, Plant for details.

This is a good time to transplant bleeding heart.

ROSES

June is a good time to plant potted roses. The weather is usually not too hot and dry, making it easier for plants to adjust to their new location. Plus, the plants have all summer to get established before the onset of severe winter weather. See April, Plant and September, Plant for tips on planting potted and shrub roses.

5 Mulch around the tree and shrub, taking care to pull the mulch away from the tree trunk and shrub stems. Do not create a mulch "volcano" around the plant by piling mulch up high around the trunk and stems. This creates the perfect environment for damaging pests and adventitious roots to form and eventually girdle the tree.

6 Water the tree or shrub. Check new plantings several times a week. Water thoroughly and only when the top few inches of soil are crumbly and moist. Make sure the roots of plants grown in soilless mix remain moist, but be careful not to overwater the surrounding soil. New trees don't need to be staked unless they have a large canopy and small root system, are grown in windy locations or were planted as bare root plants. It can take several years for trees and shrubs to root into the surrounding soil. Pay special attention to these and water as needed.

SHRUBS

Keep planting container and balled-and-burlapped shrubs. Both are available at nurseries and garden centers. Select healthy, well-shaped plants. Avoid shrubs with brown, speckled, or discolored leaves. These may have suffered drought stress or pest problems. Stressed shrubs take longer to establish and have a lower survival rate.

Cover plants in the truck bed or trailer with a tarp on the trip home from the nursery or garden center. The windy trip home can dry out the new growth, increasing the stress on the plant.

Keep roots of newly purchased shrubs moist until they can be planted. Cover balled-and-burlapped roots with woodchips if it will be a few days until planting.

TREES

Nurseries and garden centers still have a good supply of balled-and-burlapped and container-grown trees. Increase planting success by selecting healthy trees with green leaves free of brown spots, dry edges, or other signs of pest damage and neglect.

Protect newly emerged leaves while transporting your tree home. Wrap the canopy with a blanket or plastic tarp. Many nurseries wrap the tree canopy for you, but it is best to come prepared.

Wrap the trunk to protect it from damage. Store trees in a shaded location until you are ready for planting.

Check the trees daily. Water frequently enough to keep the roots and surrounding soil moist. Cover the rootball of balled-and-burlapped trees and containers with woodchips if the trees are stored for a long period of time.

See Planting a Tree on page 208 for more details.

VINES & GROUNDCOVERS

Keep planting, as container-grown vines and groundcovers can be planted throughout the growing season. Finish hardening off and transplanting annual vines into the garden and containers. Anchor the trellis in place before or right after the planting. Gently tie vines to the trellis to help them climb on their new support.

CARE

ANNUALS

Now is the time to mulch. Use pine needles, shredded leaves, and other organic material as mulch. A thin layer (1 to 2 inches) of mulch helps conserve moisture, moderate soil temperature, and reduce weeds.

■ *Recycle fall leaves right in the garden. Shred with mower and use as a mulch in the perennial garden.*

Finish staking tall annuals that need a little added support. Stake early in the season to reduce the risk of damaging taller, more established plants.

Remove flowers—deadhead—as they fade. Pinch or cut the flowering stem back to the first set of leaves or flower buds. Use a knife or garden shears to make a clean cut. This improves the plant's appearance and encourages continual bloom.

Ageratums, cleomes, gomphrenas, impatiens, narrow-leaf zinnias, New Guinea impatiens, wax begonias, and pentas are self-cleaning. These drop their dead blooms and do not need deadheading.

Remove begonia and ageratum flowers during wet weather to reduce disease problems.

Remove flowers on coleus as soon as they appear, to keep plants full and compact.

Pinch back leggy petunias to encourage branching all along the stem. Cut stems back above a set of leaves.

BULBS

Don't worry if you accidentally dig up hardy bulbs while planting perennials and annuals. Just pop them back in the ground. If you divided them with the shovel, consider them propagated. Replant both halves. You may be lucky and get two bulbs from one.

Mulch tender bulbs as described under the preceding Annuals section.

Stake tall bearded iris flowers for a more attractive display. Many garden centers and catalogs sell stakes specifically for this purpose; or try making your own with thin sturdy wire.

Stake tall dahlias at planting time to avoid spearing the buried tuberous root. Tall gladioli also benefit from staking. One gardener used a piece of lattice for support. She painted it white and elevated it on stakes, parallel to the ground. The gladiolus flower stems grew through the holes in the lattice. The structure helped create a beautiful picture of blooms, complete with hummingbirds feeding at the flowers.

Deadhead faded flowers to improve the plants' appearance and reduce disease problems.

Pinch the tips of dahlias when they reach 15 inches. This encourages branching and results in more flowers on each plant. You can also pinch back leggy begonias at this time.

Remove any yellow and dry foliage on spring-flowering bulbs.

EDIBLES

Thin rows of seeded vegetables. Reduce seedlings to recommended spacing, which pays off with larger, more productive plants. Recycle the seedlings in the compost pile, or try adding some of the edible ones, such as radishes and beets, to salads and sandwiches.

Harvest green onions when the greens are 6 inches tall. Leave some onions to grow and develop for dry bulbs.

Pick and use the outer leaves of leaf lettuce as soon as they reach 4 to 6 inches. Continue to harvest to encourage new tender and flavorful growth. Harvest spinach plants as the outer leaves reach 6 to 8 inches in length.

Stop picking rhubarb after eight to ten weeks of harvesting. Allow the leaves to grow and produce energy to build a strong plant for next season's harvest. Eating summer rhubarb is not harmful to you (it is not poisonous), but it can weaken the plant and reduce future harvests. Remove any flower stalks as soon as they appear.

Allow the leaves (green fluffy growth) to develop on asparagus plants when you are finished harvesting. They help replenish energy supplies and keep the plant productive for seasons to come.

Mulch herb and vegetable gardens in mid- to late June when the soil has warmed. Use shredded leaves, pine needles, weed-free straw, or herbicide-free grass clippings. A 2-inch layer helps conserve moisture, reduces weeds, and moderates soil temperature. Mulching cold soil can stunt the growth of tomatoes, melons, and other warm-season crops.

Stake or cage tomatoes at, or just after, planting, place a tomato tower over the plant and allow the plants to grow, or let your tomato plants crawl on the ground. Each method has its advantage.

If you allow tomatoes to sprawl on the ground, mulch the soil to reduce problems with insects and disease. Sprawled tomatoes are the most productive, but you may lose more to insects and big feet.

Stake plants for larger and earlier fruit but a smaller harvest. Anchor the stake in the ground next to the tomato, being careful not to damage buried stems and developing roots. Train one or two stems, removing side shoots that form above the leaves, up the stake. Loosely tie the vines to the stake with twine, strips of cotton cloth, or old nylon stockings. Remove suckers (stems that develop between leaf and main stem) as they form. Cut or snap the small shoots off by hand when they are 1 to 2 inches long. Remove wayward branches and thin as needed.

Cage plants at the time of planting. Place a tomato tower over the plant and allow the plants to grow. Remove wayward branches and thin as needed.

LAWNS

A spongy lawn surface may mean you have a thatch problem. Confirm your suspicions with this simple test. Remove several 3- × 3-inch plugs of grass from several areas throughout the lawn. Measure the thatch layer. If it is greater than ½ inch you should consider taking action in the fall.

Keep the grass 2½ to 3½ inches tall. The taller grass shades the soil, keeping grass roots cool and preventing weed seeds from sprouting. See April, Care for more information.

PERENNIALS

Put stakes and cages in place. Tuck plants in place or carefully tie them to the support as needed. Twine or other soft bindings work best. Loop the twine around the stem and then around the support.

Thin garden phlox and other overgrown perennials subject to mildew and leaf spot diseases. Remove one-third of the stems.

■ *It's best to put cages on plants while the plants are still small and manageable.*

■ *Create your own support with bamboo stakes and twine.*

Remove any dead or declining foliage on spring-blooming perennials. Continue to deadhead plants such as valerian, columbine, and other heavy seeders to prevent unwanted seedlings, prolong bloom, and improve their overall appearance.

Only remove half of the faded Siberian iris blooms. This will increase flowering next season while allowing a few seedpods to develop for fall and winter interest.

Consider removing the flowers of lamb's ear as soon as they form. This encourages better foliage.

Pinch back perennials to control height or delay bloom. Keep mums and asters 6 inches tall throughout the month.

Cut back amsonia and wild blue indigo (*Baptisia*) by one-third to prevent sprawling, open centers.

Prune back by half any Russian sage that flopped in the past.

Pinch or cut back an outer ring of stems or scattered plants of purple coneflower, heliopsis, garden phlox, balloon flower, and veronica. The pinched plants will be shorter and bloom later. They act as a living support for the rest of the plants and extend the bloom period.

Pinch out the growing tips or cut back 8-inch stems to 4 inches on 'Autumn Joy' sedum that may have flopped in your garden. Or, try moving it to a sunnier location with less fertile but well-drained soil.

Shear dead or leafminer-infested foliage on columbine. The new growth will be fresh and pest-free.

Cut back unsightly foliage on bearded iris and perennial geraniums after bloom.

Cut back bleeding heart half-way as the flowers fade. This reduces reseeding and encourages new growth that may last all season. Mulch the soil, and water to help preserve the leaves.

Mulch perennials with 1 to 2 inches of an organic material to conserve moisture and reduce weeds—but be careful not to bury the plant with mulch.

ROSES

Tie canes of climbers and ramblers to a trellis, fence, or other support.

Leave the fading flowers on spring-blooming old roses. These one-time bloomers have finished their flower show, but not their beauty for the season. The faded flowers are soon be replaced by fruits known as rose hips. The hips turn orange or red, often persisting through fall and winter. They are decorative in the landscape or floral arrangements, high in vitamin C, and attract birds to a winter landscape.

■ *Cut roses in the early morning, just as the top of the bud is starting to open.*

Deadhead repeat bloomers and hybrid tea roses. This improves the appearance and increases bloom time. Remove only individual flowers in the cluster as they fade. Once all the flowers in the cluster have bloomed, prune back the flower stem to the first five-leaflet leaf. Deadhead single-flowered roses back to the first five-leaflet leaf. This encourages stouter and stronger branch development.

Prune old garden, species, shrub, and climbing roses. Shrub and species roses are hardy and need very little pruning. They look best if allowed to grow to their normal size and shape. Do very little pruning on new plants. Once the plants have reached full size, they may need a little yearly pruning. Thin overgrown plantings by removing several of the older canes to ground level if this was not done in early spring. This is often the only pruning that is needed. You can shorten overgrown stems by one-third. This helps to contain plant growth and increase flowers for next season.

JUNE

TO PRUNE RAMBLERS

1. Deadhead flowers as they fade. Prune the flowering stems back to the third or fourth set of leaves.

2. Prune out one-third of the older canes, if not done earlier. This allows room for the new canes to grow and develop. New growth this year is the flowering wood next spring. Some of the new growth develops on older canes, so remove older canes that have very little new growth.

3. Tie new shoots to the trellis or physically wrap them around arches, fences, or pillars. Shoots bent sideways produce flowers all along the stem.

4. Remove any long and wayward canes that have outgrown the available space.

If you want attractive rose hips that add ornamental value and food for many birds, limit pruning.

Prune repeat bloomers in early spring before growth begins.

Ramblers are tough, often hardy climbing roses. They bloom once and proceed to ramble at will. Pruning helps control their growth and improve their appearance.

Once-blooming climbers also bloom on the previous season's growth but are not as vigorous growers as the ramblers. Be a little more selective in your pruning efforts with these plants.

SHRUBS

Consider removing grass and creating planting beds around shrubs and trees. Grass is a big competitor for water and nutrients. Plus weed whips and mowers can damage their stems and trunks, creating entryways for insects and disease.

Replenish mulch as needed, maintaining a 2- to 3-inch layer of shredded bark or woodchips. Do not bury the stems.

Finish pruning spring-flowering shrubs early this month. This gives the plants plenty of time to develop flower buds for next spring's display.

Shear and shape hedges after new growth has emerged. Prune so that the top of the hedge is narrower than the bottom. This allows light to reach all parts of the shrub. Better light penetration results in leaves from top to bottom. Remove damaged, dead, or insect-infested stems. See Pruning Shrubs on page 211 for more details

TREES

Continue mulching trees as needed. A 2- to 3-inch layer of mulch improves tree growth and reduces maintenance. Keep the mulch away from the trunk to avoid rot.

Consider replacing annual plantings under trees with perennial groundcovers. This means less root disturbance for the tree and less work for you.

The old saying, "Prune when the saw is sharp" applies to June. Concentrate your efforts on repair rather than shaping. Remove crossing, broken, or diseased branches. Make cuts where branches join other branches or flush to the branch bark collar.

Do not paint pruning cuts (except on oaks). Research shows that the tree recovers better without these products. Disinfect tools between cuts on diseased trees with alcohol or a solution of one part bleach to nine parts water.

Wait for the dormant season to prune oaks.

VINES & GROUNDCOVERS

Apply a 2- to 3-inch layer of mulch around vines and groundcovers. Do not bury the crowns of the groundcovers or the base of the vines. This can lead to rot and decline. Use shredded leaves, evergreen needles, woodchips, or twice-shredded bark.

Renovate overgrown and weedy groundcovers. Dig out the healthy plants and remove them from the garden. Remove or use a total vegetation killer to kill all the weeds and unwanted plants. Amend and fertilize the soil. Divide the healthy plants into smaller pieces, removing any weeds. Plant the divisions at the proper spacing, water thoroughly, and mulch.

Clip back or lightly mow bugleweed after it flowers to improve the appearance and prevent unwanted seedlings from taking over the garden.

Cut back creeping phlox if this was not done earlier. Prune foliage back halfway. This encourages new, healthy, more attractive growth. You may even be rewarded with a few more flowers later in the season.

Prune climbing hydrangea after flowering in June. For young plants, limit pruning to broken and damaged branches. These slow-growing plants do not need formative training. For established plants, prune overly long shoots and outward-facing stems. Very little pruning is needed.

WATER

ALL

Check container plantings every day. Water when the top few inches begin to dry. Water thoroughly until the excess water runs out the bottom of the container, but don't allow the pot to stand in water.

Water new plantings often enough to keep the planting area moist. Decrease watering frequency after several weeks when new rooting occurs.

ANNUALS

Check new plantings several times per week. Water whenever the top few inches of soil begin to dry. Water established annuals thoroughly, but only as needed. Adjust the watering schedule to fit the plant's needs and growing conditions. Water when the top few inches of soil start to dry.

In general, apply 1 inch of water once a week to plants growing in clay soils. Apply ½ to ¾ inch of water twice a week in sandy soils.

Apply water in early morning to reduce disease caused by wet foliage at night, leaf burn due to wet leaves in midday, and moisture loss due to evaporation.

Consider using a watering wand or drip irrigation system to water the soil without wetting the foliage. This puts the water where it is needed and helps reduce the risk of disease.

Do not be fooled by wilting plants. Drooping leaves can indicate drought stress. It is also one way that some plants conserve moisture. Wait until the temperature cools, and see if the plants recover. Always check the soil moisture before reaching for the hose.

BULBS

Keep the soil moist but not wet around new plantings. Established plants need 1 inch of water per week. If it rains, you only need to make up the difference. Water clay soils in one application each week and sandy soils in two applications of half the needed water each week.

EDIBLES

Water less frequently as your plants become established. Apply enough water to moisten the top 6 inches of soil. Allow the top 2 to 3 inches to begin to dry before watering again.

LAWNS

Be sure to provide new lawns with adequate moisture. Established lawns generally need 1 inch of water each week. June rainfall often provides enough moisture. Water established lawns only as needed. If your footprints remain in the lawn, the color turns a dull bluish gray, or the leaves start to roll, it is time to water the lawn. Water thoroughly but less frequently to encourage deep roots for drought tolerance. See July, Water for tips on allowing lawns to go dormant and caring for them during drought.

PERENNIALS

As a general rule, perennials need 1 inch of water per week. Check new plantings several times a week. Water thoroughly whenever the top few inches of soil start to dry. Established plants can tolerate drier soils.

Do not overwater new or established plantings. Perennials, like other plants, often wilt in the heat of day. This is their way of conserving moisture. As soon as the temperatures cool, the plants recover.

ROSES

Water roses as needed. Use a watering wand, drip irrigation, or a soaker hose to avoid wet foliage and splashing water that can lead to disease problems.

SHRUBS

Temperature, soil type, and mulching influence the need for water. Check plants, and water more often during hot spells and when growing in sandy soil. Reduce your workload by mulching planting beds.

New plantings are still a watering priority. Keep the top 6 to 8 inches slightly moist. Check shrubs planted in clay soils once a week and those planted in sandy soils twice a week.

Established shrubs only need supplemental water during dry periods. Water thoroughly when the top 3 to 4 inches of soil is crumbly and moist.

TREES

Most established trees need thorough but infrequent watering. Water established trees every two weeks during long dry periods. Moisture-loving trees, such as paper birch, may need to be watered once a week during dry weather. Check young trees once or twice a week, and water them thoroughly as needed.

Excess water is the cause of many tree deaths. Water trees thoroughly but only when needed. In clay soils, water the trees until the top 12 inches are moist. Check in a week. Water again when the top 4 to 6 inches begin to dry. The soil will feel moist but crumbly. Sandy soils need a thorough watering twice a week in hot, dry weather. Water thoroughly until the top 12 inches are moist. Check in four days, and water when the soil begins to dry.

Newly planted container-grown trees and shrubs may need special attention. Those growing in soilless mixes need the rootball watered more frequently than the surrounding soil.

VINES & GROUNDCOVERS

Water new plantings often enough to keep the soil around the roots slightly moist. Soak the top 6 to 8 inches of soil each time you water. Gradually decrease watering frequency. Water well-rooted plants when the top 2 to 3 inches of soil start to dry. Check plants growing in clay soils once a week and those in sandy or rocky soils twice a week.

Established and mulched plants need less frequent watering. Check during extended dry periods.

FERTILIZE

ANNUALS & EDIBLES

Consider using a slow-release fertilizer for your containers if the potting mix does not already contain some fertilizer. Every time you water, you will be fertilizing. Or you can use a soluble, quick-release flowering plant fertilizer every few weeks. Mix the fertilizer with water according to the package directions.

BULBS

Add 1 pound per 100 square feet of a low-nitrogen, slow-release fertilizer in the soil prior to planting tender bulbs. Incorporate a slow-release fertilizer into the soil of container gardens prior to planting. These pots will not need to be fertilized again for six to eight weeks or even longer. Or, use a dilute solution of any flowering plant fertilizer every two weeks.

EDIBLES

Fertilize rhubarb and asparagus plantings after the last harvest if not done earlier. Follow soil test recommendations. If these are not available, apply 2 to 3 pounds of a low-nitrogen fertilizer per 100 square feet.

LAWNS

Apply ½ pound of actual nitrogen per 1,000 square feet early this month if it was not done in late May. Consider using a low-nitrogen, slow-release fertilizer to reduce the risk of burn, especially on non-irrigated lawns.

PERENNIALS

Perennials growing in properly managed soil need very little supplemental fertilization. Let the plants be your guide. Top-dress established beds once every other year by spreading several inches of compost onto the soil surface. Supplement with a low-nitrogen, slow release fertilizer, if needed.

ROSES

Follow soil test recommendations, or apply 2 pounds per 100 square feet, or 2 heaping tablespoons per plant, of a low-nitrogen, slow-release fertilizer. Select a fertilizer with at least one-third of the nitrogen in a slow-release form. See April, Fertilize for more information.

SHRUBS

Fertilize only the shrubs that are showing signs of nutrient deficiency or when recommended by soil test results. Apply fertilizer in one application in the spring. Finish fertilization that has not yet been done.

TREES

Yellow and off-color leaves may indicate a nutrient problem. Take a soil test before you add fertilizer. The soil test tells what type and how much of each nutrient to add. Adding nutrients your tree does not need can harm the plant and the environment, as well as waste your time and money.

Frequent watering of aboveground planters washes many nutrients out of the soil. Use a slow-release fertilizer at the start of the season to replace these nutrients. Follow the manufacturer's recommendations.

VINES & GROUNDCOVERS

Do not overfertilize your plants. Too much fertilizer can result in excess leaf growth, poor flowering, disease problems, and root damage. Follow soil test recommendations, or limit fertilization to once a season and only if needed.

Fertilize vines growing in containers with a slow-release fertilizer at the start of the season or every two weeks with a diluted solution of soluble flowering plant fertilizer. Follow label directions.

PROBLEM-SOLVE

ALL

Check all plantings for signs of Japanese beetles. These small, metallic green insects emerge in late June and feed on more than 300 species of plants. The beetles skeletonize the leaves by eating the leaf tissue and leaving the veins intact. Otherwise stressed trees, like paper birch and lindens, repeatedly defoliated by Japanese beetles benefit from treatment. Apply a soil systemic in fall to trees and at least thirty days prior to the adult beetles' appearance on smaller plants.

Use an insecticide labeled for use on trees to control this beetle. Consult a tree care professional for treatment of large trees. See the July chapter for more recommendations on controlling Japanese beetles on a variety of plants.

Watch for signs of deer, rabbits, and woodchucks. Spray plantings with repellents, or use scare tactics to keep the animals away. Reapply repellents after bad weather, and vary the scare tactics to increase success.

Birds, chipmunks, and squirrels often pull out, nest in, or dig up potted plants. Spray with a repellent, or temporarily cover new plantings with bird netting.

ANNUALS

Remove spotted, blotchy, and discolored leaves as soon as they are discovered. Several fungal diseases can damage annuals. Sanitation is the best way to control and reduce the spread of disease. See the following Bulbs section for more information on diseases that can attack annuals.

Monitor the garden for insects, including some described under Edibles. Minimize your use of pesticides. The fewer pesticides used, the greater number of beneficial insects you find. Look for ladybugs, lacewings, praying mantises, and other insects that eat aphids and other troublesome pests. Also watch for bees, butterflies, and hummingbirds that come to visit your garden. Protect and encourage these visitors by minimizing your use of pesticides.

Continue pulling weeds as they appear. It is much easier to keep up with a few weeds than it is to reclaim an annual garden gone bad. Pull and destroy quackgrass, creeping Charlie, and other perennial weeds that invade the annual garden.

Protect containers and new plantings from birds and chipmunks. Cover new plantings and containers with bird netting. This encourages animals to find another place to nest and dig. Remove netting once plants are established and the threat of wildlife is passed.

BULBS

Botrytis blight and powdery mildew may be problems on tuberous begonias. The blight causes brown spots on flowers and leaves. Powdery mildew starts as a white, powdery substance on the leaves and causes them to eventually turn yellow and brown. Remove faded flowers and infected leaves to control botrytis blight. Powdery mildew is most common in shade during periods of fluctuating humidity. Properly space begonias to ensure good air circulation and light penetration. If this is a yearly problem, find a more suitable location for these plants.

Leaf spot fungal disease is occasionally found on iris. Remove infected leaves as soon as they are found. Sanitation and drier weather keep this disease in check.

EDIBLES

Pull weeds as soon as they appear. They are easiest to tame in the morning after a gentle rain or other time when the soil is moist. Or, use a hoe or cultivator between rows. Be careful not to damage the roots or weed out any vegetable plants. Apply a mulch to reduce future weed sprouting.

Continue monitoring and protecting plants from corn seed, cabbage, and onion maggots. Delay plantings, cover seedlings, and rotate crops to prevent problems. See May, Problem-Solve for more specifics.

Continue to pick and destroy asparagus beetle, flea beetle, cucumber beetle, and Colorado potato beetle (both the adult and larvae). Remove them as soon as they are found to reduce damage.

Cover broccoli, cauliflower, cabbage, and Brussels sprouts to prevent cabbage worms from reaching and feeding on the plants. These insects eat holes in the leaves and add a little unwanted protein (wormlike larvae) to the dinner table. Use a lightweight row cover to form the barrier, or treat susceptible plants with *Bacillus thuringiensis* var. *kurstaki*, sold under a number of product names, to control cabbage worms. This bacteria kills only the larvae of moths and butterflies (true caterpillars) and is safe for people, other insects, and wildlife.

Set out shallow, covered containers of beer or boards between rows to capture slugs. The slugs crawl into the beer and drown and hide under the boards in the morning allowing you to remove and destroy them.

Watch for squash vine borer. This orange-and-black, day-flying moth lays its eggs at the base of vine crops. Remove and smash any that are found. Check for sawdust-like material and holes at the base of the plant. This means the borers have entered the stem and are causing damage. Slice the stem lengthwise and kill any borers you find. Bury this portion of the stem, keep the soil moist, and hope it develops new roots. Reduce damage with three weekly applications of an insecticide to the base of the plant when the adults can be seen and are laying eggs.

See August, Problem-Solve for tips on controlling leafhoppers, aphids, and other pests.

LAWNS

Check for symptoms and monitor the occurrence and spread of disease. A cool, wet spring means you may see more problems. Proper care and drier weather often are sufficient to stop or slow down the spread of disease. Keep cutting the grass high, and wait to overseed damaged areas in late August or early September. See May, Problem-Solve for more details on lawn diseases.

Insects do not generally pose a major threat to Michigan lawns. Before reaching for insecticide, make sure insects are really the problem. You can conduct tests to determine if insects are damaging your lawn (see page 21).

Anthills may sporadically appear throughout the lawn. They generally do not harm anything but annoy some homeowners. If their activity is damaging the turf roots, or if you cannot abide their presence, you may chose to use an insecticide. Spot treat to avoid killing the good insects in the soil. Select an insecticide labeled for use on lawns to control the problem pest. Be sure to read and follow all label directions carefully.

The warm weather is perfect for most weeds. As grass growth slows, the weeds seem to appear and grow overnight. Avoid using herbicides (weedkillers)

TO TEST FOR THE PRESENCE OF LAWN INSECTS

Flotation test: This is used for chinch bugs. Remove both ends of a coffee can or similar container. Sink the can in the grass at the edge of the dead area. Fill the can with water and agitate the grass. Chinch bugs float to the surface. Test several areas. Treatment is needed if you find two or three of these insects per test.

Irritation test: This detects sod webworm larvae. Their feeding can cause thin patches, brown trails, or patchy lawns. Treat these insects only if you find more than one insect per square yard.

Mix 1 tablespoon of dishwashing detergent in 1 gallon of water. Sprinkle the soapy water over 1 square yard of lawn. Conduct the test in several areas, both damaged spots and areas adjacent to the damaged grass. Check the treated areas several times over the next 10 minutes. Treat if one or more sod webworm larvae are present.

Turf removal: This confirms the presence of grubs. Turf-damaging grubs are the immature larvae of several different beetles. They feed on grass roots, causing the turf to be uniformly thin, droughty, or dead. Cut and remove 1 square foot of turf. Check the top 4 to 6 inches of soil for white grub larvae. Replace the sample, and keep the soil moist until it reroots. Treat if three or four grubs are found per 1 square foot of turf.

Visual confirmation: Take a close look at the grass blades. Greenbugs, a type of aphid, occasionally feed on the grass under trees in southern areas. If you find thirty or more aphids on each grass blade, it is time to treat. Spray the infested areas and the surrounding 6 feet with insecticidal soap.

in the summer. They can damage your lawn when applied in hot, dry weather. Instead, dig out small numbers of weeds or those in bloom. Removing their flowers reduces future weed problems.

Dogs often cause brown spots of dead grass in the lawn. Their nitrogen-rich urine acts just like fertilizer burn. The treatment is the same. Thoroughly water the area to dilute the urine and wash it through the soil. It may not be practical, but it is effective. The surrounding grass eventually fills in these brown areas. There are mixed reports on urine-neutralizing products. Some people report great success while others find that watering works just as well. Some gardeners train their dogs to go in a specific mulched area. Contact your veterinarian for more ideas.

PERENNIALS

A cool, wet spring means lots of diseases. Remove spotted, blotchy, or discolored leaves as soon as they are found. Sanitation is the best control for disease problems. See the preceding Bulbs section for more details.

Watch for leafhoppers, aphids, spittlebugs, and mites. These insects all suck out plant juices, causing leaves to yellow, brown, and die. Control high populations with insecticidal soap. Repeat weekly as needed.

Get out the flashlight, and check your garden for nighttime feeders. Slugs and earwigs eat holes in leaves and flowers at night.

ROSES

Your best defense against pest problems is a healthy plant, but even healthy plants can be infested by disease. Sanitation and proper care are critical in pest management.

SHRUBS

Healthy shrubs can tolerate most pest problems. When the numbers get too high, you may need to step in and lend nature a hand. Treat borer-infested viburnum in early June when mockorange shrubs bloom and again ten to fourteen days later. Spray the bottom 2 feet of stems with an insecticide labeled for this use.

COMMON ROSE DISEASES

Blackspot is one of the most common and most serious fungal diseases on roses. It causes black spots and yellowing of the leaves. Once a planting is infected, it is likely to develop the disease in the future. Remove infected and fallen leaves throughout the season. Fall cleanup helps reduce the source of infection for the next season. Apply fungicides labeled to control blackspot on roses in mid-June or at the first sign of this disease. Repeat every seven days throughout the growing season. You can lengthen the time between applications during dry weather.

Powdery mildew is a fungal disease that appears as a white powder on the leaf surface. It is a common problem during periods of fluctuating humidity. Properly spaced plants grown in full sun are less likely to develop this disease. Apply fungicides as soon as the disease appears, and repeat every seven to fourteen days. Use a product labeled for controlling powdery mildew on roses. Several universities and botanical gardens have successfully used weekly applications of a mixture of 1 tablespoon of baking soda, ½ tablespoon of lightweight horticultural oil or insecticidal soap, and 1 gallon of water to control powdery mildew.

Botrytis blight is a fungal disease that causes flower buds to turn black and fail to open. It is most common on pink and white roses and occurs during wet weather. Prune off and destroy infected blossoms. Sanitation and drier weather are usually enough to keep this disease under control.

Cankers are sunken and discolored areas that develop due to weather, mechanical injury, or disease. Prune out infected canes beneath the canker. Disinfect tools between cuts. Provide plants with proper care and winter protection to minimize this problem.

Insect populations are also starting to build. Small populations can usually be removed by hand. You may choose to use an insecticide to control larger populations that are damaging the plant. Many rose fertilizers contain insecticides. Check your fertilizer and pesticide labels before applying these materials.

Aphids and mites suck out the plant juices, causing the leaves to appear speckled, yellow, and distorted. Lightweight horticulture (summer) oils and insecticidal soap are more environmentally friendly products that will control these pests.

Leafhoppers often go undetected but can cause plants to be weak and stunted. These greenish yellow insects feed on the underside of the leaves. They hop sideways when disturbed.

Budworms and other caterpillars feed on flower buds and leaves. Remove and destroy the caterpillars as they are found. *Bacillius thuringiensis* var. *kurstaki*, sold under a number of product names, will control these insects without harming other beneficial insects.

Rose slugs are really sawflies that feed on the leaves. Healthy plants tolerate the damage, but these insects annoy gardeners. Live with the damage, or use an environmentally friendly insecticide labeled for their control.

Rose chafers are most common in areas with sandy soil. These beetles eat the leaf tissue, leaving the veins intact. They feed on roses from late June through July. Small populations can be removed and destroyed by hand. Insecticides labeled to control chafers on roses may be used to control larger populations or insects on large plantings. Make sure the insects are still present prior to spraying. The damage is often noticed after the insects are gone.

Japanese beetles can be found eating and mating on flowers and leaves of roses. Knock them into a can of soapy water. Soil systemic insecticides applied in late May will reduce leaf feeding. Or, apply the organic insecticide Neem as a repellent in late May, prior to the beetles' arrival.

Check burning bush and other euonymus for signs of the euonymus caterpillar. These worm-like insects build webbed nests and feed on the leaves. Use a stick to knock out the nests and remove the insects as soon as they are found. Large populations can be treated with *Bacillus thuringiensis* var. *kurstacki*. This bacterial insecticide kills only true caterpillars and will not harm beneficial insects, wildlife, or people.

Look for white, hard flecks on the leaves and stems of euonymus. Treat these scale insects with insecticidal soap when the Japanese tree lilacs are in bloom. The bloom time and egg hatch coincide. Repeat applications two more times at ten- to twelve-day intervals.

Aphid and mite populations begin to build as the temperatures rise and the rains decline. Spray plants with a strong blast of water during extended droughts. The water dislodges many of the insects, helping to minimize their damage.

Continue to prune out phomopsis-blighted branches on juniper. See May, Problem-solve for specific information.

Watch other shrubs for twig blight. The fungal diseases that cause twig dieback are most common in cool, wet weather. Remove blighted, brown, and dying branches as soon as they are found. Disinfect tools between cuts.

TREES

Continue monitoring for pests. Fortunately healthy established trees are able to tolerate most problems.

Distorted, spotted, and discolored leaves may indicate you have an insect or disease problem from gypsy moths, mites, Eastern tent caterpillars, and aphids. See this month's Problem-Solve, All for tips on managing Japanese beetles.

Continue proper care of honeylocusts as they start to releaf and recover from leafhopper and plant bug damage.

Complete scab treatments on crabapples.

Continue branch removal of cytospora-infected spruce branches, fireblight-cankered crabapples, and phomopsis-infested junipers and Russian olives.

Rake anthracnose-infected leaves as they drop from trees. This fungal disease causes brown spots on lower leaves of oak, maple, ash, black walnut, and sycamore. Though annoying, the disease is usually not life-threatening. Sycamores may benefit from future preventative treatments.

See May, Problem-Solve for more details about tree pests.

VINES & GROUNDCOVERS

Treat euonymus scale found on wintercreeper and euonymus vines. See the preceding Shrubs section for management tips or replace with a non-invasive plant.

Check plants for mites and aphids. High populations cause leaves to look speckled, yellow, and often distorted. Spray plants with a strong blast of water. Follow up with insecticidal soap if necessary. Repeated applications may be needed.

Remove spotted leaves and stems on lily-of-the-valley and pachysandra. Fungal leaf spot and blight diseases can usually be controlled with sanitation. Remove infected leaves and stems as soon as they appear. In fall, rake fallen leaves off the plantings to reduce the conditions that increase the risk of this disease.

Check clematis for wilt. Leaves wilt, and both the leaves and areas of the stem turn black. Prune infected stems back to healthy tissue. Disinfect tools between cuts. Use a solution of rubbing alcohol or one part bleach to nine parts water.

Remove brown branches, possibly phomopsis blight, on junipers. Cut brown stems back to a healthy side shoot or main stem. Disinfect tools between cuts.

Monitor bugleweed (*Ajuga*) for crown rot. Look for patches of dead and dying plants. Remove and discard sick plants. Improve soil drainage, and avoid overhead watering to reduce future problems. Treat the infected area with a fungicide before replanting.

July

Most planting is done, and you may be ready to pack up the car or head to the airport on vacation. As you prepare for your trip, remember to arrange a sitter for your garden. Containers will need to be watered, vegetables harvested, and plants tended. Finding a qualified plant sitter can be difficult. Consider bartering with a fellow gardener; you'll tend their garden while they're away if they do the same for you. Or perhaps one of your apartment-bound friends would love the opportunity. If these aren't options, check with garden groups, technical colleges with horticulture programs, or master gardeners. They may be willing to help you for a fee.

Whoever you find, make the job easy so they are more likely to be successful and help you again. Leave directions for harvesting and care. Group containers together in a partially shaded location near a water source. It will take less time for them to water all the containers when they are grouped together, and the plants will need less frequent watering in the shade. Plus your friend won't overlook that one container tucked into the corner of the garden.

Or, purchase or create a self-watering device. Fill a 5-gallon bucket with water. Run cloth strips from the bucket to the soil of the container. As the soil dries, the cloth wicks the water from the reservoir to the container. Test it before leaving town.

If you travel a lot, consider self-watering pots. They can extend the time between waterings. Or, plant individual specimens of canna, papyrus, and elephant ears in nursery pots filled with water garden potting mix. Set them into large decorative containers without drainage holes. The potted plants sit in water in the large pots to create a mini water garden. This is a great container solution for busy gardeners and those who travel a lot.

Consider installing soaker hoses or drip irrigation systems for the water lovers in your landscape. Your plant sitter will be able to water with just a turn of the faucet. Add a timer, and all they have to do is check to make sure everything is working properly. This addition may also make your gardening easier.

And give directions for storing or using the produce from your garden. Your plant sitter may find this a great bonus, and you will be happy to know your fresh produce is being enjoyed.

PLAN

ALL

July is a great time to plan. Everyone's gardens look good, and it is a great time to get some new ideas. Visit botanical gardens, participate in community garden tours, and take a walk through the neighborhood. Bring your garden journal, camera, or sketchpad to record planting schemes and combinations you want to try. Evaluate the sun and shade patterns, and make sure plants are receiving the amount of light they need. Make notes on what is working and what needs to be redesigned for next year. Jot down a few possible solutions based on your recent tour of gardens.

Monitor your plantings for pest problems. Some plants seem to struggle every year no matter what you do. These may be good candidates for replacement. Continue to look for opportunities for adding bulbs in a new perennial garden or shrub bed. Keep recording bloom times, evaluating, and photographing your summer gardens.

ANNUALS

Look for areas to add a few more annuals. Many garden centers now carry fresh new plants for midsummer and fall planting. A few new annuals can freshen up the summer garden and cover up any early season losses.

BULBS

Order spring-flowering bulbs now for fall delivery.

EDIBLES

Start a list of seeds and plants needed for mid- and late-summer plantings. Select vegetables that will mature and produce in the remaining frost-free days of this season. Or, plan to have some frost protection handy in the fall.

LAWNS

Make plans for lawn care while on vacation. If you plan on being gone more than a week, you need someone to cut the grass. Vacationing during the hot, dry months of July and August may mean you need someone to water the lawn, or just let it go dormant for this portion of the growing season.

PERENNIALS

Gather a few bouquets from your perennial garden and maybe even a friend's. Try new flower combinations. If the plants look good together in the arrangement and require the same growing conditions, they will likely look good together in the garden. Use this technique to help you plan new plant combinations for future changes in the garden.

ROSES

Roses often stop blooming in the heat of the summer. Make a note to add a few annuals or summer-blooming perennials for more color during these down times in rose bloom.

SHRUBS

Create planting beds by joining several isolated trees and shrubs together into one large garden. Fill the space with additional shrubs and perennials. Larger beds mean less mowing and eliminate the need for hand trimming around individual trees.

TREES

The heat of the summer is a good time to make sure your shade trees are working for you. Check tree locations and their impact on your environment. Consider adding trees to the east and west side of your home to reduce cooling costs. And if room permits, plant a windbreak to reduce energy spending in winter. Make notes in your journal and on your landscape plan.

VINES & GROUNDCOVERS

No room for trees to provide shade for your air conditioner or patio? Consider a vine-covered trellis. Start looking now for solutions to these and other narrow spaces that need shade or screening.

PLANT

ALL

There is still time to plant. Stop by your favorite garden center, as many offer late-season plants for replacements or late additions. You might even find a bargain or two worth adding to the garden. Give July transplants extra attention during hot, dry spells. Check plants more often during very hot and dry weather. Mulch new plantings to conserve moisture and keep soil temperature cool.

■ Rudbeckia *(left). zinnia (center) and* Echinacea *(right) are all heat- and drought-tolerant plants.*

ANNUALS

Use heat- and drought-tolerant plants, such as zinnia, moss rose, gazania, lantana, dusty miller, sunflower, and cleome, for the hotspots in your landscape.

BULBS

Lilies are potted, blooming, and available in many garden centers. Plant them in areas that receive at least six hours of direct sun with well-drained soil.

Plant autumn crocus and surprise lilies (*Lycoris squamigera*) as soon as they are available. They produce leaves in spring and will surprise you with flowers this fall.

You can start digging and dividing iris in mid- to late July, about six to eight weeks after bloom. Cut leaves in a fan shape back to 6 inches. This makes them easier to handle, reduces water loss, and improves their appearance. Dig rhizomes, and check for borers. Kill the borers, and remove old and damaged rhizomes. Plant the healthy rhizomes back to back with growing points facing out or 5 inches apart in a properly prepared location. The rhizomes should be positioned just below the soil surface with the leaves and buds facing upward.

EDIBLES

Add seeds and transplants to the garden. Use vacant spots and harvested rows for these late additions. See the planting chart on page 52 for ideas.

■ *It's not too late to fill in open spaces in your vegetable garden.*

LAWNS

You can still lay sod. Use fresh sod, and install it as soon as possible. Stored sod can overheat and damage or kill the grass plants. Once installed, the new lawn needs extra care during this often hot, dry month. Make sure the soil surface stays moist until the sod roots into the soil below. Once rooted, it still needs thorough, though less frequent, watering.

PERENNIALS

Dig and divide or take root cuttings of spring-blooming poppy, bleeding heart, and bearded iris.

ROSES

Fill a vacant spot with a container or potted rose. See April, Plant and September, Plant for details on planting roses.

SHRUBS

Summer plantings need special attention. The warm temperatures slow down rooting and dry out soil. Mulch newly planted shrubs with a 2- to 3-inch layer of woodchips or bark. This keeps roots cool and conserves moisture.

TREES

Keep planting container-grown and spring dug balled-and-burlapped trees. Summer planted trees will need extra attention during the hot part of the season. Or, store them in a shaded location convenient to a water source until the weather cools.

VINES & GROUNDCOVERS

Dig and divide overgrown and declining plants. Midsummer transplants need extra attention to help them through the summer heat. Mulch and water whenever the soil around the roots begins to dry. Reduce watering as the plants become established.

Keep planting. Always prepare the soil before adding groundcovers and vines.

CARE

ALL

Mulch the soil. Mulching helps keep roots cool and moist, while reducing weeds and improving the soil. Keep mulch away from the crown of the plant. Burying plants can lead to disease problems.

Shredded leaves and evergreen needles make attractive mulches in flowerbeds, edible gardens and more. Weed-free straw and herbicide-free grass clippings are less attractive but just as effective and work well in vegetable gardens and fruit plantings. Woodchips and shredded bark are great around trees, shrubs, and on pathways.

HERE'S HOW

TO HARVEST FLOWERS FOR FRESH USE OR DRYING

1. Cut the flowers early in the morning for the best quality. Use a sharp knife or garden shears to cut the stem above a set of healthy leaves.

2. Recut the stems just prior to placing the flowers in the vase.

3. Wait until midday to harvest flowers for drying. Pick flowers at their peak. Remove the leaves and gather a few stems into a bundle. Secure with a rubber band.

4. Use a spring-type clothespin to hang the bundle from a line, rack, or other structure in a dry, dark location.

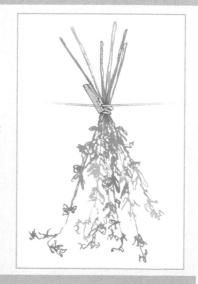

Spread a 1- to 3-inch layer of organic mulch over the soil surface. The finer the material, the thinner the layer of mulch.

ANNUALS

Continue staking tall plants that tend to flop. Loosely tie plant stems to the stake. Use twine or cushioned twist ties to secure the plants to the stake.

Harvest flowers for fresh indoor enjoyment.

Deadhead flowers for continual bloom and beauty. Pinch back leggy plants to encourage branching and more flowers.

Cut back lobelia and heat-stressed alyssum. Cut plants back halfway, continue to water, and wait for the weather to cool.

Stagger pinching and pruning within each flowerbed to display flowers all the time.

Compost annual trimmings. As the stems break down, they turn into compost, which can be used to prepare future planting beds.

BULBS

Stake and tie dahlias, lilies, and gladiolus as needed. Be careful not to spear the bulb while installing the stake. Allow enough space between the plant and stake to accommodate the bulb. Avoid this problem next year by staking tender bulbs at the time of planting, or surround tall plants with slightly shorter and stiffer plants that will serve as a living support.

Disbud dahlias for fewer but larger flowers. Remove at least two pairs of side buds that develop below the terminal (tip) bud. Remove three pairs of buds if you want giant dahlias.

Deadhead summer-flowering bulbs as needed. This increases flowering, reduces disease, and improves the overall appearance.

Remove discolored leaves and those with brown spots, holes, or soft areas. Cleanup is one of the most effective and environmentally friendly ways to control pests. Discard, do not compost, pest-infected foliage.

■ *Pinch off coleus flower stalks when they sprout so that the plant stays neat and tidy.*

EDIBLES

Blanch celery and cauliflower to keep the stems and flowers white and flavor less bitter. (To "blanch" means to block out the sun.) Cover stems of celery with soil or cardboard to block out the sunlight. Many cauliflower cultivars are self-blanching. The leaves naturally fold over the flower bud, blocking the light. You need to lend a hand for the other types. Start blanching when the flower bud is about 2 inches in diameter. Tie the outer leaves over the center of the plant. It will be ready in seven to twelve days when the head is 6 to 8 inches in diameter.

Harvest spinach when the outer leaves are 6 to 8 inches long. Remove the whole plant as days get longer and hotter and the plants get larger.

Continue picking leaf lettuce as the outer leaves reach 4 to 6 inches. Replant for a fall harvest.

Pick summer squash, such as zucchini, when the fruits are 6 to 8 inches long, or 3 to 6 inches in diameter for the round scalloped types. Keep picking to keep the plants producing.

Dig or pull radishes and beets when the roots are full size. Proper thinning and well-drained soil are important for root development. No roots? Use the greens to spice up your salads.

Check broccoli every few days once the flower buds (the part we eat) form. They quickly go from quarter size to harvest size. Harvest when the head is full sized but before the yellow flowers appear. Cut the stem 6 to 7 inches below the flower. Leave side shoots that will develop into smaller heads for later harvest.

Pick herbs as needed. Regular harvesting will keep plants compact and well-branched. Use garden scissors or hand pruners to cut short pieces off the ends of the stem. Make the cut just above a set of leaves. It looks neater, and the plant recovers faster. Wait until the plants just start blooming for the most intense flavor. Preserve this flavorful harvest for later use. See page 139 in August in the chapter introduction for tips on drying herbs, as well as Here's How to Harvest Flowers for Fresh Use and Drying.

LAWNS
Keep the grass 3 to 3½ inches tall. Taller grass is more drought-tolerant and better able to compete with pests. Warmer, drier weather means you probably need to mow less frequently.

As the heat increases and the weather turns dry, decide how to manage your lawn through droughts. You may choose to let your lawn go dormant. Stop watering and let the lawns shut down and turn brown. As the weather cools and the rains return, the lawn greens up and begins to grow again. Once dormant, leave it dormant until nature gets it growing again. Minimize foot traffic, and do not fertilize or herbicide dormant lawns. Do water ¼ inch of water every three to four weeks during extended drought. This is sufficient to keep the crown of the plant alive without breaking dormancy.

PERENNIALS
Finish staking. Carefully maneuver plants around trellises and onto stakes.

Continue deadheading and pinching back straggly plants, such as lavender.

Prune back silver mound artemisia before flowering. Prune back to fresh new growth to avoid open centers.

Cut old stems of delphiniums and diseased leaves of hardy geraniums to the fresh growth at the base of the plant. This encourages new growth and a second flush of flowers.

Prune back yellowed foliage of bleeding heart to ground level.

Stop pinching fall-blooming perennials at the beginning of the month.

ROSES
Continue to deadhead roses. Remove only individual flowers in the cluster as they fade. Once all the flowers in the cluster have bloomed, prune back the flower stem to the first five-leaflet leaf. Deadhead single-flowered roses back to the first five-leaflet leaf. This encourages stouter and stronger branch development.

Tie up new growth on climbing roses. Use string, cloth, or other flexible material to loosely tie stems to the trellis, fence, or other support structure.

SHRUBS
Watch for insects. Wilted leaves may be a sign of borer damage. Check the base of the stems for holes and sawdust debris. Prune out borer-infested stems as they are found.

Lightly prune arborvitae, yews, and junipers once the new growth has expanded. Clip stems back to a healthy bud or side shoot to contain growth. See Pruning Shrubs on page 211 for more details.

Maintain junipers' natural form by removing dead and damaged branches. Prune back to a healthy stem deep in the plant to hide cuts. Disinfect tools with a solution of one part bleach to nine parts water. Remove overly long branches back to shorter side shoots to control size.

Prune hedges and sheared shrubs when new growth expands so that the bottom of the plant is wider than the top. This allows light to reach all parts of the plant. Lightly shear summer-blooming spirea to remove faded flowers and encourage a second flush of bloom.

TREES
Remove weeds and other unwanted plants from the bases of your trees.

Prune off dead and damaged branches as they are found. Save large tree pruning for professionals. They have the equipment and training to do the job safely.

VINES & GROUNDCOVERS
Mow goutweed, also known as snow-on-the-mountain, and bishop's weed back to 6 inches several times during the growing season. This prevents flowers, reduces reseeding, and keeps the foliage fresh. Or, prune back once when foliage declines or scorches (it has brown edges). Cut the plants back to 6 inches, and wait for new and improved growth. Or, consider replacing this invasive plant with something more suitable to the landscape and environment.

Cut off wayward and overgrown stems on vines and groundcovers. Prune back to a healthy bud or side shoot. Make the cut within the outline of the plant to mask the pruning job.

Deadhead summer-blooming sedum. It improves the appearance and can encourage repeat bloom.

WATER

ALL
Check frequently, and water as needed. Water plants thoroughly but less frequently. This encourages deep roots that are more drought-tolerant.

Established plantings need about 1 inch of water each week. You may need to supplement natural rainfall. Adjust the amount of water based upon rainfall and temperatures. You need to check plants and water more often in extremely hot weather and less frequently in cooler temperatures. Provide

water in one application on clay soils and in two applications on sandy soils. Check plants growing in sandy and gravelly soils twice a week and those in clay soils once a week.

New plantings need water often enough to keep the roots and several feet of surrounding soil moist for the first several weeks of planting. Reduce frequency as the root system develops.

Check container plantings every day. Water thoroughly when the top few inches begin to dry.

LAWNS
Improperly watered lawns suffer more problems than those that depend on rainfall as the sole source of water.

Do not water and bring the lawn out of dormancy unless you can maintain a regular watering schedule throughout a drought. Allowing the lawn to go in and out of dormancy several times during the season will stress and even kill the grass.

■ *Soaker hoses are a good way to distribute low volumes of water where you need it.*

TO MEASURE WATER

1. Set several straight-sided cans under the sprinkler to measure the water applied.

2. Once the cans are filled with the required amount of water, turn off the sprinkler and move it to the next location.

3. Note the water pressure used and the time it took to apply the needed water. This will provide an idea of how long you need to sprinkle to apply the needed water.

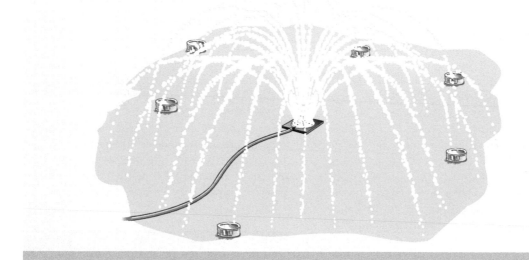

Irrigated lawns need to be watered when your footprints persist, the grass turns bluish gray, or the grass blades start to roll.

Growing lawns need 1 inch of water per week. In clay soils give lawns a good soaking once a week. Lawns in sandy soils should be watered ½ to ¾ of an inch twice a week. During an extended drought of three or more weeks, water dormant lawns ¼ inch. This is enough water to prevent the plants from drying, while still keeping them dormant. Once the rain returns, the lawn turns green.

Water early in the day for best results. Watering early reduces disease problems and water lost to evaporation.

ROSES AND SHRUBS

Roses need about 1 inch of water (5 to 6 gallons per plant) per week. Supplement rainfall as needed. Apply all the needed water in one application to clay soils. For sandy soils, make two applications of half the needed water each week.

TREES

See August, Water.

ANNUALS

Do not fertilize annuals where you used a slow-release fertilizer, which is still providing annuals with the nutrients they need.

Avoid high-nitrogen, quick-release fertilizers during hot, dry weather. These can burn heat- and drought-stressed plants.

Avoid overfertilizing cosmos and nasturtiums. Too much nitrogen prevents blooming and encourages floppy growth.

BULBS

Container bulb gardens need regular fertilizer applications. Those with a slow-release fertilizer incorporated into the soil at planting do not need additional fertilizer for one to three months. Container gardens with other types of plants also benefit from regular applications of a flowering plant fertilizer. Avoid overfertilization, especially during hot, dry weather.

Only fertilize inground plantings if needed. Use a low-nitrogen, slow-release fertilizer to avoid burn during the hot, dry summers. Plantings fertilized with a slow-release fertilizer when transplanted are likely fine and don't require additional fertilization at this time.

EDIBLES

Fertilize leafy vegetables, sweet corn, and root crops when they are half their mature size. Apply fertilizer to tomatoes, peppers, cucumbers, beans, and vine crops when they have started producing fruit.

Sprinkle small amounts of fertilizer in a band on the soil about 6 inches from the plant. Use about 2 cups of a low-nitrogen fertilizer for every 100 feet of row.

LAWNS

Only irrigated and highly managed lawns can be fertilized this month. Use a low-nitrogen, slow-release fertilizer to avoid burn. Do not fertilize dormant or non-irrigated lawns. This can damage and even kill the grass.

PERENNIALS

Avoid overfertilizing your plants. Most perennials can get all the nutrients they need from properly prepared soil and topdressing of compost.

Consider fertilizing perennials cut back for rebloom. Use a low-nitrogen, slow-release fertilizer to avoid burn.

ROSES

Fertilize hybrid tea roses, waiting at least four to six weeks after the last application.

Fertilize container roses once or twice a month if a slow-release product was not used at the start of the season. Follow fertilizer label directions.

■ *Apply a side-dressing of compost, aged manure, or low-nitrogen fertilizer if needed to give vegetables a midseason boost.*

SHRUBS

Do not fertilize. Summer fertilization can harm the roots in hot, dry weather.

TREES

Wait until next spring to fertilize newly planted trees. Fertilizing now may damage newly forming roots. Continue fertilizing trees growing in aboveground planters. Follow label directions. Monitor established trees for signs of nutrient deficiencies. Wait until fall, once the trees are dormant, to add any needed nutrients.

VINES & GROUNDCOVERS

Only fertilize plants showing signs of nutrient deficiency. Look for stunted growth, poor flowering, and lack of vigor. Consider taking a soil test before adding any fertilizer. Otherwise, supplement the spring fertilization with a small amount (3 to 4 pounds per 1000 square feet) of a low-nitrogen fertilizer. Apply the fertilizer beside the plants on the soil surface.

Fertilize vines growing in containers if a slow-release fertilizer was not applied at the start of the season. Follow label directions.

PROBLEM-SOLVE

ALL

Pull weeds as they appear, or use a hoe to lightly cultivate these invaders. Be careful not to injure the roots of your plants. Mulching reduces weeds.

Continue monitoring and controlling Japanese beetles. Pick by hand and destroy small populations of these small, metallic green-brown beetles. Use an environmentally friendly insecticide labeled for control of Japanese beetles on shrubs to control larger populations. Don't use traps to control this pest. They draw more insects into your garden.

July and early August are usually the hottest part of our growing season. Extreme heat can cause plants to stop blooming, decline, and even die. Reduce the stress to your plants by mulching the soil with shredded leaves, pine needles, or other organic mulch. A thin layer of mulch helps keep the soil and plant roots cool and moist.

Stop fertilizing during extremely hot, dry weather. This can damage already stressed plants.

Keep applying repellents to discourage troublesome deer, rabbits, and woodchucks. Make sure fencing is secure and still doing its job.

ANNUALS

Keep watching for plantbugs. These insects suck out plant juices, causing speckling, yellowing, and browning of the leaves. Repeated applications of insecticidal soap will help reduce the damage.

Check plantings for signs of leafhoppers. These wedge-shaped insects hop off the plant when disturbed. Their feeding can cause stunting and tip burn on the leaves. These insects also carry the aster yellow disease that causes sudden wilting, yellowing, and death of susceptible plants. Prevent the spread of this disease by controlling the leafhoppers. Several applications of an appropriate product may be needed for control.

Sanitation is usually sufficient to keep flower diseases under control. Pick off spotted leaves as soon as they appear. Deadhead flowers during rainy periods to reduce the risk of botrytis blight. Thin out plantings infected with powdery mildew. This increases air circulation and light penetration to help slow the spread of the disease.

BULBS

Check limp and pale irises for borers. Dig up rhizomes, cut off soft and borer-infested portions of the rhizome, and replant. Make a note on your garden calendar to cut back and clean up iris foliage in the fall.

Stalk borers feed inside stems of various flowers and cause them to wilt and die. Remove infested stems, and kill the borers if they are still present (smashing or chopping in half works well). Mark your calendar and watch for this pest next season.

Earwigs, aphids, and mites are common pests found on a variety of plants, including bulbs. Earwigs often feed on flower petals. They can be trapped and killed or treated with an insecticide. Just be aware that these chemicals also harm beneficial insects. Aphids and mites can be controlled with insecticidal soap.

Thrips cause a scratched appearance on the leaves and distorted flowers on gladioli and occasionally on dahlias. Repeated applications of insecticides can help minimize the damage. Badly infested gladiolus corms should be treated or discarded prior to storage.

Powdery mildew, leaf spot, botrytis, and anthracnose are often seen in wet summers. These cause leaves to be spotted or discolored. Bulbs of diseased plants should only be saved if the bulb is firm and free from streaking and discoloration.

Remove infected leaves and faded flowers to reduce botrytis blight, leaf spot, and anthracnose disease. Sanitation and improved weather are usually sufficient control.

Lilies are a favorite of rabbits and deer. Increase success by treating with repellents, or secure scare tactics before the plants start blooming and the animals start eating.

EDIBLES

Monitor the garden for the following pests: cabbage worms, root maggots, Colorado potato beetles, squash vine borers, picnic beetles, slugs, aphids, leafhoppers, and plantbugs. Also see June, Problem-Solve for more information.

Check the lower leaves on tomato plants and vine crops for discoloration, yellowing, and spotting.

Do not be discouraged if the bottoms of your first few tomatoes are black. Blossom end rot commonly affects the first set of fruit. Cut off the damaged portion and eat the rest.

See August, Problem-Solve for more information on all these issues.

LAWNS

Proper care is the best defense against pests. Always properly identify the pest, determine if control is needed, and evaluate your options before treating.

Grub damage becomes obvious during the dry

months of July and August. Their feeding causes the turf to be uniformly thin, appear droughty, or die. Treat only if you find three or four grubs per 1 square foot of turf.

Small patches (2 to 4 inches) of dead grass may indicate billbug damage. Check the soil for the larvae before treating.

Watch for pale or yellowing turf under trees. Greenbugs, a type of aphid, can cause this type of damage. Treatment is only needed when you find thirty or more greenbugs per grass blade.

See May, Problem-Solve and June, Problem-Solve for more on disease and insect pests.

To control weeds, continue to mow high. Taller grass is better able to out-compete the weeds. Crabgrass is just starting to appear. Mark locations of problem areas on your lawn map to make it easier to target pesticide applications next spring, reducing the amount of synthetic chemicals you use.

PERENNIALS

Continue removing spotted and diseased leaves as soon as they are found. Deadhead plants during wet weather to further reduce the risk of disease.

To control insects, check the leaf surfaces and stems for aphids and mites. Spray plants with a strong blast of water to dislodge these insects. Use insecticidal soap to treat damaging populations. This is a soap formulated to kill soft-bodied insects, but it is not harmful to the plant or the environment.

Check for plantbugs whenever you see speckled and spotted leaves and stems. Insecticidal soap or other environmentally friendly insecticides labeled for controlling plantbugs on flowers can be used. Monitor for spittlebug, earwigs, and slugs.

ROSES

Repellents, fences, and scare tactics may provide some relief from deer and rabbits.

Continue monitoring plants for pests on a weekly basis. Early detection and sanitation can reduce pest populations with fewer pesticides. Always read and follow all label directions whenever using any chemical. Wear gloves, goggles, and long sleeves. To reduce spray hazards, spray early in the morning when the air is still and there is less activity in the yard.

Watch for blackspot, powdery mildew, and canker diseases. Aphids, mites, leafhoppers, caterpillars, and beetle populations are starting to reach damaging levels. See May, Problem-Solve for more details.

■ *Keep an eye out for blackspot on your roses.*

SHRUBS

Healthy shrubs can tolerate most pests in the landscape. When weather conditions favor the pests, check with your local Extension service, a botanical garden, or a garden center for help with your diagnosis.

Control large populations of aphids and mites with a strong blast of water from the garden hose. Treat shrubs with insecticidal soap if the populations grow and damage is severe.

Check shrubs for leucanium scale. This hard-shelled insect attacks a wide range of shrubs. Treat with an ultra-fine oil or insecticide labeled for use on this pest when the hills-of-snow ('Annabelle' type) hydrangeas are in full bloom and again in two weeks.

Check the base of wilted stems for signs of borers. Sawdust and holes indicate borers are present. Prune out and destroy borer-infested branches. Regular renewal pruning is usually sufficient control.

Look for swellings at the base of viburnum, euonymus, and spirea. The disease-induced galls eventually girdle and kill the stem. Prune out infected stems below the gall. Disinfect tools between cuts.

Rake and destroy spotted leaves as they fall to reduce the source of disease next season.

Monitor lilacs and other shrubs for powdery mildew. Infected plants survive, but their appearance declines as the season progresses. Reduce problems by increasing the light and air circulation. Thin overgrown plantings during the dormant season (or right after spring bloom) to increase light and air flow and to decrease disease.

No flowers on your Endless Summer hydrangeas? Keep soil moist spring through early summer, and apply Milorganite® in spring. As the microorganisms release nutrients from this fertilizer, they also release some of the phosphorous and potassium bound to the soil. The phosphorous promotes bloom is this and other flowering plants.

TREES

Monitor all trees for signs of insects and disease. Proper care and sanitation (the removal of infected plant parts) helps minimize damage and reduce future problems.

Aphid and mite populations may explode during hot, dry weather. Have you ever parked your car under a large tree and returned to find the windshield spotted with a clear, sticky substance?

This is honeydew secreted by aphids. These small, teardrop-shaped insects can be green, black, white, or peach in color. As these insects suck out plant juices, they secrete the excess as honeydew. Occasionally a black fungus known as sooty mold grows on the honeydew. The fungus blocks sunlight, causing leaves to yellow and even drop. Lady beetles often move in and eat the aphids before this pest is even discovered. If not, you may need to step in with a strong blast of water from the garden hose. Insecticidal soap controls aphids and removes the sooty mold.

Check gypsy moth-infested trees for pupal cases (cocoons). Look in bark crevices and protected areas of the tree trunk. Destroy any that are found.

Bare crabapples are a common sight in summers following a cool, wet spring. The cause is probably apple scab. Rake and destroy leaves as they fall.

This will reduce the source of disease next season. Consider replacing disease-susceptible crabapples with newer scab-resistant cultivars. See April, Problem-Solve for information on chemical controls for apple scab.

Anthracnose, a fungal disease, can cause spotting and eventually leaf drop on oaks, maples, ashes, black walnuts, and sycamores. Healthy trees survive this damage. Sprays are not effective at this time. Rake and destroy fallen leaves to reduce the source of infection for next season.

Continue to prune out dead and cankered branches. Disinfect tools with rubbing alcohol or a solution of one part bleach to nine parts water. Avoid pruning oaks at this time.

■ *Keep an eye on phlox and other shrubs for powdery mildew.*

■ *Lady beetles are a good organic solution to aphids.*

August

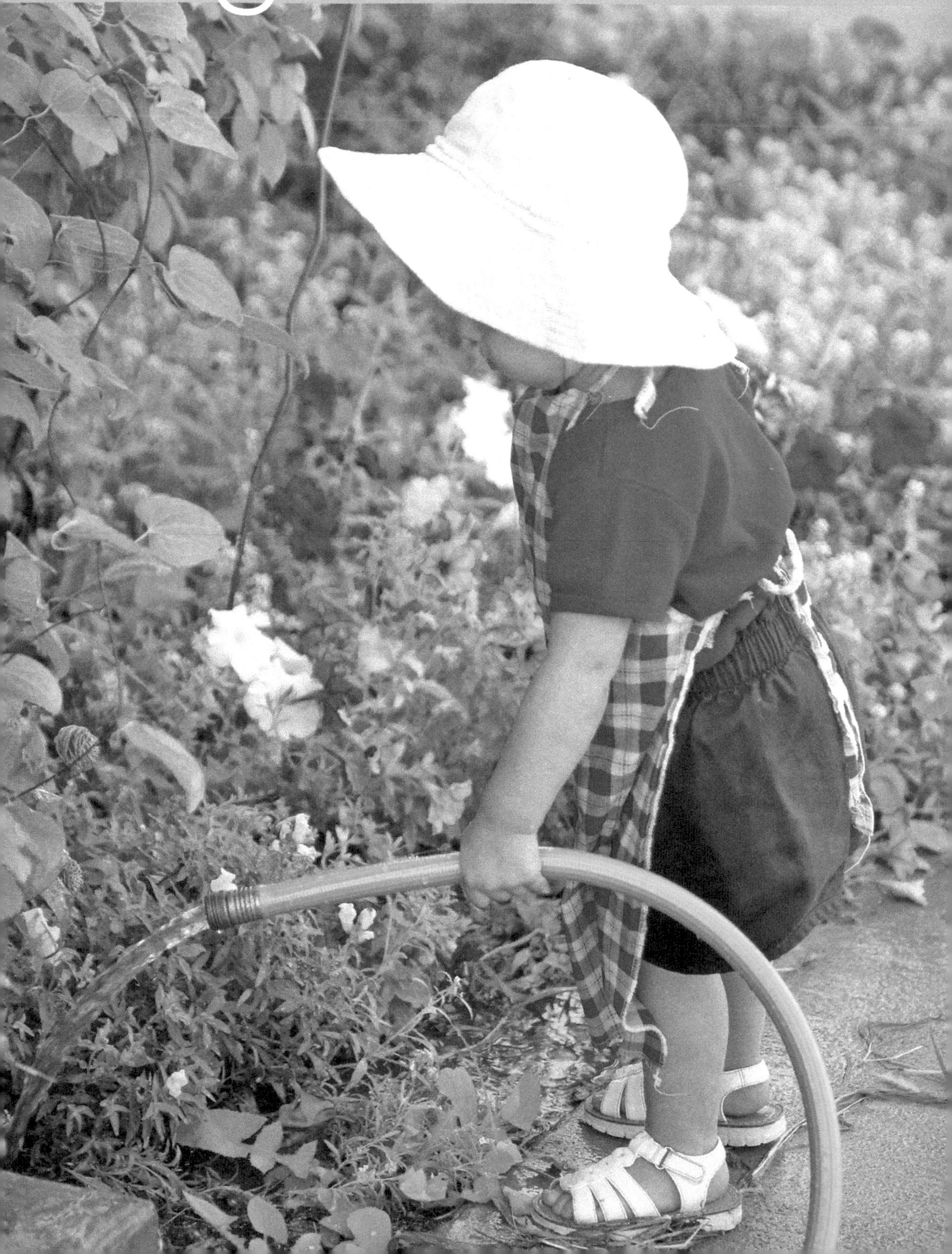

Early August is often the peak of hot, dry weather. You may spend much of your gardening efforts watering and mulching, but hopefully you will spend a bit of time harvesting fresh vegetables and flowers.

Harvest flowers in the morning. Take a bucket of water with you, and place cut flowers in the water while collecting the remaining flowers. Remove their lower leaves and recut the stems just prior to arranging. Keep the vase full of fresh water.

To harvest flowers for drying, wait until midday. Remove leaves and combine in small bundles. Use rubber bands to hold the stems together. As the stems shrink, the rubber bands contract, holding the stems tight. Use a spring-type clothespin to attach drying flowers to a line, nail, or other support. Dry in a warm, dark, and airy location.

Preserve the flavor of herbs for year-round enjoyment by gathering herbs in the morning after the dew has dried. If possible, harvest right before the plant begins flowering, when the buds are formed but not open. You'll get the greatest concentration of oil. Discard any damaged or diseased parts. You can remove up to 75 percent from an established plant. Then select the preservation method that suits your needs.

Dry herbs as described or spread them on a cookie sheet and place in the oven on its lowest setting. Prop the door open to increase air circulation. Stir occasionally. Remove the leaves when thoroughly dried. They will crumble when pinched and rubbed.

You can also spread a cup of herbs on a paper plate covered with one paper towel and place in the microwave. Set the microwave on high about 1 to 2 minutes. Experiment to find the best time for your machine. Heat an additional 20 seconds if the herbs are not yet dry. Stop when the herbs feel brittle and easily pull off the stems. Store dried herbs in airtight containers.

Or, spread the herbs on a cookie sheet in the freezer for several hours. Once frozen, place in freezer bags or containers for later use. Blanch (dip in boiling water) basil prior to freezing. Most other herbs do not need to be blanched to preserve their flavor and quality.

You can also chop the herbs as you would when using fresh herbs. Put a tablespoon of herbs in each ice cube tray compartment. They are now premeasured for future use. Fill the cube with water and freeze. Pop the frozen cubes out of the tray, and store in the freezer. Enjoy!

PLAN

ALL

Wear a hat and long sleeves to protect eyes and skin from the sun's rays. Try gardening in early morning or evening to avoid the extreme heat. And watch out for the mosquitoes!

Keep visiting botanical and public gardens. Participate in their educational events, field days, and garden tours. This is a great way to find out if certain plants do as well in our area as the catalogs claim.

Take advantage of the heat. Grab a cold drink, sit under the shade of one of your lovely trees, and write in your journal. Record details on your new plantings, the weather, pest problems, and plant care. This information helps you prepare for next season. Create or add to your planting wish list. Write down the plant name, variety, bloom time, and other features that caught your attention. Use this list when planning changes and additions to next year's garden.

HERE'S HOW

TO TAKE CUTTINGS FROM ANNUALS

1. Coleus, geraniums, wax begonias, browallia, impatiens, fuchsia, annual vinca, and herbs are commonly saved this way: Take a 4- to 6-inch cutting from the tip of a healthy stem. Remove any flowers and the lowest set of leaves.

2. Dip the cut end in a rooting hormone to encourage rooting and discourage rot. Place the cutting in moist vermiculite, perlite, or a well-drained potting mix.

3. Place in a bright location away from direct sun. Keep the rooting mix moist.

4. Plant rooted cuttings—usually ready in two weeks—in small containers filled with a well-drained potting mix. Move them to a sunny window and care for them as houseplants.

ANNUALS

It's never too early to start preparing for winter. Start taking cuttings from annuals you want to overwinter indoors. Your garden plants are healthy and will root faster now than later in the season.

BULBS

Finish ordering spring flowering bulbs from catalogs. Order early for the best selection. Consider growing some autumn crocus or surprise lilies this year. Find a location that tolerates their early spring leaf growth but isn't subject to deep cultivation over summer. Autumn crocus mixes well with groundcovers and low-growing perennials.

Time to harvest ripe peppers and tomatoes.

EDIBLES
Plan a harvest party, and share your fresh produce with friends and relatives. Visit the farmer's market. This is a great source of fresh vegetables and a good place to try some new vegetables you may want to grow next season.

LAWNS
Mid-August through mid-September is the best time to repair, replace, or start a new lawn. Consider replacing lawns with 60 percent or more weeds and bare spots. Those with compacted soils, some weeds, or bare spots would benefit from renovation and repair. See September, Plant for details.

PERENNIALS
Look for bare areas for new plants or planting beds. Late summer is a great time to add new plants or prepare the soil for new perennial gardens.

ROSES
Many repeat-blooming roses are putting on their second show of the season. Take time to enjoy your roses as summer care begins winding down.

VINES & GROUNDCOVERS
Annual and perennial vines can provide quick shade, decorative windbreaks, and screening in the landscape. Consider them as an option for narrow spaces too small for trees and shrubs. This is a good alternative to columnar buckthorn, which has become an invasive weed in our landscapes. Use groundcovers under trees where the surface roots make it hard to mow or the shade makes it impossible to grow grass.

Plants grown in containers can be moved into the shade to protect them from the August heat.

PLANT

ANNUALS
Replace weatherworn annuals with fall bedding plants. Purchase pansies, flowering kale, and other cool-weather annuals to spruce up the garden for fall. You may have to wait until late August, when transplants are available.

BULBS
Finish digging and dividing irises. Cut leaves in a fan shape back to 6 inches. Dig rhizomes, and check for borers. Kill borers, and remove old and damaged rhizomes. Plant the healthy rhizomes back-to-back with growing points out or 5 inches apart in a properly prepared location. The rhizomes should be just below the soil surface with the leaves and buds facing upward.

EDIBLES
Keep planting seeds of short-season crops that can be harvested before the first killing frost. Calculate the number of days left before the first killing frost, and compare it to the needed growing dates for the crop. See the late planting chart on page 218.

■ *Oakleaf hydrangea (above) and butterfly bush (below) are both beautiful summer-blooming shrubs.*

LAWNS

Begin seeding lawns in mid- to late August as the weather starts to cool. The soil is warm, so the seeds germinate quickly. The temperatures are cooling and perfect for growing grass. See May, Plant for details on seeding a lawn.

This is also a good time to lay sod. The cooler temperatures promote rooting, and you will need to water less frequently than with lawns sodded in July. See April, Plant for details on installing sod.

Bare areas can also be repaired. Remove dead grass, amend soil as needed, and roughen the soil surface. Purchase a lawn patch kit or make one yourself. Mix one handful of a quality lawn-seed mix into a bucket of topsoil. Sprinkle this over the soil surface, rake smooth, and mulch. Water often enough to keep the soil surface moist.

Overseed thin lawns. Creating a denser stand of turf helps reduce weeds, fight pests, and improve the overall appearance. See September, Plant for directions.

PERENNIALS

Keep making additions to your perennial gardens. Dig and divide overgrown iris, poppies, and other spring-blooming perennials.

ROSES

Finish planting potted hybrid teas early in the month. The later you plant, the greater the risk of winterkill. See May, Plant for details on planting potted hybrid teas. You can plant hardy shrub roses throughout August and early fall; see September, Plant for details.

SHRUBS
Consider adding a summer-flowering shrub to brighten up any drab, lifeless areas in your yard.

Bottlebrush buckeye (*Aesculus parviflora*) is a large shrub that produces white spikes of flowers in July.

Butterfly bush (*Buddleja davidii*) is a sub-shrub that dies back to the ground in most winters. It is suited to warmer parts of the state or for overwintering in an unheated garage. Just be patient, as this plant can be late to emerge, especially in a cool spring. Fragrant flowers in white, pink, lavender, or yellow cover this plant from midsummer to fall.

Summersweet (*Clethra alnifolia*) produces lightly fragrant white flowers in summer and golden foliage in fall on up to 5-feet-tall plants. This summer beauty attracts butterflies and is hardy to zone 4.

Hydrangeas (*Hydrangea* spp.) are good summer bloomers, with various choices for sun and shade locations. 'Annabelle' types produce white, snowball-like flowers in July. The pink-flowered (no matter the soil pH) 'Invincibelle' and 'Bella Anna' produce large blooms and are reliably hardy in zone 3. 'All Summer Beauty', 'Penny Mac', or 'Endless Summer' produce blue (in acidic soil) or pink (in alkaline soil) flowers in July and August. See July, Problem-Solve if this has not been your experience. Panicle hydrangeas such as 'Vanilla Strawberry', 'Limelight', and 'Little Lamb' offer white, pink, or chartreuse flowers that fade to pink and brown from August through September.

Potentilla (*Potentilla fruticosa*) is covered with yellow, white, orange, or pinkish flowers from June through fall.

Spirea (*Spiraea japonica*) is a popular summer-blooming plant with white, pink, rose, or lavender blooms.

TREES
Late summer and fall are excellent times to plant trees. Many stores have sales on plants at this time

Keep mulch a few inches away from the base of trees to reduce the risk of disease and rodent damage.

of the season. Some stores offer trees at reduced prices. Make sure you are really getting a bargain. Drought-stressed and poorly maintained trees are not a bargain. These are slow to establish and may never fully develop into healthy landscape specimens. After several years of struggling, you may end up replacing the tree. Not only have you spent money and time buying and planting two trees, but you have also lost valuable tree-growing time.

VINES & GROUNDCOVERS

Keep planting groundcovers and vines. There is still time for plants to establish roots before winter sets in.

HERE'S HOW

TO PLANT GROUNDCOVERS UNDER TREES

1. Do not cover the tree roots with soil or till deeply. Cultivation damages the fine feeder roots located in the top 12 inches of soil.

2. Use an edger or sharp shovel to edge the new planting bed. Cut the grass short and cover with newspaper or cardboard and mulch. Or, carefully remove grass with a sod cutter, or kill it with a total vegetation killer.

3. Leave the dead grass (if killed with an herbicide) intact to serve as your first layer of mulch. You may cover it with a decorative mulch after planting. You can cut through the grass, cardboard, and mulch or let things decompose for several months or overwinter for easier planting

4. Dig a hole twice the width but the same depth as the groundcover. Remove the container, and set the groundcover in the hole at the same depth as it was growing in the pot.

5. Fill with soil. Water to help remove air pockets and settle the soil.

6. Mulch the area with woodchips, evergreen needles, or shredded leaves.

Minimize the impact on established trees when planting groundcovers beneath their canopy.

CARE

ALL

The heat usually continues and often peaks this month. Protect your plants and yourself from heat stress. Mulch plants to keep the roots cool and moist. Place a thin layer of shredded leaves or other organic material on exposed soil around the plants.

ANNUALS

Watch for heat stall. Purple alyssum, snapdragons, lobelia, garden pinks, French marigolds, and others stop flowering during extremely hot weather. Wait for the weather to cool for these plants to start flowering. If this is a yearly problem, find a cooler location for these plants. Next year, replace them with zinnia, gazania, moss rose, sunflowers, lantana, and other more heat-tolerant plants.

Continue to deadhead faded flowers. Cut back to the first set of leaves or flowering offshoots. Pinch back leggy plants for a fresher look. Use a sharp knife or hand pruners to prune the plant one-fourth to halfway back. Cut just above a bud or set of healthy leaves. The remaining plant looks better and recovers faster.

BULBS

Leave foliage on tender and summer bulbs as long as possible. Dig gladioli only after foliage has yellowed and dried naturally. Allow lily foliage to yellow and die naturally. Cut, do not pull, the leaves.

Continue to disbud and tie tall dahlias as needed. See July, Care for details.

Continue cutting gladioli and dahlias for indoor enjoyment.

EDIBLES

Check late plantings for overcrowding. Remove excess plants so the remaining seedlings have enough space to reach mature size.

■ *Onions ready to harvest.*

Protect ripening melons and the fruit of other vine crops from rot. Slide a downturned plastic lid or mulch the soil under the fruit.

Harvest potatoes as the tops die and tubers reach full size. Dig carefully to avoid damage. Gently remove excess soil and store surplus potatoes in a cool, dark location.

Dig onions when the tops fall over and begin to dry. Use those started from sets first; they do not store as well as those started from seeds or plants. Cure the bulbs you plan to store. Braid the tops and hang them to air dry, or spread them on a screen in a dry location. Give them one to two weeks to dry before storing in a cool, dry location.

Pick peppers when the fruits are firm and fully colored. Separate the hot and mild peppers during harvest and storage to avoid surprises.

Harvest tomatoes when they are fully colored. Leave ripe tomatoes on the vine for an extra five to eight days to enhance their flavor. Continue removing unwanted suckers on staked tomato plants. Check the plants every five to seven days and remove the side shoots (suckers) that form between the stem and leaf.

Harvest cucumbers based on their use. Pick for sweet pickles when they are 1½ to 2½ inches long, dill pickles at 3 to 4 inches in length, and slicing cucumbers when 6 to 9 inches long. Harvest burpless cucumbers when they are 10 to 12 inches long.

LAWNS

Dormant lawns should be left dormant until the drought conditions pass. Minimize foot traffic and do not fertilize or use herbicides on dormant lawns. Give them ¼ inch of water during extended (three- to four-week) drought periods. This keeps the grass alive while allowing it to remain dormant.

■ *If heavy foot traffic is killing your grass, consider replacing it with steppers or a mulched path.*

Keep the grass 3 to 3½ inches tall. Start cutting newly sodded lawns as soon as they are well rooted.

PERENNIALS

Continue deadheading for aesthetics, to prevent reseeding, and to prolong bloom. Leave the last set of flowers intact to allow the formation of seedpods that add interest to the winter landscape.

Cut back declining plants to improve appearances. Remove insect-damaged, declining, and dead foliage.

Do not prune sub-shrubs such as butterfly bushes (*Buddleja*), blue mist spirea (*Caryopteris*), and Russian sage (*Perovskia*). Enjoy their late-season blooms, and allow plants to start hardening off for winter.

Cut back short-lived perennials such as blanket flowers (*Gaillardia*) and 'Butterfly Blue' pincushion flower (*Scabiosa*). Late-season pruning stimulates root growth and may help extend the plant's life.

ROSES

It is not too late to mulch roses. A 2- to 3-inch layer of organic matter can help conserve moisture and suppress weeds. Weed the garden prior to mulching. Avoid piling the mulch around the crown of the plant.

Hybrid tea roses are often disbudded to increase flower size. Remove side buds that form along the stem. This allows the plant to send all its energy to one flower. The result is one large, long-stem flower. Harvest or deadhead this back to the first five-leaflet leaf.

Other roses, such as grandifloras and floribundas, produce several flowers in a cluster. Remove all but one bud for a single large bloom, or allow the cluster to develop so you have several smaller blossoms. Deadhead the individual flowers as they fade. Cut the whole stem back once all the flowers in the cluster have faded.

Remove suckers that appear at the base of roses. Cut them off below ground to reduce the chance of re-sprouting. These canes are growing from the hardy rootstock and can diminish the vigor and beauty of the desired, grafted rose.

Prune off any cankered, dead, or damaged canes. Between cuts, disinfect tools with a solution of one part bleach to nine parts water. This reduces the spread of diseases.

Continue to harvest or deadhead flowers on shrub roses. Regular deadheading keeps the plants producing more flowers.

SHRUBS

Avoid late-season pruning that can stimulate late-season growth.

Finish touchup pruning on sheared plants as soon as possible. Remove only wayward branches. Save major pruning for the dormant season.

TREES

Pull mulch away from the trunks of the trees.

Check new plantings and remove any labels, wires, twine, or other materials that can eventually girdle the trunks.

Inspect all trees for trunk damage. Expand planting and mulch beds to protect trees from weed whips and lawn mowers.

Watch for early signs of fall. Trees that color up early are letting you know they are in distress. Construction damage, girdling roots, root rot, and decline can cause all or part of your tree to turn fall color prematurely. Proper watering and care may help a stressed tree. Other problems need to be addressed by a certified arborist.

Save major pruning chores for fall. Late-season pruning can stimulate late-season growth that may be damaged in the winter. Avoid pruning honeylocusts and oaks. The open wounds increase the risk of disease.

VINES & GROUNDCOVERS

Watch for brown leaf edges that can indicate scorch. Pay special attention to hostas and other shade lovers grown in sun. Water is not always the solution. Often the plants are unable to take the water up fast enough to replace what they lose during extreme heat. Mulch the soil, water properly by moistening the top 6 inches whenever the top 3 to 4 inches start to dry, and consider moving plants to a more suitable location in the future.

Remove badly scorched leaves.

WATER

ALL
Let the weather and your plants determine your watering schedule. Water garden beds whenever the top few inches of soil start to dry. Mulched and shaded gardens need less frequent watering. Check plantings several times a week during extremely hot, dry weather.

Pay special attention to moisture-loving plants. Consider moving them to areas that tend to stay moist for longer periods.

Water your gardens early in the morning to reduce the risk of disease and water loss to evaporation. Use a soaker hose or watering wand to get the water to the soil and roots where it is needed.

Check container plantings every day. They usually need a thorough watering once a day. Apply enough water so that the excess runs out the bottom. Water the soil, not the foliage, to minimize disease problems and moisture lost to evaporation. Use a watering wand or other hose attachment that allows you to place the water on the soil where it is needed. These tools also help extend your reach, making watering an easier and drier experience.

Check new plantings several times a week. Water thoroughly and often enough to keep the top 4 inches of soil slightly moist. Most established plants need about 1 inch of water per week. Apply needed water in one application in clay soils and in two applications in sandy soils.

Water established, mulched, and drought-tolerant plantings thoroughly but less frequently.

LAWNS
Grub-infested, disease-damaged, or stressed lawns should be watered. Watering helps reduce stress and masks pest damage.

An established irrigated lawn should receive 1 inch of water when it shows signs of wilting.

New lawns should be watered often enough to keep the soil surface moist. Reduce watering frequency once the sod has rooted into the soil and the grass seed begins to grow.

Give dormant lawns ¼ inch of water every three to four weeks during extended drought periods. This keeps the grass alive while allowing it to remain dormant.

ROSES AND SHRUBS
See July, Water.

TREES
Don't forget to water established trees and moisture lovers during extended droughts. Mature trees need about 10 gallons of water for each diameter inch of the tree. Hand watering with a hose takes approximately five minutes to produce 10 gallons of water. Double-check this amount with your

■ *Commercial gators are useful tools for watering newly planted trees.*

Spot spray to minimize pesticide use and avoid killing plants you wish to preserve.

watering setup. Once calibrated, multiply the tree diameter times five minutes (or time for your system) for total watering time.

Or create your own watering system with five-gallon buckets. Punch several ¼-inch-sized holes in the bottom of five-gallon buckets. Place several buckets throughout the area under the canopy of your trees. Fill as many times as needed to provide sufficient water.

FERTILIZE

ALL

Stop fertilizing inground plantings. Late applications of fertilizer encourage late season growth that becomes more susceptible to winter injury.

Early in the month, avoid fertilizing gardens during hot, dry periods. Adding fertilizer when water is limited can damage plant roots.

Stop fertilizing any plants in containers that spend their winter outdoors.

Container plants that won't be overwintered can still be fertilized using a quick-release fertilizer according to label directions. Check the fertilizer needs of any containers that had a slow-release fertilizer mixed into the soil. If the plants appear less vigorous and foliage is pale, you may need to fertilize.

HERE'S HOW

TO APPLY TOTAL VEGETATION KILLER EASILY

1. Remove the top and bottom of a plastic milk jug.

2. Cover the weed with the plastic milk jug.

3. Spray the total vegetation killer on the weed inside the milk jug. The jug protects the surrounding plants from the harmful weed-killer. Remove the jug after the herbicide on the weed dries.

PROBLEM-SOLVE

ALL

Ground ivy, quackgrass, and bindweed are perennial weeds that can quickly take over your garden. Hand pulling does not usually work on these deeply rooted plants.

Cultivation just breaks the plants into smaller pieces that can start lots of new plants. Use a total vegetation killer to control these pesky weeds. These products kill the tops and roots of the weeds and any growing plant they touch. Several applications may be needed.

Paint, sponge, or wipe the total vegetation killer on the weed leaves. The chemical moves through the leaves, down the stems, and into the roots.

Include hand pulling, cultivation, and mulching as part of your ongoing weed control. Try to eliminate weeds before they flower and set seed.

Watch for powdery mildew. This fungal disease looks as if someone sprinkled baby powder on leaves. Remove infected leaves as soon as they appear. Neem-based fungicides are considered organic. Or try the baking soda mix tested by Cornell University. Mix one tablespoon baking soda with one-half tablespoon insecticidal soap or an ultrafine horticulture oil in a gallon of water. Regular applications are needed.

Fall cleanup reduces the source of infection next season. Review the growing conditions and make needed adjustments in next year's design. Severe infestations block the sunlight, causing leaves to yellow. Increased sunlight and air circulation reduces this problem.

Japanese beetles are finishing their aboveground feed. They soon enter the soil and lay their eggs for the next generation. Knock the adults in a can of soapy water to help reduce future populations. Larger numbers can be controlled with an environmentally friendly insecticide labeled for use on shrubs to control Japanese beetles.

Watch for signs of deer, rabbits, and woodchucks. Apply repellents, vary scare tactics, and check fencing in plantings that have been constantly plagued by these animals.

ANNUALS

Continue monitoring plants for insects and disease. Mites and aphids are big problems during hot, dry weather. Watch for slugs and earwigs in shaded locations and during cool, wet weather.

Remove leaves with spots and discolored flowers. Sanitation is often the most effective treatment for fungal diseases in the garden. Discard infected plant parts to reduce the spread of disease.

BULBS

Monitor plants for pest problems. Properly identify the cause and all control options before treating. Your local county office of the Michigan State University Extension Service or their website are good sources for help.

Viruses and aster yellows can cause poor flowering and distorted flower spikes on gladioli. There are no chemical cures for these diseases. Remove infected plants as soon as they are found. This helps reduce the risk to nearby healthy plants. Control aphids and leafhoppers feeding on the plants. These insects carry the diseases from sick to healthy plants. Controlling the insects reduces the spread of these diseases. Discard the corms of any diseased gladioli.

Monitor plants for thrips, aphids and mites. Thrips are tiny and difficult to control. Repeated applications of Neem, insecticidal soap, or an insecticide labeled for this pest may reduce problems. Treat or discard thrip-infested gladiolus corms prior to winter storage. Damaging populations of aphids and mites can be controlled with a strong blast of water or insecticidal soap.

EDIBLES

Continue removing and destroying cucumber beetles, Colorado potato beetles, and cabbage worms as soon as they are found. See June, Problem-Solve for more control options.

Monitor and control squash vine borer. Remove and destroy infested vines this fall as cleanup will help reduce next season's population. See June, Problem-Solve for tips on managing animals, slugs, and this pest.

Keep picnic beetles out of the garden with timely harvest. These ¼-inch beetles, black with four yellow dots, do not harm the fruits, but they are attracted to overripe or damaged fruits. Attract them with a mixture made of 1 cup water, 1 cup dark corn syrup, one cake of yeast, and a spoonful of vinegar. Place the mixture in a container outside the garden. Use it to attract the beetles away from the garden, trap, and drown them.

Watch for signs of aphids, leafhoppers, and tarnished plantbugs. These insects suck out plant juices, causing the leaves to yellow and bronze. Severe damage can stunt plant growth. Use several applications (five to seven days apart) of insecticidal soap to treat these pests.

Check the lower leaves of tomatoes for yellowing and brown spots. Septoria leaf spot and early blight are common causes of these symptoms. Remove and destroy infected leaves as soon as they are found. Fall cleanup, proper spacing, staking, and full sun reduce the risk of these diseases, as does sterilizing tomato cages from year to year. Regular applications of a fungicide, labeled for use on vegetables, can be used to prevent the spread of this disease, if cleanup and sanitation haven't worked. Look for and select more environmentally friendly products when possible.

Late blight can be devastating. Do not replant areas or preventatively treat tomato plantings if late blight has been a problem in the past. Your local university Extension service usually keeps gardeners informed of the potential threat of this disease.

Be patient when dealing with blossom end rot. The blackened ends of fruit are caused by a calcium deficiency. Do not add calcium; our soils have plenty. Instead, avoid root damage caused by late staking and cultivating. Mulch the soil to keep it consistently moist, and wait. Once the soil moisture is consistent, the plants will adjust and the remaining fruits will be fine. Cut off the black portion and eat the rest.

Reduce problems with powdery mildew by growing vine crops on trellises or fences to increase light and air flow and to reduce disease problems.

LAWNS

Insects may be more of a problem if the summer has been hot and dry. Continue monitoring for grubs, billbugs, sod webworms, and greenbugs. Make sure the insects are present and the damage is severe enough to warrant treatment. See June, Problem-Solve for more details.

Skunks, raccoons, and moles can damage lawns by digging and tunneling in search of fat, tasty grubs.

Continual damage means they found a food source and plan to stay. Get rid of the grubs to solve the problem. Squirrels also dig in the lawn. They are storing nuts and seeds for future meals. The damage is irritating, but not a threat to the health of the lawn. Gently tamp down disturbed areas.

Drought-stressed and newly seeded lawns are often infected with rust. This fungal disease causes the grass to turn yellow, orange, or brown. You may notice an orange residue on your shoes after walking across the lawn. The symptoms will soon disappear and the grass will begin to recover on its own. Treatment is usually not needed.

Powdery mildew often occurs in August. Like rust, it is more of an aesthetic problem than a threat to the lawn's health. See May, Problem-Solve for more information on lawn diseases.

PERENNIALS

Continue to monitor perennial gardens for disease and insect problems. Catching the problems early may mean the difference between removing a few sick leaves and spraying the whole garden.

Make a note in your journal to use mildew-resistant plants and correct growing conditions next year. Susceptible annuals include zinnias and begonias. Perennials susceptible to powdery mildew include bee balm and garden phlox. Try 'Marshall's Delight', 'Gardenview Scarlett', 'Vintage Wine', and other mildew-resistant

■ *Grubs can attract animals that dig into your lawn, so it's best to remove the grubs (and the food source).*

cultivars of bee balm (*Monarda didyma*). Choose mildew-resistant cultivars such as 'Bright Eyes', 'David', or 'Star-fire' of garden phlox (*Phlox paniculata*) or substitute the mildew-resistant wild sweet William (*Phlox maculatum*).

ROSES

Blackspot and powdery mildew may be causing significant damage. Most fungicides are preventatives and won't cure what is already infected. Make a note to start treatment earlier next season if this was a problem in your garden.

If the weather is hot and dry, insect populations are thriving. Watch for aphids, mites, and leafhoppers. Rose chafers have done their damage for the year, and Japanese beetles are starting to disappear. See June, Problem-Solve for more information.

SHRUBS

Watch for aphids and mites. Summer thunderstorms often help keep these insects in check. You can create your own summer showers with the garden hose. Spray plants with a strong blast of water to help knock many of these pests off the plants. Try insecticidal soap when the populations start damaging the plants.

Rake and destroy spotted and discolored leaves to reduce damage caused by the disease this season and next. Make notes regarding problem plants. Plan on making changes in the location or pruning practices to help relieve chronic disease problems.

TREES

Watch for aphids and mites that can continue to be a problem during the hot months of August. These small insects suck out plant juices, causing leaves to discolor and eventually turn brown. Let lady beetles and other predacious insects take care of these pests. High populations can be reduced with a strong blast of water from the garden hose.

Inspect the landscape for Japanese beetles that are finishing their aboveground feeding. Heavy infestations may be treated in fall with a soil systemic. This will kill next year's beetle population as they feed on treated trees.

Check tree trunks for female gypsy moths. The white, flightless moths crawl up the trunk to mate and lay eggs. Remove and destroy the female and egg masses as they are found.

Continue to rake and dispose of diseased leaves as they fall from the trees.

Continue to remove any cankered and diseased branches. Prune 9 to 12 inches below the cankered (sunken or discolored) areas of the branch. Disinfect tools with rubbing alcohol or a solution of one part bleach to nine parts water. Continue to give trees proper care to reduce the adverse effects of the disease.

VINES & GROUNDCOVERS

Check honeysuckle vines for aphids. Dislodge the insects with a strong blast of water. Use several applications of insecticidal soap or Neem if populations reach damaging levels.

Capture and destroy slugs eating holes in the leaves of hostas and other shade lovers. Set out shallow tins, sunk into the ground, filled with beer. The slugs crawl inside and drown. Or, place beer in an empty soda or beer bottle and lay on its side. This gives you a built-in cover to prevent the beer from being diluted by the rain. Tuck bottles under the plants for a tidier look.

September

September is a time of transition. Our gardens are recovering from summer stresses and preparing for the winter ahead. The same goes for gardeners.

You will be harvesting vegetables, planting, and winterizing, all at the same time. Make the most of it by looking for ways to double, or even triple, the benefit of any activity.

Fall leaves are a perfect example. Many municipalities encourage citizens to rake leaves to the curb for the city to pick up. It always seems to rain, washing many leaves into the sewer. The city then sends a crew to clean out the sewer. In many cases the city pays a private contractor to haul away the leaves. This company composts, bags, and sells our leaves back to us in the form of compost. Seems like we are spending too much time and money to get our leaves back in a different form.

So put away the rake and break out the mower. As you mow you shred the leaves, saving time raking and money spent on soil amendments. Shred the leaves and leave the small pieces on the lawn, or shred, bag, and spread them as mulch or use as an amendment in annual planting beds.

Our gardens seem to reach their peak this month, right before the first fall frost. Protect the plants from the first frosty days of fall for an additional week or two of warm weather. Those few extra days of flowers mean a lot when the snow begins to fall.

A blanket can provide relief from a frosty night or two. Make the task easier with the help of floating row covers. These spun fabrics let air, light and water through while trapping the heat and protecting plants from frosts. See this month's Care section for more details.

Many gardeners like to extend their gardening enjoyment by moving plants indoors for winter. I prefer to let most of my annuals die a quick death at the hands of Jack Frost. But there are always a few plants I just cannot part with each year. These may include the unusual hibiscus cultivar, scarlet, white or striped mandeveilla, or Gryphon begonia. I overwinter some from cuttings and others as plants.

Share your abundant harvest with the less fortunate in your community. More than 13 million children have substandard diets or depend on emergency food programs. Your fresh produce can make a difference by providing garden-fresh nutritional food to hungry families in your community.

PLAN

ALL

Your garden has filled in and is starting to reach its peak. It always seems to happen just before the first killing frost. So get out the camera and start taking pictures. This visual record of your garden makes it easier to plan future gardens. Continue to record successes, challenges, and new ideas in your journal. Add to your wish list of plants for next year's garden. Record bloom time, care, and other plant features. Good records help you repeat your successes, not failures.

BULBS

Visit your favorite garden center to purchase spring-flowering bulbs. Buy a few extras for forcing. Purchase full-sized bulbs that are firm and free from soft, dry, or discolored spots and pests. Store your bulbs in a cool, dark place until planting. The basement, spare refrigerator, or similar location will work. Avoid storing bulbs in a refrigerator that contains ripening fruit (this interferes with flower development) or can be accessed by children who might accidentally eat the bulbs. Always select the bulb best suited to the growing location. They should fit the light, soil, and other growing conditions of the planting site. Shop early for a greater selection of varieties and healthier bulbs.

EDIBLES

Plan to extend the season using cold frames, hot caps (milk jugs will work), and season-extending fabrics. Protection on those first frosty nights can extend the harvest through the warm weeks that always follow. Or, let nature end the season with the first killing frost. Use this as an excuse to end a troublesome growing season full of insects, disease, and weeds. Then you can start planning for next year's garden.

LAWNS

Labor Day marks the beginning of increased lawn care activity. Cooler temperatures and regular rainfall make this a good time to start a new lawn or repair an existing one.

PERENNIALS

Fall is for planting and planning. Evaluate your fall perennial garden. Do you need more mums, asters, or fall-blooming anemones? Note the results of

■ *Pansies, stock and snapdragons can be planted as colorful fall annuals.*

pinching back tall sedums, coneflowers, and other fall bloomers.

ROSES

Enjoy the beauty and fragrance roses provide. Make notes on the health and attributes of the roses in your garden.

TREES

Continue writing about your trees in your garden journal. Make sure planting records are complete. Evaluate and record pest-management strategies. Record fall color in your landscape. This may be a feature you want to improve in the future.

VINES & GROUNDCOVERS

Time to start preparing for winter. Locate a sunny location or space under lights for tropical vines that will soon move indoors. Decide how to manage any perennial vines growing in containers that need some winter protection. These can be planted in the ground, stored in an unheated garage, or given extra protection for the winter.

PLANT

ANNUALS

Garden centers are filling with pansies, ornamental kale, and other fall annuals. These plants tolerate the cool fall temperatures and extend your garden enjoyment even after frost. Plant cold-hardy pansies now for two seasons of enjoyment. These bloom in fall, survive the winter, and provide another floral display in spring. Plant them in bulb gardens as groundcover around tulips, daffodils, and hyacinths. Their colorful flowers make a nice addition to blooming bulbs and help mask the declining foliage.

BULBS

Always prepare the soil prior to planting. Bulbs need well-drained soil for best results. It is easier to prepare the soil correctly in the first place than to try to fix it after the bulbs are planted. See the Introduction for more information.

Bulbs planted early are more likely to sprout during a warm fall. Wait until late September in the northern part of the state and early October in the southern part to start planting. You have plenty of time—until the ground freezes—to get these bulbs into the ground.

You can still dig, divide, and transplant bearded iris. The later you plant, however, the greater the risk of winter injury. See the July, Plant or August, Plant sections on planting bulbs for details. Start transplanting existing bulbs. This spreads out

■ *Cut back iris leaves (top), and remove rotted, damage and old non-flowering sections of the rhizome (bottom) when transplanting.*

planting time and helps you with the final spacing and placement of your new additions.

EDIBLES

Add short-season and frost-tolerant plants to the garden. You can still plant lettuce, greens, spinach, and onion sets. Try growing them in containers that can be moved in and out according to the weather, or have some frost protection handy for covering on cold nights.

Dig and pot parsley and chives to bring indoors and grow for winter, or start new plants from seed for even better success.

Take cuttings of oregano, rosemary, sage, marjoram, mint, and winter savory for your indoor winter herb garden. Take 3- to 4-inch cuttings from healthy plants. Stick the cut end in moist vermiculite or perlite. Keep the vermiculite moist and the plant in a bright, but not sunny, location. Plant the rooted cutting in a small container of moist, sterile potting mix.

Plant garlic in the first half of this month. Fall planting is risky but can reward you with a larger and tastier harvest next season. Plant the cloves in an upright position, 3 to 5 inches apart and 1 inch deep. Protect the young plants with winter mulch. With some luck, they will grow in early spring.

LAWNS

Whether you are renovating an existing lawn, starting a new one, or just patching bare spots, early to mid-September is the best time to plant grass seed. The warm soil speeds up germination, while the cooler air temperatures aid in growth and development. Avoid late seeding (after September 20) that may not have time to establish and may be winterkilled.

Replace or overseed lawns that contain more than 60 percent weeds. Starting over gives you quicker and more effective results. Reclaiming a weed-infested lawn often requires more pesticides and gives poor results over a long period of time. Kill the existing weeds and grass, properly prepare the soil, and seed or sod to replace an existing lawn. See April, Plant and May, Plant for tips.

HERE'S HOW

TO RENOVATE A LAWN

1. Cut the grass shorter, 2 inches, just during this process. Grass acts as a living mulch. Rake off and compost long clippings if needed.

2. Remove the thatch layer if it is greater than ½ inch thick. Use a vertical mower to lift the thatch. Set the revolving blades to slice into the top ½ inch of soil. This removes the thatch while creating grooves or slits in the soil surface. These slits make a good seedbed. Rake up and compost the debris. Alternatively, you can core aerate compacted soil in several directions to improve drainage and seeding success. This is less stressful on the lawn and you.

3. Spread grass seed over the renovated area using a broadcast or drop-type spreader. Use 3 to 4 pounds per 1,000 square feet of sunny grass-seed mixes or 4 to 5 pounds per 1,000 square feet of shady mixes. Apply half the total amount in one direction and the remainder at right angles to the first. Rake for good seed-to-soil contact.

4. Fertilize renovated lawns next month.

5. Raise the mower back to the recommended 3- or 3½-inch mowing height. Cut the grass once it reaches 4 inches.

Overseeding is the last step before replacement. Use this method on lawns that are thin, have lots of bare spots, or are full of weeds. Consider hiring a professional for large jobs.

PERENNIALS

Keep adding perennials to your garden and landscape. The warm soil and cooler air temperatures are great for planting and establishing new perennials.

Move self-sown biennials to their desired location. Transplant early in the month so the seedlings will have time to reestablish before winter.

Transplant peonies now until after the tops are killed by frost. See October, Plant for detailed instructions.

Add mums to the fall garden. Fall-planted garden mums are usually not hardy and will likely not survive our winters. Many botanical gardens and estates use them as annuals for fall interest. Increase your success by purchasing and planting mums in spring. Try Mammoth™ and other hardy mums introduced by the University of Minnesota.

Consider planting your bulbs and mums at the same time. Dig a hole for the bulbs in late September or early October. Place the bulbs in the bottom of the hole and lightly cover with soil. Set the mum in the same hole above the bulbs. Make sure the mum will be planted at the same depth as it was growing in its container. Backfill with soil and gently tamp. Water and enjoy the fall display. Or, consider using the sunken-pot technique. Sink empty planting pots, with drainage, in groundcover and other planting areas. Set potted mums in the sunken pot. This method eliminates the need to dig and disturb surrounding plant roots.

Finish digging and dividing perennials as soon as possible. Northern gardeners should try to finish this task early in the month. Those in southern areas should try to finish by the end of the month. Wait until spring to divide Siberian iris, astilbe, delphinium, or other slow-to-establish perennials.

It's a good time to prepare soil for new garden areas. Edge the new garden bed. Cut the grass short and cover with newspaper or cardboard and organic mulch. The grass and paper will decompose over winter, and the garden will be ready for planting in spring. Or, kill the existing grass with a total vegetation killer or remove with a sod cutter. Take a soil test, and amend the soil as needed. Shredded fallen leaves make a great soil amendment. Spade several inches of this free material into the top 12 inches of soil. They disintegrate over the winter and improve the drainage and water-holding capacity of your soil.

ROSES

Wait until next spring to plant and transplant hybrid teas for best results. Planting early gives them several months to establish a healthy root system before winter.

Hardy shrub and landscape roses can be planted spring through fall. Make sure they get proper post-planting care to reduce transplant shock and speed up establishment.

SHRUBS

Always start with a call to 811, the free utility-locating service. Or, contact MISS DIG at 800-482-7171 or www.missdig.net. Allow three business days for a response.

HERE'S HOW

TO PLANT SHRUB AND LANDSCAPE ROSES

1. Prepare the soil in the planting bed by working the needed organic matter and amendments into the top 12 inches of soil. Sprinkle the area with water, or allow the soil to settle for several days before planting.

2. Dig a hole at least twice as wide and just as deep as the container. Hardy shrub roses are not grafted and should be planted at the same depth they are growing in the container.

3. Move the rose near the planting hole, and cut off the bottom of the container.

4. Place the rose, pot and all, in the planting hole. Adjust the planting depth so the top of the pot is even with the surrounding soil surface.

5. Slice the side of the pot and peel it away. Slice through any girdling (circling) roots.

6. Backfill the planting hole soil. Water to eliminate air pockets and help settle the soil.

7. Mulch the soil with a 1- to 3-inch layer of woodchips or shredded bark.

Start transplanting shrubs as the leaves begin to drop and the plants go dormant. Moving large established shrubs can be tricky and heavy work. Replacing overgrown or misplaced shrubs may be easier, cheaper, and more successful.

Continue planting balled-and-burlapped and container-grown shrubs. Planting can continue until the ground freezes. The sooner you get the plants in the ground, the more time the shrubs will have to adjust before winter.

Complete planting evergreens this month.

TREES

Fall is for planting. The cooler temperatures mean less watering for you and an easier time for trees to get established. As with shrubs, call 811 three business days before planting, for marking of underground utilities. See October, Plant for a list of trees to avoid for fall planting.

Trees are sold as bare-root, balled-and-burlapped, or container plants.

Bare-root trees are cheap and lightweight, but they often have the poorest survival rate. They must be planted as soon as possible after digging. This makes them a less-than-ideal choice for most homeowners. They are frequently used by municipalities, parks, and other organizations for large-scale plantings. Bare-root plants are easier to find in spring and are only available from a few sources.

Balled-and-burlapped trees are dug in early spring before growth begins, or during fall after leaf drop. The trees are dug with a small portion of the root system intact. They are more expensive and heavier, but they have a greater rate of survival than bare-root trees.

Container-grown trees are planted and grown in pots for several years. The smaller root system and pots make them easier to manage. They are moderately priced and can be planted spring through fall.

No matter what type of planting stock you select, make sure it is a healthy tree. Look for trees with straight trunks, a strong central leader (main stem),

or appropriate growth habit. Avoid trees with damaged trunks, wilted or scorched leaves, and signs of insect and disease damage. See Planting a Tree on page 208.

Give your healthy tree a safe ride home. Use a pickup, trailer, or large vehicle to move the plant. Loosely tie the branches to minimize breakage. Cover the canopy with plastic or fabric if leafed out. Carefully lay the tree on its side. Wrap the trunk with carpet or fabric anywhere it comes in contact with the vehicle to prevent damage. Tie the tree in place, and do not forget the red flag for trees that extend 3 feet beyond the vehicle. Many nurseries will help.

You may want to spend a little extra money to have the experts deliver your tree. They have the staff and equipment to handle and move large trees. Many nurseries will even place the tree in a pre-dug planting hole for you. Consider the delivery charge as an insurance policy on your initial investment.

Once your tree is home, follow these tips for planting:

Store trees in a cool, shaded location until they can be planted. Cover the roots of bare-root and balled-and-burlapped trees with woodchips. Water all planting stock often enough to keep the roots moist.

Locate the root flare on the tree by gently pulling the soil away from the trunk. The root flare is the area where the roots gradually flare away from the trunk. This area is often covered by soil. Measure the distance from the root flare to the bottom of the rootball. This is equal to the depth of your planting hole.

Dig a hole the same depth as the rootball (flare to bottom) and at least two to preferably three or more times wider than the root system. Make a wide, shallow, saucer-shaped planting hole. Research has shown that the roots will be better able to penetrate the surrounding soil.

If you want to transplant trees in your yard, wait until the leaves drop and the trees are dormant.

HERE'S HOW

TO PLANT TREES

For container-grown trees:

1. Roll the pot on its side or push on the container to loosen the roots.

2. Cut away the bottom of the container.

3. Place the tree in the planting hole so that the root flare is at or slightly above the soil surface.

4. Slice and peel away the container. Loosen circling (girdling) roots by hand or with a sharp knife.

For balled-and-burlapped trees:

1. Place the tree in the planting hole so that the root flare is at or slightly above the soil surface.

2. Remove the twine and cut away the burlap and wire cages. These materials do not decompose in most soils and can interfere with root growth and eventually girdle parts of the tree.

For all trees:

1. Use your shovel to roughen the sides of the planting hole. This prevents glazing (smooth sides) in clay soils, which keeps the roots from growing into the surrounding soil.

2. Fill the planting hole with existing soil. Highly amended soils discourage root development into the surrounding soil. Water or gently tamp to help settle the soil and remove air pockets.

3. Mulch the soil with a 2- to 3-inch layer of woodchips or shredded bark. Keep the chips away from the trunk to avoid disease problems.

4. Water the planting hole and the surrounding soil thoroughly after planting. Water frequently enough to keep the top 12 inches of soil moist, but not wet. Most trees are killed with kindness from overwatering.

5. Remove only broken and damaged branches. Major pruning will be done in two to four years.

Loosely tie lower branches to prevent damage and keep them out of your way. Dig a trench around the tree slightly larger and deeper than the desired rootball. Undercut the rootball with your shovel. A sharp spade makes the job easier. Use hand pruners and loppers for larger or tougher roots. Slide a piece of burlap or canvas under the rootball. Have several friends lend a hand. Extra hands and strong backs will make the job easier and reduce the risk of dropping the tree and damaging the rootball. Set the tree in the prepared hole (wider but same depth as the rootball). Carefully cut or slide the tarp away from the tree. Backfill the hole with existing soil, water, and mulch.

VINES & GROUNDCOVERS

Keep planting. Fall is a great time to add new plants to the landscape. Be cautious when planting under established trees. See August, Plant for tips.

1. Start planting once the site is prepared. Dig a hole at least two to three times wider, but no deeper, than the container.

2. Gently push on the container sides to loosen the roots. Slide the plant out of the pot. Do not pull it out by the stem. Place the plant in the hole so that the rootball is even with the soil surface.

3. Fill the hole with the existing soil. Water to settle the soil and eliminate air pockets.

Plant autumn crocus in groundcover beds. These bulbs sprout leaves in spring. The leaves fade in 6 to 8 weeks, and you will be surprised with pink, white, or lavender flowers in the fall.

CARE

ANNUALS

Get out row covers, blankets, and other frost protection. September frosts are common in the northern and even southern parts of the state. Apply frost protection in late afternoon when the danger of frost is forecast. Cover plants with row covers (season-extending fabrics) or blankets. Remove blankets in the morning once the temperature is warm. Recover plants each night

there is a danger of frost. Row covers can remain on the plants day and night during threatening weather. These products let air, light, and water through while trapping heat near the plants.

Move containers into the house, porch, or garage when there is a danger of frost. Move them back outdoors during the day or when warmer weather returns.

Move hibiscus and other tropical plants to their winter indoor locations. These plants need bright light. Place them in a south-facing window or under artificial light for best results.

Many gardeners like to bring annuals indoors and keep them for next year's garden. Here are a few ways to keep plants for the winter. Pick the method that works best for the type of plant and the time and space you have available.

Take cuttings of browallia, coleus, fuchsia, geranium, impatiens, wax begonia, annual vinca, herbs, and other plants you plan to overwinter indoors. This method takes up less space and minimizes the risk of bringing insects and diseases inside. See the August, Plan for details.

You can also transplant flowers from the garden into a container or bring outdoor planters inside. Isolate these plants for several weeks before introducing them to your indoor plant collection. Unwanted insects often move inside with the plants. Place plants under lights or in a sunny window. Water and care for them as you would your other houseplants. Do not be alarmed if the leaves begin to yellow. These leaves often drop and are replaced by new, more shade-tolerant leaves. You can cut back the plants or leave them intact. The more leaves on the plant, the more energy is produced to help it through the transition.

Dig geraniums and store them in the basement in a cool, dark area. Unfortunately, we do not always have the same cool basements and root cellars our grandparents possessed. It is difficult to keep these plants from growing or drying out while in storage. This is the least successful method. If it is your only option, it is worth a try, as they will die if left outside.

Continue to harvest flowers for fresh arrangements and drying. Collect extra flowers to dry and use later for holiday decorations and gifts.

BULBS

Move amaryllis indoors before the first fall frost. Store the bulb in a cool, dark location or continue

HERE'S HOW

TO OVERWINTER TENDER BULBS

1 *Carefully dig up tender bulbs. Allow plenty of digging room for the additional bulbs that have formed over summer.*

2 *Prepare (cure) bulbs for storage. Set them in a warm, dry place out of direct light. See the Storage Chart on page 162 for specific recommendations. Gently brush off (do not scrub) excess soil and trim off dried foliage and stems.*

3 *Place cured bulbs in a box or flat filled with peat moss, sawdust, or other storage material. Gladioli prefer to be stored dry and uncovered. Label the type and color of the bulb. Move to a cool, dark location for the winter.*

SEPTEMBER

SPECIFIC STORAGE REQUIREMENTS FOR TENDER BULBS			
BULB	*CURE TIME*	*STORAGE*	*STORAGE TEMPERATURE*
Begonia, tuberous	several days	dry peat	50 degrees Fahrenheit
Caladium	several days	dry peat	50 degrees Fahrenheit
Calla lily	1 to 2 days	peat moss or perlite	50 degrees Fahrenheit
Canna	overnight	peat moss	45 to 50 degrees Fahrenheit
Dahlia	several hours	dry peat or sawdust	45 degrees Fahrenheit
Gladiolus	2 weeks	dry/uncovered	40 degrees Fahrenheit

to grow it indoors. See the January chapter for information on reblooming.

Caladiums, calla lilies, and tuberous begonias can be grown indoors for the winter. Move container plants inside prior to the first killing frost. Dig up in-ground plants, pot up, and move indoors. Care for them as you would your other houseplants.

Yellowing foliage or the first fall frost means it is time to dig, cure, and store tender bulbs for winter.

Leave Siberian iris leaves and seedpods intact for fall and winter interest.

EDIBLES
Store leftover seed in their original package in an airtight container in the refrigerator. The controlled environment will help keep the seeds viable for next season.

Prune out the stem tips on tomato, squash, and melon plants early this month to allow the plant to expend its energy on ripening the existing fruits instead of producing more fruits that don't have time to mature.

Harvest eggplants when the fruits are 6 to 8 inches long and glossy. Use a knife or pruning shears to cut the fruits off the plant.

Pick muskmelons when the fruit stem starts to separate from the fruit. Wait for the crack to appear all around the stem for a fully ripe, great-tasting melon.

Harvest watermelons when the fruits are full-sized, dull-colored, and the portion touching the ground

changes from white to cream. Check the tendrils nearest the fruit for confirmation. These curl and dry when the fruit is ripe.

Continue harvesting tomatoes, peppers, and squash.

Take one fall harvest of rhubarb before the first killing frost. The stalks are safe to eat and the plant has had ample time to replenish its energy supply. Cut the rest of the stalks back after a hard freeze.

Keep cutting, using, and preserving herbs. Cut short pieces off the ends of the stem. Make the cut just above a set of leaves. It looks neater, and the plant recovers faster.

Prepare for the first fall frost. Move tender potted plants indoors.

Cover plants with sheets or season-extending fabrics whenever frost is predicted. See the preceding Annuals section for details.

Leave ferny asparagus leaves and stems standing for the winter. The standing stems help capture snow that insulate the roots for winter.

LAWNS
Keep mowing high.

Now is the time to correct compacted soils and thatch problems. Both problems interfere with root growth and result in thin lawns. Removing the thatch or removing plugs of soil (core aerating) allows water and fertilizer to reach the roots. Actively growing grass quickly recovers from the stress of these operations. See May, Care for more information on dethatching and core aeration.

■ *A core aerator will leave little plugs all over your lawn. These eventually decompose. Speed this up by chopping with your mower or using a core aerator that grinds the cores in place.*

PERENNIALS

Winter is quickly approaching, especially for those in the north. Make note of new and tender plantings that need winter protection. Look for sources of weed-free straw, marsh hay, evergreen branches, or other winter mulch materials. Wait until the ground freezes to apply them over the plants and soil.

Stop deadheading plants you want to develop seedpods for winter interest, such as fall-blooming rudbeckias, coneflowers, astilbes, Siberian iris, and sedums.

Continue deadheading to prevent seed set on perennials that are overtaking your garden.

Cut back any summer-blooming plants that have faded. This improves their appearance and opens up space for the fall flower display.

ROSES

Focus your management strategies on encouraging plants to start hardening off for winter. Avoid late-season fertilization and pruning that stimulate new growth.

HERE'S HOW

TO ACCLIMATE ROSES TO THE INDOORS

1. Locate a cool, sunny area to grow the plants over winter.

2. Over the next few weeks, gradually reduce the amount of light the plants receive.

3. Quarantine (isolate) the roses for several weeks. Watch and control insects prior to introducing them into your indoor plant collection.

4. Move plants to their permanent indoor location. Keep soil slightly moist and continue to watch for insects and disease.

Some gardeners move planters of miniature and tree roses indoors for winter. Start acclimatizing any roses you plan on wintering indoors.

Stop deadheading after the final wave of flowers or in the latter part of the month. This allows rose hips to form and the plants to start hardening off for winter. Limit pruning to removal of dead, diseased, and damaged canes.

SHRUBS

Fall cleanup begins.

Rake leaves out of shrub beds to eliminate unwanted animals' habitat and potential damage to surrounding plants.

Remove and destroy leaves from diseased shrubs to reduce the source of disease next season.

Remove any damaged or pest-infested branches. Wait until late winter to do major pruning to take care of winter damage and regular pruning at the same time.

TREES

Instead of raking, consider recycling your leaves to save work and improve the landscape. Shred leaves with the mower and leave them on the lawn. As long as you can see the grass blades through the shredded leaves, the lawn is fine. In fact, the leaves quickly break down, adding nutrients and organic matter to the soil. Shred leaves with your mower, and dig them into annual vegetable and flowerbeds. The leaves break down over winter, improving the soil for next year's garden.

Bag leaves and tuck them next to your home. The bagged leaves add insulation to the house. In summer, use the leaves as mulch in flower and vegetable gardens.

Shred leaves with the mower, and throw them in a heap to decompose. Composting really is that easy.

As the leaves drop, it is a good time to start pruning. The bare trees make it easy to see the plant's structure and determine which branches stay and which ones go. See the Introduction for more pruning details.

■ *Use your mower to shred leaves, which will add nutrients and organic matter to the lawn.*

Contact a certified arborist for professional help training young trees and pruning large trees. Contact the Arboriculture Society of Michigan (www.asm-isa.org), or Trees are Good (www. treesaregood.com) for a list of certified arborists in your area.

VINES & GROUNDCOVERS

Move tropical vines indoors for winter as the temperatures cool but before the first killing frost. Prune tropical vines back just enough to make them manageable for their indoor home. Isolate these plants from your other houseplants for several weeks. Monitor for insects, such as mites, aphids, and whiteflies. These insects cause the leaves to appear speckled, yellow, and often distorted.

Spray infested plants with insecticidal soap to treat mites and aphids. Repeat weekly until the pests are under control. Use yellow sticky traps placed near plants to reduce whitefly populations. Remove damaged and diseased leaves and stems. Wait until late winter or early spring for routine pruning.

WATER

ALL

Keep watering container gardens. Check them daily and water whenever the top 2 to 3 inches of soil are slightly dry. Water thoroughly so that the excess runs out the drainage hole.

Check soil moisture before watering gardens. Only water when the top few inches of soil begin to dry. Continue to water thoroughly but probably less frequently. Cooler fall temperatures and rain showers often take care of this job for you.

ANNUALS

Remember to check late additions to the garden. Newly planted fall annuals and fall containers will need more attention than established plants.

BULBS

Reduce or stop watering amaryllis that are to be stored dormant during the fall.

Thoroughly water new plantings that need additional irrigation during a dry fall.

EDIBLES

Water new plantings often enough to keep the soil slightly moist. Ensure maximum productivity with proper watering and care for mature plants.

LAWNS

Water new plantings often enough to keep the soil surface moist. Reduce watering frequency once the grass seeds sprout or the sod roots into the soil below.

PERENNIALS

Mulch new plantings and monitor soil moisture. Proper watering will speed establishment and increase winter survival.

ROSES

Mulching, proper watering, and care are the best way to ensure healthy, beautiful plants. This is especially true for roses.

SHRUBS

Make sure all new plantings and evergreens receive a thorough watering as needed throughout the fall and before the ground freezes.

TREES

Evergreens, new plantings, and transplants survive winter better when they receive sufficient moisture throughout the fall.

VINES & GROUNDCOVERS

Water new plantings as needed. Keep soil moist around recently planted vines and groundcovers. Allow the top 3 to 4 inches of soil to start to dry before watering plants that have been in the ground for several weeks.

FERTILIZE

ALL

Most gardens do not need to be fertilized this late in the season.

Keep fertilizing annual container gardens that did not have a slow-release fertilizer incorporated at planting. Follow label directions on the container.

Do not fertilize aboveground tree, shrub, and perennial planters that will be overwintered.

Fall is a great time to take a soil test. It gives you time to read the report and plan your fertilization program for next season. Excess nutrients can cause floppiness, poor flowering, and other problems, and applying less fertilizer saves you money.

ANNUALS

There's no need to fertilize. Consider adding shredded leaves, compost, or other organic matter to annual beds in fall to improve drainage in clay soils and water-holding ability in sandy soils.

BULBS

Follow soil test recommendations or incorporate 1 pound of a low-nitrogen fertilizer per every 100 square feet at planting.

EDIBLES

Enjoy the harvest. Make notes for any changes in your fertilization program that are needed for next season.

LAWNS

Apply 1 pound of actual nitrogen per 1,000 square feet around Labor Day, when the temperatures start to cool. This is equivalent to 20 pounds of a 5-percent and 10 pounds of a 10-percent-nitrogen fertilizer. Consider using a slow-release formulation to avoid burn and encourage slow, steady growth. September fertilization helps lawns recover from the stresses of summer. Use phosphorous-free or organic fertilizers unless your soil test shows this nutrient is lacking.

Incorporate fertilizer in the soil prior to seeding or sodding a new lawn.

PERENNIALS

Topdress with compost every other year to provide most of the nutrients your perennials need. This can be done whenever you have time and compost is available.

Siberian squill (left), and daffodils and hyacinths (right), are all good animal-resistant choices.

ROSES

Do not fertilize. Late season fertilization can delay dormancy and reduce wintering success.

SHRUBS

Fall, after plants are dormant, or early spring, before growth begins, are good times to fertilizer shrubs. Established shrubs need infrequent fertilization. Wait a year to fertilize new plantings.

TREES

Fall, after the trees are dormant, is a good time to fertilize established trees. Let the plant and a soil test be your guide. Trees usually receive sufficient nutrients from decomposing mulch, lawn fertilizers, and grass clippings left on the lawn. Contact your Michigan State University Extension Service or their website for soil test information.

Check trees for signs of nutrient deficiencies. Poor growth and off-color leaves may indicate the need to fertilize. Wait a year to fertilize new tree plantings. They have been well tended in the nursery and fertilizer may harm the new, developing roots.

PROBLEM-SOLVE

ANNUALS

Remove all diseased and insect-infested plant material during fall cleanup. This reduces the potential for problems next season.

Powdery mildew often peaks in fall. Make a note to replace susceptible plants or use slightly shorter plants in front of infected plants to mask the discolored foliage.

Remove weeds as they appear and before they have a chance to set seed.

Watch for squirrels digging in the garden. They love to store their nuts in gardens where the digging is easy. Tolerate the disturbance or discourage them with scare tactics and repellents.

BULBS

Prevent iris borers by removing old iris leaves and debris. Fall sanitation eliminates the sites for iris borer adults to lay their eggs. Without eggs, there will be no borers next season.

Thrips overwinter on the corms of gladiolus. Discard thrip-infested corms or treat with an insecticidal dust prior to storage. Label the bulbs as treated with insecticide as a reminder to wear gloves when handling the corms next spring.

Remove and discard disease-infested leaves. Do not store any tender bulbs that show signs of rot or disease.

Squirrels, voles, and chipmunks look forward to digging bulbs. Commercial and homemade repellents may provide relief. Apply them as soon as there is potential for damage. Hot pepper, human hair, and highly scented soaps are just a few of the home remedies. There are many commonly found commercial repellents.

Scare tactics include white bags and balloons on sticks, clanging pans, and radios. Vary the tactics used for better results. Urban animals may be so accustomed to the noise and smell of people that these tactics do not work.

Create a barrier with chicken wire. Dig the planting hole to the proper depth. Place and properly space bulbs in the planting hole. Cover bulbs with 1 inch of soil. Lay the chicken wire over top of the bulbs. Fill the hole with the remaining soil. The wire screening keeps out voles, chipmunks, and squirrels. Bend the screening down around the sides to further discourage wildlife, or purchase a bulb cage. Set the cage at the proper depth, set bulbs in place, and fill the hole and cage with soil.

Use soil grit, some coarse-textured stone, mixed with soil placed over the bulbs. This is supposed to discourage digging.

Or, avoid the problem by planting daffodils, hyacinths, snowdrops, grape hyacinths, fritillaria, squills, and winter aconites, which tend to be resistant to animal damage.

EDIBLES

Keep pulling weeds and removing insects and diseased leaves as soon as they are discovered. See the June, July, and August Problem-Solve sections for ideas on managing insects and disease.

Remove and destroy all pest-infested plant debris in fall. A thorough cleanup is your best defense against insects and disease. Do not compost pest-infested material unless you have an active compost pile that reaches 160 degrees. Contact your local municipalities for disposal options.

LAWNS

A healthy lawn is your best defense against pests. Review your maintenance practices to be sure you are mowing, fertilizing, and watering correctly. If not, make needed adjustments.

Fall is the best time to control perennial weeds such as dandelions and plantain. Chemicals are usually most effective, and the actively growing grass quickly fills in the empty spaces. Minimize your cost and the negative impact on the environment by spot treating, or try some of the natural products that continue to be introduced. Broadleaf weedkillers with the active ingredient Hedta and Fehedta are effective against many common broadleaf weeds.

Add a wetting agent to liquid herbicide mixtures. The wetting agent breaks down the surface tension of the water, providing better coverage. Even pesticide coverage helps in the control of waxy-leafed, hard-to-eliminate weeds, such as clover and violets. Control violets in the lawn with a broadleaf weedkiller for difficult weeds. Make the first application in mid-September. Repeat in late October if weeds are still present.

Wait for a hard freeze to treat creeping Charlie.

Grubs are starting to move deeper into the soil for winter. Complete all grub treatments by September 15. Only treat lawns diagnosed with a real problem.

The cool, wet weather of fall increases the risk of disease. Watch for leaf spot, mildew, and rust. Fall fertilizations and proper care are usually enough to control these diseases. See May, Problem-Solve for more on turf diseases.

Skunks, raccoons, and moles damage lawns in their search for food. Continual damage means they have found some tasty grubs and plan to stay. Get rid of the food—the grubs—and you solve the problem. Squirrels can also be found digging in the lawn. They are storing nuts and seeds for future meals. The damage is irritating but not a threat to the health of the lawn. Gently tamp down disturbed areas.

PERENNIALS

Continue weeding all gardens. Removing weeds now can reduce the amount of weeds next year.

Monitor plants for insects and disease. Fewer harmful insects are present during the cool temperatures of fall. See July, Problem-solve for more details on pests and their control.

Continue removing spotted and diseased leaves as soon as they are found. Water early in the day or use a watering wand or drip irrigation to reduce moisture on the leaves. This helps reduce disease problems. Make note of mildew-infested plants. Consider thinning plantings in early spring to reduce mildew, moving susceptible plants to a sunnier location or replacing them with mildew-resistant plants.

Remove plants with rotting roots and stems. Amend the soil to improve drainage, adjust watering, and replace with a plant more suited to the location.

Let healthy insect- and disease-free plants stand for winter. You'll add winter interest, feed the birds ,and increase winter hardiness.

ROSES

Continue to monitor and control pests. Maintaining a healthy, relatively pest-free plant throughout the season is the best start to winter protection. Remove canes with sunken or discolored areas. Remove and rake away any diseased foliage. Continue fungicide treatments as needed.

Insect populations are still present. Monitor and treat only when damage occurs.

Weed control continues as long as weeds appear. Cleaning up weeds now reduces future weed and pest problems.

SHRUBS
Watch for the last few pests of the season. Cooler temperatures usually mean fewer aphids and mites.

If your landscape suffered severe feeding damage from Japanese beetles, some borers, and other pests, and the plant's health is compromised, check out soil-applied insecticides. Use one labeled for these pests in the fall for control next season.

Leaf spots and blotches are common problems in cool, wet seasons. Do not bother to spray the plants now; it won't help. Remove small numbers of infected leaves as soon as they appear. Rake and destroy disease-infected leaves. This reduces the source of infection next season.

Note any plants covered with a white powdery substance. Powdery mildew fungus is a common problem on lilacs and many other plants. The plant will survive; it just looks bad. Thin out overgrown shrubs next spring to increase light and air circulation and to reduce disease problems.

Remove weeds from planting beds. Unwanted plants can compete with shrubs and host unwanted diseases.

TREES
Check tree trunks for gypsy moth egg masses. The eggs are covered with a yellow hairy substance. Each cluster can contain more than 600 eggs. Remove and destroy any egg masses found.

Fall applications of soil systemic insecticides can be made for bronze birch, emerald ash, and other life-threatening borers. These products also control spruce galls, birch leaf miners, Japanese beetles, gypsy moths, plantbugs, and several other pests. Keep in mind overuse can lead to resistance and secondary pest outbreaks.

VINES & GROUNDCOVERS
Continue monitoring for insects and disease. Remove and discard spotted and discolored leaves as soon as they are discovered to reduce the source of disease next season.

Insects should be less of a problem as the weather cools. Note scale insects that can be treated by professionals in the fall with a soil-applied insecticide, or mark your calendar so that you remember to control them in winter with a dormant spray or next season with an insecticide.

■ *If you suspect your ash tree has emerald ash borer, call 1-800-292-3939. For more information visit www.emeraldashborer.info.*

October

Hopefully the weather has been mild, and the gardens are in their glory. October days can fluctuate from warm and mild to wintery, almost overnight. Take advantage of mild weather to plant trees, shrubs, and bulbs. The soil is warm, air temperatures are cool (good for the plant and the person planting), and plants are in place and ready to start growing as soon as spring arrives.

Watch for and record overlooked fall color on perennials. Hostas, balloon flower, and willow amsonia turn a lovely yellow; bergenia and geraniums turn a reddish purple; barronwort is tinged in red; and Angelina sedum is a burnt amber. Continue to watch as some of these (Angelina, bergenia, geranium) as well as hellebores, creeping phlox, and coral bells, will hold onto their leaves through milder winters or when mulched with snow. It is refreshing to the spirit to see a bit of color as the snow recedes after a long winter.

You can begin dormant pruning, but I prefer to wait until late winter. The plants recover quicker from the pruning, and the stems, fruits, and dried flowers remain intact for winter interest. For low input (not lazy!) gardeners, try to get the most out of every chore. Late winter pruning allows you to repair winter and animal damage while shaping the shrubs and creating a strong framework for your trees. It also means one time spent pruning versus two!

Wait until spring to clean up perennial beds. Just remove and destroy disease- and insect-infested material in the fall. Many plants, such as coneflowers, rudbeckias, liatris, astilbe, and baptisia, provide winter interest for you, habitat for beneficial insects, and seeds for wildlife. Try leaving the flower stems of hostas standing for winter interest, and watch as juncos feast on the seeds.

In fall you will be busy with a wide range of tasks to be accomplished in the few remaining days or weeks before the snow begins to fall. By late March or April, as the snow recedes, you will be ready to get back out in the garden. It is a great time to stretch your gardening muscles, evaluate winter damage, and start looking for signs of life in the garden.

Take a few minutes to clean out the spare refrigerator or invest in an additional energy-saving model. A colleague once said, "Every gardener should have a spare refrigerator. Not just for beer and soda, but for storing bulbs."

OCTOBER

PLAN

ALL

Enjoy the change of season. Take pictures and video the colorful parts of your yard. Carve out a few minutes to record the highlights and challenges of this growing season. Use this information, garden reviews, and pictures to plan future improvements and reduce pest problems. Be sure to include both successes and failures. Write down all those new plants and great ideas you want to try next season.

This is a good time to list plants you wish you had in your fall garden. Note any that didn't live up to their early season performance.

Consider preparing new perennial gardens now, when the list of garden chores is much shorter.

Start making a list of plants that need winter protection from cold, snow, and animals.

ANNUALS

Note your plants that are frost tolerant. Pansies, snapdragons, ornamental kale, alyssums, and pinks tolerate frost. Plan to include these in future spring and fall gardens.

Record the locations and flowers that are first to freeze. Coleus, impatiens, and begonias are killed by the first frost and often leave a big hole in the garden. Use these in areas where their early demise is no problem, or plant them under trees, near the south side of the house, or in other areas that are the last to freeze.

BULBS

Create impact in your landscape with bulbs. It may be a splash of color at your front door to welcome visitors or a mass of daffodils visible from the kitchen. Plant virtual pathways and rivers of bulbs through your landscape. A ribbon of color interests and leads visitors through your yard. Don't forget to add minor bulbs. These small-stature, early bloomers provide petite bursts of color in even the smallest yard.

ROSES

Roses survive the first frost and continue to be beautiful. Hybrid teas are still blooming, and rose hips provide additional interest. Most grafted roses, including hybrid teas, benefit from winter protection. Hardy shrub and species roses survive with little or no winter protection. Find detailed descriptions of several methods of winter protection in the Care sections of the fall chapters.

PLANT

ANNUALS

Flowering tobacco, cosmos, alyssum, snapdragons, and cleome are a few of the annuals that may reseed in the garden. Most are lost to fall cleanup and soil preparation. These volunteers fill empty spaces in mixed, annual, perennial, and shrub gardens. Pull out plants, but do not cultivate the soil. Sprinkle any remaining seeds over the soil surface. Next spring, wait for the surprise. You may want to turn only a few small spaces over to nature, and save the rest for spring planting.

BULBS

October marks the peak of fall bulb planting. Soil preparation is the important first step. Work the soil when it is dry or only slightly moist. Bulbs need well-drained soil for best results and to prevent rotting. Follow your soil test recommendation or add at least 2 inches of organic matter and 1 pound of a low-nitrogen, slow-release fertilizer per 100 square feet. Dig the fertilizer and amendments into the top 8 to 12 inches of soil.

Bonemeal, a traditional amendment, is generally not needed and can attract bulb-eating rodents. Most of our soils already have enough of the phosphorus that bonemeal provides. Select a fertilizer with little or no phosphorus and potassium (the second and third numbers on the fertilizer bag) unless otherwise indicated by your soil test.

Planting earlier than October increases the risk of bulbs sprouting prematurely during a warm fall. Keep planting bulbs until the ground freezes. There are even some tricks that can be used after the ground freezes. See November, Plant for some ideas.

Daffodils, tulips, crocus, and other spring-flowering bulbs are generally planted at a depth of two to

HERE'S HOW

TO BUILD A COMPOST PILE

■ *Build a compost pile by layering green materials and brown materials like you'd make a lasagna. Start with chopped up dried leaves (you can run over them with the lawn mower). Then add herbicide-free grass clippings and plant based kitchen scraps, and keep layering. The smaller the pieces you add to the pile, the faster they'll decompose. Add soil or compost to inoculate the pile with the microorganisms that do the composting. Moisten to the consistency of a damp sponge. Make the pile at least three feet tall and wide for faster results.*

■ *You can continue adding new ingredients to the pile but this slows down decomposition. Or create a holding pile for raw materials until you accumulate enough to make a second compost pile. Shredded newspapers, the stems of broccoli, last summer's dead annuals, and your Halloween pumpkin are just a few of the items you can include. Do not add meat, bones or dairy products that attract rodents. Don't add weeds gone to seed or perennial or invasive weeds such as bindweed, quackgrass and purple loosestrife. Keep the pile "cooking" (a properly constructed pile will heat up) by using a pitchfork or garden fork to turn the pile when it starts cooling. Move the less decomposed materials from the outside of the pile to the center and more decomposed material from the outside to the center. Repeat.*

■ *If your pile smells, turn to aerate and add dry material. If it is not decomposing fast enough, add some soil and fertilizer, turn and lightly moisten.*

HERE'S HOW

TO PLANT LARGE GROUPS OF BULBS

1. Start by raking the mulch off the planting area. Amend the soil, if needed, by adding organic matter to the top 8 to 12 inches of soil. Then create the planting hole to the depth of 2 to 3 times the height of the bulb.

2. Set the bulbs in the planting area. For a natural look, mix several types of bulbs together in a bucket and then scatter them on the ground. Fix the bulbs so the pointy end is up.

3. You can sprinkle the ground with a homemade or commercial repellent if animals have been a problem. Read and follow label directions. Or cover bulbs with an inch of soil. Then lay chicken wire over the area. Bend the wire down over the edges of the planting area to discourage animal digging.

4. Fill the planting hole with the amended soil you removed. The bulbs will be 2 to 3 times their height deep and the planting area will be level with the surrounding soil.

5. Use a shrub rake or hard rake to spread mulch over the planting area for a finishing touch. You can use the same mulch that you use in the rest of the planting bed for this step. Remember to water the bulbs after you're done planting them.

three times the vertical diameter. Plant 2 to 3 times the diameter apart or according to label directions.

Transplant and move existing bulbs as needed.

Plant last year's hardy forced bulbs outdoors if this was not done in spring. They probably will not bloom until the second spring after planting.

Force spring-flowering bulbs for a touch of spring indoors. Daffodils, tulips, and hyacinths are often used for forcing. Select shorter cultivars or those specifically recommended for forcing. Plant several bulbs in a 4- to 6-inch container filled with a well-drained potting mix. Water thoroughly and move to a cold location (35 to 45 degrees Fahrenheit) for thirteen to fifteen weeks.

Store potted bulbs in a spare refrigerator. Do not store fruit with the bulbs, and make sure the family knows this is not some new cooking trend.

Place bulbs in a root cellar, attic, or other areas where the temperatures stay cold but above freezing.

Bury potted bulbs in a vacant garden area outdoors. Dig a trench the same depth as the containers. Place the containers in the trench and fill with soil. Cover the area with evergreen branches or straw after the ground begins to freeze.

One gardener gets double duty from his pond. Once the pond is drained for winter, he fills it with potted bulbs. He covers the pots with dry leaves and the pond with a piece of plywood.

Another gardener buys Styrofoam cut-flower containers from a wholesale florist. He fills them with potted bulbs and stores them in his unheated garage for winter. The unheated garage gives the bulbs the cold they need and the insulated container prevents them from freezing in extremely cold weather.

EDIBLES
Finish planting garlic cloves. Place them in an upright position, 3 to 5 inches apart and 1 inch deep. Protect the young plants with winter mulch.

Start a windowsill herb garden for fresh seasonings all winter. Try oregano, thyme, parsley, and sage in small individual pots or planted together in a larger container.

Finish planting perennial herbs outdoors early in the month so that the plants have a chance to root before winter. Grow mint in a container in-ground with the lip at least two inches above the soil or as a container plant to prevent it spreading and overtaking the garden. Overwinter container plantings in an unheated garage or mulch into a garden for winter.

Plant annual rye, oats, or buckwheat as a green manure crop. These plants provide a green ground-cover for the winter garden. Dig or till these plants into the top 6 inches of soil next spring. They add nutrients and help improve the soil.

LAWNS
You can still lay sod to establish new lawns or to repair existing ones. Weed removal and soil preparation are important whether you are repairing a small area or installing a 1-acre lawn. See the lawn-starting tips in April, Plant. Once in place, water the sod often enough to keep the soil surface moist. Reduce watering and begin mowing the sod after it has rooted into the soil below.

PERENNIALS
Finish planting early in the month. The later you plant, the less time your perennials have to get established, thus the greater risk of winterkill. Limit late planting to hardier perennials suited to our cold winters.

Locate a place to overwinter less hardy transplants and those scheduled for spring planting. Sink the pots into the ground. Once the soil freezes, mulch with evergreen branches or weed-free straw for extra protection.

Collect and sow seeds of coneflower, rudbeckia, and other late summer- and fall-blooming perennials. Spread the seeds outdoors on well-prepared soil.

Dig and divide peonies after the tops have been killed by frost. Use a spading fork to dig the rhizomes. Dig a hole wider than the plant to avoid damaging the root system. Cut the clump into smaller pieces, leaving at least three to five eyes per division. Prepare the planting site by adding several inches of compost into the top 12 inches of soil. Replant the divisions, keeping the eyes no more than 1 to 2 inches below the soil surface.

ROSES

There may be time to finish planting hardy shrub and landscape roses if you plant them as soon as possible. Make sure they get proper post-planting care, which will help reduce transplant shock and speed up establishment. See September, Plant for detailed instructions.

SHRUBS

Good weather conditions mean less stress on both the transplants and the planter. Start with a call to your utility-locating service. Allow three business days before you start digging. Call 811 or contact MISS DIG at 800-482-7171 or www.missdig.net.

You can transplant shrubs as soon as they are dormant. See March, Plant for tips or more information, and use this chart to help determine proper sizing:

RECOMMENDED ROOTBALL SIZE		
SHRUB SIZE	MINIMUM DIAMETER	MINIMUM DEPTH
2 feet	12 inches	9 inches
3 feet	14 inches	11 inches
4 feet	16 inches	12 inches
5 feet	16 inches	12 inches
6 feet	16 inches	12 inches

Finish planting evergreens early in the month. This gives the plants a little more time to put down roots before winter arrives.

TREES

Small trees can be transplanted once the leaves drop. See September, Plant for tips, and review the following chart for details on transplanting trees.

RECOMMENDED ROOTBALL SIZE FOR TRANSPLANTING		

TREE DIAMETER AT CHEST HEIGHT	ROOTBALL DIAMETER	ROOTBALL DEPTH
(SIZE IN INCHES)		
½	14	11
¾	16	12
1	18	14
1¼	20	14
1½	22	15
1¾	24	16
2	28	19

Purchase healthy balled-and-burlapped and container-grown plants from local nurseries and garden centers.

Plant evergreens by early October to give their slow-growing roots time to establish before the ground freezes.

Avoid planting trees that are slow to root. Wait until next spring and summer to plant:

Acer rubrum (red maple)
Betula species (birch)
Crataegus species (hawthorn)
Gleditsia triacanthos inermis (honeylocust)
Liriodendron tulipifera (tulip tree)
Magnolia species (magnolia)
Malus species (crabapples and apples)
Nyssa sylvatica (black gum)
Populus species (poplar)
Prunus species (ornamental and edible
   plums and cherries)
Pyrus (Pear)
Quercus species (oaks)
Salix species (willows)
Tilia species (lindens)

VINES & GROUNDCOVERS

Finish planting early in the month to give plants time to start rooting into surrounding soil before the ground freezes. Wait until next spring to plant tender and borderline-hardy plants.

Store unplanted hardy groundcovers and vines for winter. Find a vacant garden space in a protected area. Sink the pots into the ground. This insulates the roots from below-freezing temperatures. Do the same for hardy vines growing in containers. Mulch after the ground freezes or move potted vines into an unheated garage for winter. Place in a corner as far from the door as possible. Pack the pots with Styrofoam peanuts or other insulating material. Water whenever the ground thaws and is dry. A third option: Move the planters to a sheltered location. Pack bales of straw around the pot for added root insulation.

CARE

ANNUALS

Keep frost protection nearby to keep your annuals going. Cover plants in late afternoon when there is a danger of frost. Remove the coverings when temperatures warm.

Move containers into the garage, porch, or house when there is a danger of frost. Move them back outdoors when warm weather returns.

Hibiscus, bougainvillea, oleander, and other tropicals need to move indoors for winter if you want to use them next season.

Call it quits when you are tired of gardening or the

meteorologist says cold weather is here to stay. But wait, you're not done yet! Shred fallen leaves with your mower, and work them into the top 6 to 12 inches of garden soil. The leaf pieces decompose over the winter, improving the drainage of heavy clay soils and the water-holding capacity of sandy soils.

Do not till areas where you want annuals to reseed.

BULBS

Dig, cure, and store tender bulbs after a light frost. See September, Care for specific details.

EDIBLES

Move rosemary, sweet bay, and other tender herbs indoors. Place them in a bright, sunny window or under artificial lights for the winter. Keep the soil moist but not too wet.

Cover tender plants left outdoors in late afternoon whenever there is a danger of frost.

Don't let green tomatoes go to waste. Pick mature green tomatoes when the blossom end is greenish white or unripe tomatoes that are showing color before the tomato plants are killed by frost. Ripen these tomatoes indoors for added enjoyment. Store

HERE'S HOW

TO OVERWINTER TROPICALS

1. Start by bringing them into the garage, screened-in porch, or an indoor room away from your houseplants. Keep them isolated for several weeks. Check for insects, and use insecticidal soap to treat mites and aphids you discover. Handpick and destroy caterpillars, slugs, earwigs, and beetles.

2. Move the plants indoors to a warm, sunny location. A south-facing window, Florida room, or atrium works well. Or, add an artificial light to improve the light conditions found in most of our homes.

3. Continue to water thoroughly whenever the top few inches of soil start to dry. Do not fertilize until the plant adjusts to its new location and shows signs of growth.

4. Prune only enough to fit the plant into its winter location. Do not worry about the falling leaves. The plant will replace the fallen leaves as soon as it adjusts to its new location.

5. Continue to watch for pests, and water as needed. Enjoy the added greenery and occasional flowers.

6. Prune overgrown plants in late February. Pruning later will delay summer bloom.

7. Wait until March to start fertilizing with a dilute solution of flowering houseplant fertilizer.

unripe tomatoes in a 60 to 65 degree Fahrenheit location. Spread them out on heavy paper so that the fruits do not touch, or wrap each one in newspaper if they must touch in storage. They will ripen over the next few weeks. Speed the process by moving a few tomatoes to a bright, warm location a few days prior to use. You can also use green tomatoes to make relish or fried green tomatoes.

Dig radishes, beets, and turnips when they reach full size. Leave some carrots, turnips, and parsnips in the garden for winter storage. Mulch the plantings after the soil is a little crunchy with frost. Harvest them throughout the winter.

Harvest pumpkins when the fruits are full size, the rind is firm, and the spot touching the ground turns from cream to orange. Cleaning pumpkins helps extend their longevity. Dip harvested pumpkins in a solution of 4 teaspoons bleach per 1 gallon of water. Allow the pumpkin to dry and cure at room temperature for one week. Move it to a cool location. With some luck, it should last at least two months.

If you haven't already, take one fall harvest of rhubarb before the first killing frost. The stalks are safe to eat and the plant has had ample time to replenish its energy supply. Cut the rest of the stalks back after a hard freeze.

Cut back and remove pest-infested vines and stalks from the garden to reduce the risk of reinfesting next year's garden.

Check stored vegetables during the fall and early winter. Discard any damaged or rotting fruit. One bad apple, onion, or squash does spoil the bunch.

LAWNS

Put away the rake and break out the mower. Shredded leaves make a great amendment for gardens and lawns. Shred leaves with the mower the next time you cut the grass. And yes, you need to keep cutting the grass as long as it keeps growing. Remove no more than one-third of the total height at each cutting.

You may need to make several passes with the mower during peak leaf drop. As long as you can see the grass blades, the lawn is fine.

Mow and collect any herbicide-free clippings and leaves to add to a compost pile or vacant garden. Spade this mix into the top 6 inches of an annual or vegetable garden this fall, or use them to mulch the soil around your perennials. Don't use chopped leaves as a winter mulch on top of plants, because they mat down, hold moisture, and lead to disease. Mulch instead with straw and evergreen branches.

Store dry leaves in bags over winter for use next spring. Do not store wet leaves. The weight can be difficult to manage, and the smell that develops in the bag turns most gardeners' noses. Tuck the leaf-filled bags behind the bushes next to your home's foundation. This is an out-of-the way storage area that provides added insulation.

Gardeners in the southern part of the state can still core aerate the lawn. You get the best results when the lawn has at least four weeks of good growing weather to recover. Do not dethatch the lawn using a vertical mower at this time of the year. The lawn does not have enough time to recover before winter.

PERENNIALS

Clean up and remove any diseased or insect-infested leaves, stems, and flowers. You need to decide what look you want for your winter garden. Some gardeners like a neat and tidy look and prefer not to have standing dead stuff. Others leave perennials for winter interest and improved hardiness. Many plants, such as salvia and mums, overwinter better when the dead stems are left standing.

Cut back the foliage of peonies and hostas to reduce the risk of fungal leaf disease in next year's garden.

Carefully blow or rake tree and shrub leaves out of your perennial gardens. Large leaves get wet, mat down, and provide poor insulation for your plants. Do use shredded leaves as a soil mulch around the plants.

Collect dried pods, grasses, and other materials for fall and winter arrangements.

Remove stakes and supports as plants decline. Clean and store for next year's garden.

Start preparing the soil for next year's gardens. See September, Care for details.

ROSES

Plan and prepare for winter protection. Some years, the "do nothing method" works fine, while other years you'll lose all your less-than-hardy roses if you don't properly prepare for winter. Wait for a week of freezing temperatures to begin the process (unless otherwise specified below); try one of these for grafted and less hardy hybrid teas, climbers, and tree roses.

The Minnesota Tip Method requires work but yields consistently good results. It is the best method for overwintering climbers and tree roses outdoors.

Ramblers are usually hardy and some climbers survive with little or no protection. Those growing against the south side of your home may survive with minimal care. Mound soil over the base of the plant. Leave the plant attached to the trellis and wrap with fabric. Fill with evergreen boughs or straw for extra insulation. Remove in spring as temperatures hover above freezing.

■ *Mounding soil around the base of the rose helps protect the graft.*

HERE'S HOW

TO PREPARE ROSES FOR WINTER USING THE MINNESOTA TIP METHOD

1. Start the process in mid-October in the northern part of the region and several weeks later in the southern parts. Loosely tie together the rose canes. Do not prune climbing roses or ramblers in the fall or you eliminate the spring bloom.

2. Dig a trench from the base of the plant outward. It should be long enough and deep enough to accommodate the plant. Use a spade or garden fork to gently loosen the soil around the plant.

3. Tip the plant over and lay it in the trench. Be careful to bend the roots, not the stem. You don't want to break the graft that you are trying to protect. Cover the plant with soil.

4. Once the soil freezes, mulch with a thick layer of straw. Use chicken wire or hardware cloth to keep the mulch from blowing away. Start removing this protection in early April.

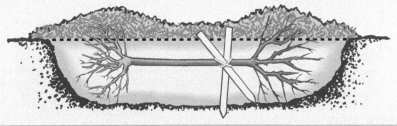

TO HARVEST AND STORE ROSES FOR WINTER ENJOYMENT

1. Line a solid cardboard box with a plastic bag. Use a 10-by-14-inch or other box of a convenient size.

2. Move the box to the basement, crawl space, or other location where it will stay cool but above 40 degrees Fahrenheit.

3. Fill the box with wet sand once it is in its permanent location. It may be too heavy to move once it's filled.

4. Pick roses that are in full bud and show a little color.

5. Remove the leaves and submerge the stems (with the flowers above the water) in warm water for 45 to 60 minutes.

6. Make a hole in the sand for the rose stem. Stand each rose in the sand so its entire stem is covered and the buds show just above the sand.

7. Remove flowers to enjoy throughout winter. Recut the stem and place in hot water.

The soil mound method has also proved effective. Stockpile and cover soil or compost that you plan to use as winter mulch. Covering prevents it from freezing so that it is workable when it is time to cover the roses. Loosely tie the rose canes. Cover the base with 8 to 10 inches of soil. Once this freezes, cover the top of the plant with evergreen boughs or straw. Some gardeners use chicken wire to contain the mulch.

Or, put those fall leaves to work, and use the "leaf mulch method." Use a 4-foot-high section of hardware cloth to create a fence around the rose garden. Sink several inches of the hardware cloth fencing into the ground to keep out plant-damaging rabbits and rodents. This must be done before the ground freezes. Prune the roses back to 18 inches after a week of freezing temperatures. Cover the roses with a 3-foot layer of tightly packed dry leaves. Use a leaf rake to gently compact the leaves around the roses. Some gardeners cover the leaves with a sheet of plastic to keep them dry. Remove the leaves in spring, and use them as mulch in the garden.

Increase success when using rose cones with proper timing and ventilation. Wait for a week of freezing temperatures before starting the process. Cover the base of the rose with soil, and prune roses as needed to fit under the cone. Once the soil mound is frozen, cover the plants with straw for extra insulation, and put the rose cone in place. Spread soil around the base of the cone. Once this freezes it will prevent the cone from blowing away. In the meantime, use a brick to secure the rose cone. Vent on warm days and be sure to remove in spring as temperatures start hovering just above freezing.

Purchase and store rose cones if you use this type of winter protection. Do not start covering roses until after a week of freezing temperatures. This is usually mid-November in the northern part of the state and the end of November or early December in the southern part.

SHRUBS

Rake and compost or recycle fallen leaves. Disease-free leaves can be shredded and left on the lawn, dug into annual gardens, or added to the compost pile. Bury or discard disease-infected leaves. These are a source of infection for the next growing season.

Prepare aboveground planters for winter. Find a sheltered location in an unheated garage or enclosed porch to store the planters for winter. Use bales of hay to insulate shrubs in planters left outside.

See November, Care for tips on preventing snowload and salt damage.

Wait until early spring to prune evergreens. Pruning now exposes the inner growth that has not been exposed to wind and sun. Fall pruning can increase winter injury. Avoid pruning spring-blooming shrubs, such as lilac and forsythia. Dormant season pruning removes flower buds needed for next spring's display. Remove only dead, pest-infected, or damaged branches at this time.

TREES

Continue recycling leaves. Shred them and leave them on the lawn, or recycle them in the garden or compost pile. See September, Care for more ideas.

Start gathering winter protection materials such as burlap for wind and salt barriers, fencing for snow loads, and fencing for animal barriers.

Prune as needed. Start by removing crossed, broken, or diseased branches. Leave healthy branches with wide crotch angles (the angle between the trunk and branch) that are evenly spaced spiraling upward around the trunk for the basic structure. Make cuts where a branch joins another branch, above a healthy bud, or flush with the branch bark collar. See Pruning on page 209 for more details.

VINES & GROUNDCOVERS

Blow or rake fallen leaves off plants. Large leaves trap moisture, block sunlight, and lead to crown rot and other disease problems on groundcovers. Or, try this technique: Cover plantings with netting to catch the falling leaves. Remove the leaf-covered netting. Drag it off or roll it up to keep the leaves on the netting until you clear the groundcover planting. Replace the netting and keep removing leaves until all of them have fallen to the ground.

Prune out diseased stems and leaves. Disinfect tools between cuts with rubbing alcohol or a solution of one part bleach to nine parts water.

Gardeners looking for a challenge might try overwintering tubers of 'Blackie', 'Marguerite', and 'Pink Frost' sweet potato vines. Dig plants after a light frost has killed the leaves. Discard any damaged or diseased tuberous roots. Remove foliage, and allow the tuberous roots to dry overnight. Pack them in peat moss and store in a cool, dark location.

WATER

ALL

Cooler temperatures mean less watering. Supplement natural rainfall when the top 2 to 4 inches of soil start to dry. Continue to monitor new plantings and water often enough to keep the top few inches of soil slightly moist. Water plants as needed until the ground freezes.

ANNUALS

Keep watering container gardens. Water annuals moved indoors whenever the top few inches of soil start to dry. Water thoroughly. Empty any excess water that collects in the saucer, or use a gravel tray as described in the following Vines & Groundcovers section.

BULBS

Thoroughly water new bulb plantings. Water potted bulbs before placing them in cold storage. Check occasionally to make sure the soil is still moist.

EDIBLES

Keep the roots of indoor young seedlings moist. Check daily and water when the soil starts to dry. Reduce watering frequency once the seedlings root. Water windowsill gardens thoroughly until the water runs out the bottom. Pour off excess water or use a gravel tray as described in the following Vines & Groundcovers section. Wait for the top few inches of soil to dry slightly before watering again. Check small pots and young plants every few days. Larger containers may go a week or more between being watered.

LAWNS

Keep the soil surface moist under newly laid sod. Continue to water thoroughly, but less frequently, once the sod is rooted into the soil below. Fall-seeded lawns benefit from regular, thorough watering. Established irrigated lawns should be watered when they show signs of wilting.

OCTOBER

ROSES, SHRUBS, & TREES

New plantings, evergreens, and aboveground planters need the most attention. Water these plants thoroughly before the ground freezes. This will help minimize winter damage.

VINES & GROUNDCOVERS

Water tropical vines growing indoors whenever the top few inches of soil begin to dry. Water

■ *Install winter protection to protect your plants from hungry animals and winter winds.*

thoroughly so that the excess runs out the bottom. Place a saucer filled with pebbles (gravel tray) under the pot. Allow excess water to collect in the pebbles while the pot sits above the water. This increases the humidity around the plant, while eliminating the need to pour excess water out of saucer.

Check potted vines wintering outdoors. Water when the soil is thawed and dry. Water thoroughly so that the excess runs out the bottom.

FERTILIZE

ALL

Take a soil test of new and existing gardens. Test the soil of older gardens every three to five years or whenever you suspect a nutrient problem. Alternate years for testing to help spread out the cost. See the Introduction to this chapter or contact your local County Extension Service office or visit their website for soil test information. Send the sample in now so you have the results for winter planning and spring soil preparation.

Wait until spring to fertilize most plants except lawns and established trees. Late-season fertilization can lead to late-season growth that can be winterkilled.

BULBS

Follow soil test recommendations, or add 1 pound of a low-nitrogen, slow-release fertilizer per 100 square feet of garden bed at planting.

LAWNS

Late October is the most important time for fertilizer application. Apply 1 pound of actual nitrogen per 1,000 square feet. This can be obtained by applying 20 pounds of a 5-percent-nitrogen or 10 pounds of a 10-percent-nitrogen fertilizer per 1,000 square feet. Use an organic or phosphorous-free fertilizer unless your soil test directs otherwise.

Use a slow-release nitrogen fertilizer for best results. Actively growing plants use some of the nutrients now. The unused nitrogen remains in the frozen soil over winter. As soon as the ground thaws, the grass will begin growing. This fertilizer will be available for the grass early in the season.

PERENNIALS

Top-dress the soil with compost or organic matter, if you have not done so recently. Consider using shredded fall leaves as a soil amendment for new garden beds. Work the shredded leaves into the top 12 inches of soil in empty gardens. These break down over winter and improve the soil for future planting. Or spread the shredded leaves on the soil surface for soil mulch around the plants. Do not use leaves to cover the plants for winter protection as they mat down, ice up, and can weaken or kill the plants.

TREES

Fall, after the trees go dormant, is a good time to fertilize established trees. Fertilize only if the soil test results or plant growth indicates a nutrient deficiency. Wait a year to fertilize new tree plantings.

Do not fertilize trees growing in aboveground containers.

PROBLEM-SOLVE

ALL

A killing frost signals the end of the growing season and the start of fall cleanup. Remove all insect- and disease-infested plants. Discard or bury—do not compost—these plants. Fall cleanup is the best way to reduce the risk of insects and disease in next year's garden. Disinfect tools between cuts.

Record pest problems, control methods used, and successes and failures. These records help you anticipate and reduce future pest problems through proper planning and plant selection.

Fall cleanup is an important key to pest control. Remove diseased or pest-infected foliage. This reduces the source of insects and disease for next season.

Monitor plantings, secure fencing, and use scare tactics to keep animals from nibbling plants. Whirly gigs, plastic owls, and noisemakers may provide some relief. Commercial and homemade

Consider fall foliage when designing your landscape.

repellents may also help. Make sure that whatever you use on edibles is safe for people. Avoid rotten eggs and other homemade remedies that could cause a health risk to your family.

Start putting animal barriers in place, especially around new plantings, fruit trees, and euonymus. A 4-foot-high fence buried several inches into the soil helps keep voles and rabbits away from the base of the plants. Some gardeners choose to cut down their gardens in fall to eliminate the vole's habitat. Others depend on nature, hawks, owls, temperature extremes, and the neighbors' cats to control these rodents.

If animals have been a problem, stock up on repellents. Early applications, before feeding starts, appear to be more effective. Reapply repellents after harsh weather and as recommended on the label.

Continue to pull or hoe weeds. Removing weeds now reduces the number in next year's garden. Remove diseased leaves and insects prior to applying winter protection.

ANNUALS
Watch for mites, aphids, and whiteflies on annuals moved indoors.

BULBS
Check on tender bulbs in storage. Remove and discard any soft, discolored, or rotting bulbs.

Treat or discard thrip-infested gladioli corms prior to storage. These tiny insects overwinter in the corms.

Remove old iris foliage and debris. This eliminates the egg-laying habitat for the adult moth. The moth (adult iris borer) will look for a more suitable patch to lay her eggs.

EDIBLES
Monitor seedlings for damping off. This fungal disease causes seedlings to collapse and die. See February, Problem-Solve for details.

LAWNS
If desired, apply a broadleaf herbicide (weedkiller) to creeping Charlie and other difficult-to-control weeds in mid- to late October after a hard frost.

Do not be alarmed if treated creeping Charlie begins to grow next spring; it dies back quickly. Make a second application to violets if needed. Consider natural products when available, and spot treat problem areas to reduce the amount of chemicals needed.

Mushrooms and moss can drive turf enthusiasts to distraction. There is no miracle cure for either. As with all weeds, once we find the cause of the problem, we have also found the cure.

Mushrooms are the fruiting bodies of fungi. They typically appear after a period of cool, wet weather. The underground fungus feeds on decaying tree roots and wood in the soil. Once the food source is gone, the fungus disappears. Rake and break up the mushrooms to prevent kids and pets from eating them. Time is the only cure.

Moss also thrives in moist conditions. It is commonly seen in shaded areas with compacted and poorly drained soils. Change the poor growing conditions, and you eliminate the moss.

Increase the amount of sunlight reaching your trees by having a certified arborist thin out the tree canopies. Add organic matter to improve drainage, and try planting shade-tolerant grass and groundcovers.

If the moss returns, you may have to look for alternatives to grass. Try mulching the area with woodchips or shredded bark. Better yet, add a few steppingstones, and call it a moss garden!

SHRUBS
Call a professional to manage severe and ongoing insect problems. Some pests can be controlled with a soil-applied systemic insecticide that is applied in fall to control a variety of leaf-feeding and boring insects next summer.

TREES
Fall soil applications of systemic insecticides can still be made for preventing damage from bronze birch borer, emerald ash borer, spruce galls, birch leaf miners, Japanese beetles, gypsy moths, and several other pests. Only treat trees that have suffered severe damage in the past.

Install cankerworm traps if these voracious insects caused repeated defoliation of oaks, elms, apples, crabapples, and many other trees. Use a band of fabric treated with a sticky material around the trunk of trees that were severely defoliated the previous season. Put sticky traps in place in mid-October and remove in December.

Reduce damage from deicing products. Salts applied to walks and drives can wash into the soil and damage plants. Road salts can spray on nearby plants, causing damage to twigs and needles. Salt damage causes stunted or distorted growth, leaf burn, poor flowering and fruiting, and premature fall color. Repeated exposure to deicing salts can kill plants.

Shovel first and then apply only traction materials or melting compounds to walks and drives.

Use sand or some of the newer environmentally friendly deicing products, such as magnesium chloride or calcium magnesium acetate.

Create physical barriers between the plants and salt spray. Decorative fencing, burlap screens, or salt-tolerant plants can all protect salt-sensitive plants from injury.

Thoroughly and repeatedly water salt-laden soils in spring.

A few salt-tolerant (soil and spray) trees include:

Cockspur hawthorn
Eastern red cedar
Ginkgo
Hackberry
Hedge maple
Honeylocust
Kentucky coffeetree

■ *Allow moss to remain in shady locations. It makes a great groundcover under trees and shrubs.*

November

The growing season is not over! You still have a few things to harvest and much more to do to prepare for winter. Make an end-of-the-season to-do list. Prioritize what must be done before the snow flies and what can wait if you run out of time.

Don't let a lack of space prevent you from getting the most out of your garden. Preserve your harvest with a makeshift root cellar in a corner of the basement as far from the furnace as possible. Use the two outside walls for storage. Then take a Styrofoam cooler or insulating material to create the ceiling and remaining walls. Check periodically on stored vegetables, and use as needed.

Check the yard, porch, and other areas where your tools tend to collect. Clean and sharpen them if you have time, and store them in a dry place for winter.

Replace damaged or old hand-pruner blades that can no longer be sharpened. High-quality pruners have replacement blades, while cheaper pruners must be replaced when damaged. Replacement blades are available through garden supply catalogs and many garden centers. Use a three-cornered (tapered) metal file to sharpen the cutting edge of your hand pruner. Take the pruners apart for easier sharpening. Sharpen away from the blade for safety or toward the cutting edge for a sharper edge—just be careful. Smooth off any burrs that form along the edge. Make a test cut to check for sharpness. Clean the blades with a lightweight oil. Spray to lubricate the working parts and prevent rust.

Empty pots and flats you plan to reuse next spring. Wash with one part bleach to nine parts water. Share extra pots with school groups, master gardeners, and community gardeners. Contact your municipality, garden center, or botanical garden to see if they recycle surplus or damaged flats and containers.

Start a compost pile. You do not need anything fancy. Remember, the compost bin is just a structure to contain and hide your pile from view. It should allow easy access and be large enough to hold your materials. All you need are discarded pallets, chicken wire, and lattice to do-it-yourself or just some space to pile green plant debris and let it rot.

Take a moment to reflect and dream. You spent the season evaluating the beauty of your garden, but take some time now to evaluate the amount of work spent to keep the garden looking good.

NOVEMBER

PLAN

ALL
Finish your journal entries for this growing season. Once the snow flies and holidays arrive, it will be hard to remember the useful details of the past summer.

ANNUALS
It is never too soon to start planning for next season. Take inventory of all your tools, seeds, and gardening equipment as you pack them away for winter storage. Start a list of replacement tools and supplies that you need for next year.

BULBS
Looking for more places to plant bulbs? Tuck them in vacant or annual garden areas. Dig a trench the proper planting depth. Fill the trench with bulbs spaced a few inches apart. This acts as a temporary holding location until space becomes available.

■ *You can keep planting bulbs until the ground freezes so hard you can't get a shovel in. Think how beautiful these alliums would be in your garden.*

Transplant these bulbs in spring once the foliage dies or in fall during the normal planting season.

Force bulbs for indoor enjoyment or gifts. See October, Plan for details.

Scatter bulbs of daffodils, crocus, grape hyacinths, snowdrops, or squills and plant them where they fall. This creates a more informal or natural appearance.

Plant bulbs along the woodland or shade garden's edge. These areas usually receive sufficient sunlight in spring before the trees leaf out.

Plant squills, grape hyacinths, or crocus in the lawn. These add a bit of color to the sea of green. Wait until after they're done flowering to cut the grass. Then mow the grass as high as possible to allow the leaves to grow and replenish the bulb's energy. Just be sure you like the look, because it will be challenging to eliminate their beauty. Anything that kills the bulbs will kill your grass.

EDIBLES
Look for plans to build a cold frame. This is a great winter project that can help you get an earlier start and a later finish to the growing season. Face the front of the cold frame south for maximum light and heat. Face the back of the cold frame north to provide screening from the wind and offer a little additional heat from the foundation.

LAWNS
It is almost time to pack away your lawn care equipment. Make notes on any needed changes, improvements, or repairs.

Purchase a good snow shovel or snow blower and plant-friendly deicing salt. Removing the snow before salting saves you money and reduces salt damage to the lawn.

PERENNIALS
Consider maintenance and year-round interest as you add plants to your wish list.

ROSES
This is a busy month for rose care. As soon as the weather stays consistently cold, you need to tuck your roses away for winter.

■ *Evergreen boughs can provide a natural protection for your overwintering plants.*

■ *Be sure to wait until the weather is consistently cold before covering up your rose bushes.*

SHRUBS

Pull out your journal and review problems encountered last winter. Check notes you made on winter protection needed to prevent plant damage this season. Locate and gather materials needed. Make a visit to the garden center to purchase needed supplies.

TREES

You can do a lot to maintain the health of your trees, but sometimes it may be necessary to call in a professional. Ask friends and relatives for recommendations. Check online or contact The Arboriculture Society of Michigan (www.asm-isa.org) or Trees Are Good (www.treesaregood.com) for a list of certified arborists. These tree care professionals have voluntarily participated in an international program that certifies a standard of tree care knowledge.

VINES & GROUNDCOVERS

Consider adding a few vines to crawl through the perennial garden or up the trunk of a tree. Avoid fast-growing, twining vines that can strangle other plants. Climbing hydrangea climbs trees without girdling the trunk. Use twining vines, such as clematis and hardy kiwi to disguise downspouts and mailboxes. Mix two different clematis vines or an annual such as hyacinth bean vine with a trumpet vine for added bloom and interesting foliage effect.

Try the same tactic with groundcovers. Mix several sedums for color and texture variation. Use solid and variegated cultivars together. The lighter foliage contrasts nicely against the solid green leaves. Always select partners that are suited to the growing conditions and are equally aggressive. Otherwise, you will end up with only one plant—the stronger of the two—in the end.

PLANT

ANNUALS

Finish soil preparation as the last few leaves drop and before the ground freezes. Take a soil test now if you did not get around to it last month. Test the soil every three to five years, or whenever soil conditions change or plant problems develop.

Store leftover seeds as described in October.

BULBS

Keep planting spring-flowering bulbs until the ground freezes. Plant bulbs at a depth two to three times the vertical diameter.

You can *still* plant spring-flowering bulbs once the ground lightly freezes. It just takes a little extra effort and creativity.

TO PLANT SPRING FLOWERING BULBS LATE IN THE SEASON

1. Use a shovel to break through the frost and outline small planting areas.

2. Slide the shovel under one edge of the outlined area and pry off the frozen soil. It will lift off just like a manhole cover.

3. Plant the bulbs at the proper depth and space.

4. Water the newly planted bulbs and replace the soil lid. The frozen soil makes it difficult for squirrels to reach the bulbs.

Plant bulbs in pots for forcing. Store them in a cold, 35- to 45-degree-Fahrenheit storage area for thirteen to fifteen weeks. Plant bulbs in early to mid-November for March and April flowers. See October, Plant for forcing details.

EDIBLES

Consider planting an indoor herb and vegetable garden. Leafy crops such as lettuce and spinach, root crops such as radishes, as well as herbs such as oregano, rosemary, sage, mint, winter savory, and marjoram survive most indoor growing conditions.

LAWNS

Dormant seeding is risky. You might want to risk a little seed and some time on small areas, but think twice before seeding large areas or new lawns. The goal is to get the seed in place before the ground freezes but after the soil is 40 degrees or colder so the seed can't germinate. If the seed sprouts in late fall it will most likely be killed by the harsh winter conditions.

Sprinkle seed over bare or thin areas of the lawn. The fluctuating winter temperatures will help work the seed into the soil. Don't worry about the snow; it makes the best winter mulch. Hope for consistently cold weather until spring.

Unseasonably warm weather can extend the landscaping season. Sod can be laid as long as the ground is not frozen and the sod is available. Keep the soil surface moist until the sod roots into the soil below. Make sure it is well watered before the ground freezes. Poorly rooted sod is subject to winter drying.

Snowfall is the best protection for late-season plantings.

PERENNIALS

It is too late to plant perennials. Every gardener occasionally pushes the limit and plants later than they should, but you are taking a risk. Increase your success by overwintering transplants for spring planting.

Collect and save seeds of coneflowers, black-eyed Susans, and other perennials you want in new locations. Plant in fall or collect, store, and plant seeds next spring. Remove seeds from the seedpod and allow them to dry, and then place the seeds in an envelope. Write the seed name and the date they were collected on the outside of the envelope. Place the envelope in an airtight jar in the refrigerator.

TO OVERWINTER PERENNIAL TRANSPLANTS

Outdoors

1. Find a vacant planting space in a protected location. Look for areas near your house, shed, or fence that are sheltered from winter wind and sun.

2. Sink pots into the soil in this protected location. The soil insulates the roots.

3. Once the ground freezes, cover with evergreen boughs or weed-free straw for added insulation.

Indoors

Store in an unheated garage. Set transplants on boards and surround the pots with mulch, potting mix, or other items for added insulation. Water whenever the soil is thawed and dry.

This gives the seeds a needed cold treatment while storing them at a consistent temperature. The seeds will be ready to plant next spring.

ROSES

Wait until next spring to plant. You need to protect any roses you purchased that did not get planted. Find an unused garden area in a protected location. Sink the pot in the soil. Once the ground freezes, protect this rose just like all the others. Plant it in its permanent location once the ground is workable next spring.

SHRUBS

Continue planting and transplanting as long as the ground is workable. Wait until spring to plant evergreens. This gives the plants a chance to put down roots and get established before the harsh winter weather arrives.

Late purchases can be protected until spring as described for roses. For added protection, enclose plants in a cylinder of hardware cloth 4-feet high and sunk several inches into the soil to protect the plants from voles, rabbits, and deer. Fill with evergreen boughs or straw for added protection.

TREES

Finish planting deciduous trees as soon as possible. This gives plants a little time to adjust to their new locations.

Consider having large tree additions made over winter. Some nurseries dig the rootball (leaving the tree in place) in fall. Once the rootball freezes, they move the tree to a pre-dug hole in its new location. The success rate has been good. It is expensive, but it's one way to get an instant tree.

Planning on having a living Christmas tree this holiday season? Dig its planting hole now before the ground freezes. Cover the hole with a board or fill it with mulch. Cover the soil to prevent freezing, making winter planting easier.

VINES & GROUNDCOVERS

It is too late to plant vines and groundcovers. Store unplanted vines and groundcovers for the winter. Follow the directions in the Perennials section.

Keep adding bulbs to groundcover plantings until the ground freezes.

HERE'S HOW

TO CLEAN TOOLS

1. Wash or wipe off excess soil. Use a narrow putty knife to remove hardened soil, or soak soil-encrusted tools in water, and scrub with a wire brush.

2. Remove rust with a coarse grade of steel wool or medium-grit sanding paper or cloth. Add a few drops of oil to each side of the tool surface. Use a small cloth to spread it over the metal. This protects the surface against rust.

3. Sharpen the soil-cutting edges of shovels, hoes, and trowels to make digging easier. Use an 8- or 10-inch mill file to sharpen or restore the cutting angle. Visit your local hardware store for all the necessary equipment. Press down and forward when filing. The file only cuts on the forward stroke. Lift the file, replace it to the original spot, and push down and forward on the file again. Repeat until the desired edge is formed. File into or away from the cutting edge. It is safer to file away from the cutting edge. The edge will not be as sharp, but there is less risk of hurting yourself.

4. Check handles for splinters and rough spots. Use 80-grit sandpaper on rough, wooden-handled tools. Coat with linseed oil.

5. Make sure the handles are tightly fastened to the shovel, hoe, or rake. You may need to replace or reinstall missing pins, screws, and nails. It is cheaper to replace a problem tool than to pay the medical bills when the shovel flies off the handle.

CARE

ALL

Move all garden chemicals to a safe location for winter storage. Create a lockable storage area to keep chemicals safely away from children and pets. Store chemicals in a cool, dry location. Properly stored chemicals, organic and synthetic, will last for years. Liquid pesticides lose their effectiveness if exposed to freezing temperatures and sunlight. Granular chemicals will not perform well after they are wet. Always leave pesticides in their original containers. It is illegal—and unwise—to transfer them to a different container. Never store chemicals in containers in which they can be mistaken for food.

Dispose of empty pesticide containers properly. Check the label for specific instructions.

Clean hand tools, shovels, rakes, and hoes before putting them in storage for the winter. It is easier to do the job now than to wait until spring when the rust and hardened soil are harder to remove.

ANNUALS

Check on geraniums and other annuals in dormant storage. Move plants to a cooler, darker location if they begin to grow. If growth continues, pot them and move them to a sunny window or under artificial lights.

Most of the plants moved indoors are spending their energy adjusting to their new location. They are trying to survive, and very little new growth appears. Things will improve as the days lengthen and light intensity increases.

BULBS

Check on tender bulbs and amaryllis in winter storage. Look for signs of rot, mold, or softening. Discard any diseased bulbs. Throwing out one bulb will prevent the rest from going bad.

Check on bulbs in cold storage. Make sure the soil is still moist. You will need to move them to a cooler location if sprouting occurs.

Mulch after the ground freezes. This is usually around Thanksgiving in the southern part of the region and a few weeks earlier in the north. A layer of evergreen branches, straw, or hay works fine. Do not worry if it snows before you get the mulch in place. Snow is the best mulch available, and it is free. Mulch insulates the soil, eliminating fluctuating soil temperatures. Keeping the soil temperature constant prevents early sprouting. Mulched soil stays frozen, and the bulbs stay dormant even during a winter thaw. This layer of insulation also prevents heaving that is caused by the freezing and thawing of the soil. The shifting soil can dislodge and even push bulbs or other plants right out of the soil.

EDIBLES

Continue frost protection for cool-season crops that you are trying to save.

Trim herbs growing indoors as needed for cooking. Allow young plants to establish themselves before harvesting large amounts.

Harvest lettuce when the outer leaves are 4 to 6 inches long. Dig radishes, carrots, and turnips when the roots are full size. Make one last, crispy, fresh salad for family and friends to enjoy.

Mulch carrots, parsnips, and other root crops left in the garden for winter storage. Cover the lightly

■ *Prepare your mower for winter storage.*

frozen (crunchy) soil with straw or evergreen branches. This insulates the soil, protecting the vegetables and making it easier to harvest in winter.

Mulch fall-planted garlic for winter protection. Cover young plants with straw or evergreen branches after the ground lightly freezes.

Finish cleanup and start preparing the garden for next spring. Read how to use leaves to improve the soil in October, Care.

LAWNS

Rake and remove leaves from the lawn. If left on the lawn, large leaves block the sunlight and trap moisture, increasing the risk for disease and turf death.

Better yet, shred them with your mower. Even maple and oak leaves can be left on the lawn once shredded with the mower. See October for more details.

Keep cutting the grass as long as it keeps growing or until the snow starts flying. Your final cut does not need to be shorter.

Once the mowing season is over, clean up and pack away the mower until next spring. Empty the gas tank by running the engine until it stalls, or add a gas preservative and run the engine for a few minutes to distribute it throughout the gas. Disengage the spark plug wire for safety. Drain and replace the oil. This should be done at least once a year. Check the owner's manual for specific information. Clean off any dirt and matted grass. Sharpen the blades or make a note in your journal to do that before the next mowing season begins. Buy replacement belts, spark plugs, and an air filter as needed, and store them for spring.

PERENNIALS

Soil preparation can be done until the ground freezes. Spread a 2- to 3-inch layer of organic matter on the soil of your perennial gardens now or in the spring. Do this every two to four years.

Apply winter mulch over late plantings, borderline hardy plants, or perennials subject to frost heaving after the ground freezes. This occurs after a week of freezing temperatures. The goal of winter mulch is to prevent the freezing and thawing of the soil. Apply the mulch anytime after the ground freezes and before the winter thaw occurs. Waiting until after the soil freezes gives the wildlife a chance to find another place to spend the winter—as opposed to under your mulch and near your plants for easy feeding.

Do not worry if it snows before you put the mulch in place. Snow is the best mulch. Keep the other materials handy for late applications needed when the winter thaw melts the snow. Apply the mulch after the snow melts and before the soil thaws.

Place planters in an unheated garage, porch, or other protected area where temperatures hover near freezing. Insulate the roots with packing peanuts or other material. Water whenever the soil is thawed and dry. Or, sink the containers into a vacant garden area for the winter. This is perfect for double-potted containers. Slide the ugly inner pot out of the decorative planter. Bury the ugly pot in a protected area of the landscape. Next spring, lift the pot out of the soil, repot or divide as needed, and place in the decorative container.

Leave the stems or place markers by balloon flower, butterfly weed, and other late-emerging perennials. Plant bulbs next to these perennials to mark their locations and prevent accidental damage in early spring.

ROSES

Timing is an important factor in successful winter protection of non-hardy roses. Wait until after a week of freezing temperatures to finish your winter protection. Mulching and covering too early can lead to heat buildup, disease problems, and death of plants.

Cut back roses only enough to apply winter protection. The major pruning will be done in spring. Do not prune ramblers, climbers, or once-blooming shrub roses, since they bloom on old wood.

Care for indoor roses as you would your other houseplants. Grow them in a cool, sunny location. They will drop leaves as they adjust to their new location. Keep the soil slightly moist, and continue to watch for pests. Mites are a common problem on indoor roses.

SHRUBS

Dormant pruning can be done now until growth begins in spring. Prune summer- and fall-blooming plants, such as hydrangea and potentilla, or wait until late winter so that you can enjoy the winter interest these plants provide. Plus the wounds close quicker as new spring growth begins.

Wait until spring, after flowering, to prune lilacs, forsythia, and other spring-flowering shrubs. Remove damaged branches as needed.

Apply winter protection to shrubs exposed to deicing salts, snow loads, and winter wind and sun.

Give special attention to rhododendron and other broad leaf evergreens. Use a screen of burlap to cut the winter winds and shade the plants from the winter sun. Or circle the plants with a cylinder of hardware cloth several feet tall and sunk several inches into the ground. Fill with straw or the more festive evergreen branches to protect the shrubs.

Loosely tie upright arborvitae, junipers, and yews that are subject to splitting. Use strips of cotton cloth or old nylon stockings to tie the multiple stems together. Tying the stems prevents snow from building up on the plant, causing it to split and bend. Or, wrap the whole plant in bird netting. This prevents snow loads and may help discourage deer.

Do not use wraps on the trunks of trees and shrubs. Research has found they do not help and can, in fact, hurt the plants. If you feel you must use them, apply them in the fall and remove them in the spring.

TREES

Keep raking and mulching leaves as long as they keep falling. See September, Care for tips on managing leaves in the landscape.

Install wind, sun, and salt screens. Burlap, weed barrier fabrics, or other barriers can protect new plantings and sensitive plants from winter damage. Wrap arborvitae and upright junipers with strips

of cotton, old nylon stockings, or bird netting. This will prevent the snow load damage that frequently occurs.

Avoid tree wraps for winter protection. Research has shown that they do not protect the plant and can cause damage if left on the tree too long.

Move containers to an unheated garage for the winter. Water the soil whenever it is thawed and dry. Or, protect the roots of plants left outdoors by surrounding them with bales of hay or other insulating material.

Continue pruning as needed. Prune trees to repair damage or establish structure. Always prune with a goal in mind. Consider waiting until late winter for major pruning jobs. This way you can remove winter damage at the same time you improve the tree's structure.

Winter is a good time to prune oaks.

Wait one to two years before pruning newly planted trees. After that time, prune to establish a strong framework.

Wait until spring to prune evergreens. Large branches removed in the fall can be used for holiday decorations.

VINES & GROUNDCOVERS

Remove the last of the fall leaves. See October, Care for tips on making this task easier.

Remove dead and damaged branches whenever they are found. Disinfect tools between cuts on diseased plants. Use rubbing alcohol or a solution of one part bleach to nine parts water.

WATER

ALL

Water all outdoor plants thoroughly before the ground freezes. Moisten the top 6 to 8 inches of soil, and then drain and store the water hose for the winter. Pick a warm day to make the job easier and less damaging to the hose.

ANNUALS

Water annuals growing indoors. Apply enough water so that the excess runs out the drainage hole. Pour off any water that collects in the saucer, or use a gravel tray described in October, Water. Repeat whenever the top few inches of soil start to dry.

BULBS

Check on forced bulbs, and water if the soil begins to dry.

EDIBLES

Water plants in cold frames, under plastic, or under other season-extending devices whenever the top few inches of soil start to dry.

Check young seedlings daily and indoor gardens several times each week.

LAWNS

Newly planted lawns benefit from regular watering throughout the fall. Established lawns should only be watered during dry falls when they show signs of wilting. Put away the sprinkler, and stop watering when the ground freezes.

■ *Winter pruning allows you to see the overall structure of the tree.*

SHRUBS

Keep watering as needed until the ground freezes. Make sure new plantings and evergreens are thoroughly watered before the ground freezes. Once the ground is frozen, drain and store the hose until spring.

VINES & GROUNDCOVERS

Water container plants wintering indoors whenever the top 2 to 3 inches of soil begin to dry. Apply enough water so that the excess runs out the bottom. Water pots stored in the garage and outdoors whenever the soil is thawed and dry.

FERTILIZE

ALL

For outdoor plants, review plant growth, and note areas that need soil tests. Use this as your first step in correcting problems. The soil test results will indicate if a lack of nutrients or incorrect fertilization is causing the problem.

Contact your local Michigan State University Extension Service office or website for soil test information. They have information on how to take the test and bags for submitting samples to the soils lab.

Store leftover fertilizers for winter. Granular fertilizers need to be kept in a cool, dry place. Keep liquid fertilizers in a dark location in above-freezing temperatures.

ANNUALS

Indoor plants, including annuals grown indoors, need very little fertilizer. Use a diluted solution of flowering houseplant fertilizer if plants are actively growing and showing signs of nutrient deficiency. Otherwise wait until plants adjust to their new location, light intensity increases, and plants begin to grow.

BULBS

Follow soil test recommendations, or add 1 pound of a low-nitrogen, slow-release fertilizer per 100 square feet of planting space.

Established bulb plantings need little, if any, more fertilizer. Fertilize to promote vigor and good bloom. Spring, as the bulbs sprout, is the best time to fertilize. Do not fertilize after the ground freezes.

EDIBLES

Concentrate on improving the soil with shredded leaves, well-rotted manure, and other organic matter. Spade several inches of these materials into the top 6 to 12 inches of soil (if it's not frozen).

Use a dilute solution of a low-nitrogen fertilizer for seedlings and windowsill gardens. Follow label directions for rates and times of applications.

LAWNS

There is still time to apply fertilizer in early November before the ground freezes and snow begins to cover the ground. See October, Fertilize on fertilizing lawns for more information.

TREES

There is still time to fertilize. Consult your soil test results to see if your trees need any more nutrients.

VINES & GROUNDCOVERS

Give tropical vines time to adjust to their indoor home. Yellow and falling leaves are due to low light and poor growing conditions. Once new growth begins, you can start fertilizing. Use a diluted

Protect new plantings from animal damage. Place a cylinder of one-quarter inch hardware cloth around the trunk or stems. The cylinder should be at least 4 feet high with the bottom few inches sunk into the ground.

solution of any flowering houseplant fertilizer. Apply to indoor vines that are actively growing and in need of a nutrient boost.

PROBLEM-SOLVE

ALL

Make sure animal fences and barriers are in place.

Ornamental plums, euonymus, fruit trees, and arborvitae are a few wildlife favorites. Monitor these plantings for animal damage throughout the winter.

Place snow fencing around desirable plants. A 5-foot fence around a small area will often keep out the deer. Make sure they cannot reach in and feed.

Use a cylinder of hardware cloth, 4 feet tall, to protect trees and other plants from rabbits, deer, and voles. Sink the bottom few inches of the fencing into the ground before it freezes.

Start applying repellents to areas and plants that have suffered animal damage in the past. Start before feeding begins. This encourages them to go elsewhere for dinner. Reapply after heavy rains or as specified on label directions.

Squirrels and chipmunks often dig up and move the bulbs as fast as we plant. Cayenne pepper and commercial repellents labeled for squirrel and chipmunk control may provide some relief. See September, Problem-Solve for more ideas on managing wildlife damage.

Voles are also a problem. High populations can damage bulbs, lawns, and other plantings. This rodent can be killed with a snap trap baited with peanut butter and oats. Place the trap in a PVC pipe or under cover to prevent accidental harm to songbirds. Keep in mind there may be more than 400 voles per acre.

ANNUALS

Watch for whiteflies, aphids, mites, and any other insects that may have moved indoors on the plants. These pests suck out plant juices, causing the leaves to yellow and eventually brown.

High populations of aphids and mites can be controlled using insecticidal soap. Check the label before mixing and applying this or any other chemical.

Whiteflies can stress and stunt plants. These insects multiply quickly and are much harder to control. Try trapping whiteflies with commercial or homemade yellow sticky traps. They stick to the trap and die. This will not eliminate the whiteflies but may reduce the populations enough to minimize stress to plants. Whiteflies are difficult to control with pesticides. Use three applications, five days apart, of an insecticide labeled for controlling whiteflies. If you miss one application, you need to start the entire treatment process over. Apply in a well-ventilated location, and avoid using pesticides if pets or children are present.

Fungus gnats are small insects that are often found flitting across the room. They do not hurt the plants; they just annoy us. These insects feed on the organic matter in the soil, such as dead plant roots and peat moss. Keep the soil slightly drier than normal to reduce their populations.

BULBS
If your landscape has become a fine dining location for squirrels, deer, and rabbits, you may choose to plant only animal-resistant bulbs. Daffodils have been the longtime favorite for gardeners plagued by animals, but here are a few more to consider:

Autumn crocus (*Colchicum*), hyacinth, glory-of-the-snow, crown imperial (*Fritillaria*), grape hyacinth, netted iris (*Iris reticulata*), ornamental onions, squill, snowdrops (*Galanthus*), snowflake (*Lycoris*), and winter aconite (*Eranthis*) are usually left undisturbed by animals. Keep in mind that in years of high animal populations and limited food, they will eat almost anything.

EDIBLES
Clean up the garden if you have not already. Remove debris that harbors insects and diseases for next season.

Prepare for next year by evaluating the cause of problems in this year's garden.

Wilted tomatoes, dead beans, and a poorly performing garden may be caused by a nearby black walnut tree. The roots, leaves, and nuts of these trees contain a substance called juglone. This substance is toxic to many plants, including vegetables. The tree's roots can travel hundreds of feet beyond the tree, killing any susceptible plants in their way.

Avoid planting black walnut trees in small landscapes where you are trying to grow other trees, flowers, and vegetable gardens. Plant vegetable gardens at least 50 feet away, preferably farther, from these trees. Grow vegetables in containers or create a raised-bed garden. Cover the ground and inside of the raised-bed walls with weed barrier fabric. Fill with 8 to 12 inches of soil. This helps keep the tree roots out of the raised bed garden.

Do not use black walnut leaves to amend soil. Compost them until they are unidentifiable.

Consider removing the black walnut tree for long-term, not short-term, benefits. It takes five to ten years for the roots and debris to decompose and become nontoxic.

LAWNS
Work on your journal. Record all pest problems encountered this season. Evaluate the possible cause and the solutions tried. Do a little research over the winter to reduce future problems.

PERENNIALS
Cut back and remove disease- and insect-infested perennials.

ROSES
Fall cleanup will help to minimize future problems. Rake and destroy fallen leaves. Remove any disease-infested leaves.

TREES
Look for egg masses of gypsy moths and tent caterpillars. Remove and destroy them as soon as they are discovered.

December

Score points with the family and start cleaning the basement. (They don't need to know that you are making room for a new or expanded seed-starting setup.) Make a wish list of materials needed. Be sure to include seeds, flats, containers, and other supplies that you will need. Your family will now be on to you and your recent cleaning frenzy—but you can solve their gift-buying dilemmas. Consider giving the same type of gift or gardening gift certificate to your favorite gardeners.

And while you're at it, clean and pack away the tools—another planting season is over. And so is the mowing season. (There are some good things about winter!) Clean and store your mower if you have not done so already.

While storing your tools and equipment take a quick inventory of the condition and quantity of your supplies. Remember, the holidays are coming and gardening tools would make a great gift to give—or better yet, to receive. Consider sharing duplicates with friends and family who are just starting to garden. Add a gift certificate to a garden center or a bit of your time and expertise to help them get started.

The soil is usually frozen by the holidays, and we have not yet had the damaging winter thaw. Don't throw away that holiday tree! Prune off the branches and cover perennial and bulb beds, or leave the tree intact and use it as a windbreak for other plants in the landscape or a little added winter interest. The trees provide shelter for the birds that like to feed on the seeds of coneflower, rudbeckia, and liatris in the perennial garden. No holiday tree? Don't worry. Take a walk through the neighborhood, where you are sure to find discarded trees at the curb.

Watch for wildlife visiting your gardens. They can be a wonderful addition to the landscape. Their movements and antics are entertaining. Make a list of the visitors to your winter garden. Note what plants helped bring them into the landscape.

Unfortunately, some wildlife visitors do more damage than we can tolerate. Watch for tracks, droppings, and other signs of wildlife. Monitor for damage done by deer and rabbits munching on trees and shrubs, squirrels digging, and voles eating roots. Apply repellents, scare tactics, and fencing to minimize damage.

Keep exercising and stretching to keep those planting muscles toned until spring returns.

DECEMBER

PLAN

ALL

Sit back, relax, and look out the window. Get out your gardening journal and record your thoughts on the past growing season. Make a few notes about what you want to do differently and what can stay the same. Now look out the window again. Is your landscape working for you now? Make a list of additions that should be considered in next year's plan. Consider adding some plants for winter interest, attracting wildlife, or feeding your family.

Make sure your garden records are up to date. Record the varieties grown, the source, and success rates. Revise your garden plan to reflect what you really did, not just what you planned.

No plan would be complete without a wish list needed for next season. A new journal, plant labels, hand pruners, flower scissors, a harvest basket, a new shovel, a gift certificate to your favorite garden center or catalog, and a load of manure (to be delivered at a later date) all make great holiday gifts to give and receive.

■ *Enjoy the herbs you grew all summer with oils and vinegars. They also make great gifts!*

ANNUALS

Frame your best garden and flower photos and give them as gifts to friends and relatives. Use dried flowers from your garden to decorate gift packages and cards. A bouquet of dried flowers makes a great gift for any housebound person—gardener or not.

LAWNS

Ask for a new fertilizer spreader, an environmentally friendly push mower to work off the winter bulge, or just the promise of a helping hand as a holiday gift.

Make plans for dealing with shady areas under trees where grass won't grow.

The lack of sunlight and competition for water make it difficult, if not impossible, to grow grass under some shade trees. But you do not have to sacrifice shade or give up on the lawn.

Think about planting shade-tolerant grass seed mixes. They contain a high percentage of fine fescue grass. This shade- and drought-tolerant grass is the best choice for shady locations.

Or, plant shade-tolerant groundcovers in heavily shaded areas. Hostas, coralbells, *Brunnera*, barrenwort (*Epimedium*), and deadnettle (*Lamium*) are just a few of the shade-tolerant groundcovers you can try. Start with just a few plants to make sure there is enough sunlight and moisture for the groundcovers.

Mulch densely shaded areas. Spread 3 inches of woodchips under the tree. Keep woodchips away from the tree trunk. The woodchips improve the growing conditions, while keeping the lawn mower and weed whip away from the trunk of the tree.

ROSES

The holidays and garden catalogs seem to arrive at the same time. Take this opportunity to add a few new roses to your gift list. Here are a few tips for enjoying roses throughout the winter:

Harvest rose hips and include them in holiday and winter arrangements. They combine nicely with fresh evergreens and dried materials.

Enlarge and frame pictures of your favorite garden roses. These also make great gifts and greeting cards.

Purchase one of the tabletop roses available at garden centers and florists.

PLANT

BULBS

Try forcing amaryllis and paper-whites for indoor bloom. These bulbs do not need a cold treatment and are readily available at most garden centers. See February, Plant for tips on forcing paper-whites (*Narcissus*) and for potting and growing amaryllis.

Plant any leftover bulbs for forcing. These won't flower until late March or April when many of our outdoor bulbs are blooming. I use these as accent plants or in containers and windowboxes in my landscape.

EDIBLES

There's still time to start a windowsill garden. Use leftover seeds or scour the garden centers for any leftover inventory. Leafy crops, such as lettuce, do well in the low light indoors. Mix in radishes and miniature carrots for some zing. Onions, parsley, basil, chives, and other herbs are always good suggestions for indoor gardens.

LAWNS

Dormant seeding is risky. Unseasonably warm weather coaxes the seed to germinate. A quick drop

■ *You can use some of your prunings to make decorative holiday plantings.*

HERE'S HOW

TO GROW A WINDOWSILL GARDEN

1. Locate small pots for individual plants or large containers for mixed plantings. Use clean containers with drainage holes. Fill with sterile potting mix.

2. Plant seeds or rooted cuttings. Water thoroughly so that the excess water drains out the bottom. Pour off any excess water.

3. Place the garden in a sunny, south-facing window. Or place it under artificial lights for the best results. Keep lights 4 to 6 inches above the tops of the plant.

Consider making several gardens with various plant combinations. They make great holiday gifts for both cooks and gardeners.

back to normal cold can kill the young seedlings. You might want to risk a little seed and some time on small areas, but think twice before seeding large areas or new lawns. See November, Plant for details.

TREES

Live Christmas trees need to be planted as soon as possible after the holidays. Move the tree outdoors after seven to ten days indoors. Any longer and the tree may break bud and begin growing. If the tree does start to grow, you will have an indoor evergreen for Valentine's Day, Easter, and May Day.

Start the transition by moving the tree to a screened-in porch or garage for several weeks. This allows the tree to gradually adjust to the colder outdoor temperatures. Plant (in a previously dug hole), water, mulch, and shield from winter wind and sun. Then keep your fingers crossed—a little luck never hurt.

CARE

ANNUALS

Check on plants stored in the basement. The stems should be firm but dormant. Move them to a

cooler, darker location if they start to grow. If growth continues, pot them and move them to a sunny window or under artificial lights.

Care for annuals and tropicals (such as hibiscus) that are growing indoors for the winter. Keep them out of drafts and in the brightest possible location.

Pinch and clip as needed to encourage compact growth. Keep pruning to a minimum by removing only dead leaves and dead stems.

BULBS

Mulch outdoor bulb plantings with evergreen branches, straw, or marsh hay after the ground freezes if frost heaving and early sprouting have been problems.

Many garden magazines and books talk about reblooming amaryllis as if it were easy. Don't be discouraged if that has not been your experience. You are in the majority. Many frustrated gardeners grow a great crop of leaves but no flowers. Here are a few techniques for reblooming amaryllis:

The traditional approach: Keep the amaryllis growing indoors throughout the spring. Move the

Evergreen boughs provide decorative winter protection for less-hardy and grafted roses.

plant outdoors for summer. Some gardeners sink the pot in the ground to reduce the need for water. Stop fertilizing midsummer, and cut back on water in late August. Move the pot indoors. Cut back or allow the leaves to dry naturally. Store it in a cool, dark place for three months. Move the pot to a sunny window, water as needed, and wait. With some luck you should have flowers in a month.

Bare-root storage: Keep the plant growing indoors throughout the spring. Plant the bulb directly in the garden for the summer. Dig it up and move it indoors prior to the first fall frost. Allow the leaves to dry, and store the bare root bulb in a cool, dark location. Plant the bulbs in January and grow in a sunny location.

Continual care: Keep your amaryllis plant growing year-round. Leave it in the container. Move it outdoors for summer and indoors in a well-lit location for winter. This method may produce flowers in summer and winter.

EDIBLES

Thin out seedlings in your newly planted windowsill garden and continue harvesting herbs as needed for seasoning.

Remove any damaged or diseased leaves as soon as they are found.

LAWNS

All of your hard work can be damaged with a quick toss of deicing salt. A little care now eliminates the frustration and time needed next spring to repair winter-damaged turf. Shovel before applying deicing salt. This reduces the amount of salt needed to control ice on walks and drives. It also eliminates salt-laden snow from ending up on the lawn. Use plant-friendly deicing compounds. Calcium chloride is more expensive, but it is easier on your plants. Calcium magnesium acetate is also safe for both concrete and plants. Watch for new, more plant-friendly products entering the market. Apply deicing compounds down the middle of walks and drives, avoiding the grass. Consider using sand or kitty litter to provide traction and reduce the use of salt. Avoid these products in areas where they will be washed into and potentially clog

drains and sewers. Note the areas most affected by deicing salts. Water these areas in spring to dilute the salts and wash them through the soil.

PERENNIALS

Don't worry if you have waited too long and the snow has buried all your good intentions. Wait until the first winter thaw to mulch borderline hardy perennials, late plantings, or those subject to frost heaving. Use evergreen branches, straw, or marsh hay for winter mulch.

Even in December you can enjoy fresh green edibles with a kitchen window herb garden.

ROSES

Complete winter protection after a week of freezing temperatures. Prune only enough to apply winter protection. The canes need to be short enough to fit under the protective covering but long enough to increase winter survival. Since rose canes die from the tip back, the longer canes have a better chance of surviving our tough winters.

Check on winter protection already in place. Make sure rose cones and mulches are secure.

Check roses growing in containers in winter storage.

SHRUBS

Check winter protection, and make sure it is securely in place—keeping out the animals or protecting the plants from harsh winter weather and deicing salt.

Continue dormant pruning on summer- and fall-blooming shrubs. Wait until after shrubs bloom to prune spring-flowering shrubs. Once the snow falls, limit your pruning to repair damage.

Prune off a few branches of red twig dogwood, juniper, winterberry, arborvitae, and yews. Add these to your indoor or outdoor holiday décor.

Carefully add holiday lights to the winter landscape. Do not wrap branches with strands

of lights. Drape the lights over the branches or loosely secure the lights to the stems. Remove lights in spring. If left in place, the ties can damage fast-growing shrubs. Plus, the wires quickly dull your saw blades.

TREES

Keep the roots of living Christmas trees moist at all times. Minimize its time inside to maximize your chance of success. If the tree begins to grow, you are stuck with a big houseplant until next spring.

Wait until late winter or early spring to do the majority of evergreen pruning. You can remove large branches that block walks and drives. These can be used for holiday decorations.

Be careful when hanging holiday lights on trees and shrubs. Always use lights made for outdoor use. Loosely attach the lights to the tree branches and trunks. Remove lights in spring before growth begins. Tightly wrapped lights can girdle a tree in one season. Use a sturdy ladder, and work with a buddy; or consider hiring a professional. Many landscape companies now install lights and other holiday décor.

VINES & GROUNDCOVERS

Check on vines stored in the garage or protected area for winter. Adjust the location or winter mulch if needed. Use evergreen boughs to protect European ginger and other tender plants from winter injury. Use your discarded holiday tree to create shade and windbreaks for tender vines. Evergreen vines often suffer leaf burn from winter winds.

WATER

ALL

It is usually not necessary to water outdoor gardens. In mild years, the ground may not freeze until late December. Wait to put the hose away so that you can water thoroughly before the ground does freeze. When it does, make sure the garden hose is safely stored for winter. Turn off the water or insulate outside faucets to prevent freezing.

Use loppers to extend your reach when pruning.

Add a layer of gravel to a plant saucer to increase humidity and fill it with water to keep the pot from sitting directly in water.

ANNUALS

Water indoor plants whenever the top few inches of soil start to dry. Water so that excess water runs out the bottom. Pour off any water that collects in the saucer, or create a gravel tray.

BULBS

Check bulbs in cold storage for forcing. The soil should be moist (like a damp sponge) but not wet. Keep the soil around amaryllis and paperwhites moist as well. Check these plants every few days, and water as needed.

EDIBLES

Check indoor plantings several times a week. Keep the soil moist for seedlings. Allow the top 1 or 2 inches of soil to slightly dry before watering small pots. Allow the top 3 inches of soil to slightly dry before watering larger containers.

Water thoroughly until the excess runs out the bottom of the pot. Water often enough to meet the plants' needs.

ROSES

Water roses growing in containers in winter storage anytime the soil is dry and not frozen.

Keep the soil slightly moist on indoor roses.

SHRUBS & TREES

Check soil moisture in aboveground planters. Water planters anytime the soil thaws and dries.

VINES & GROUNDCOVERS

Water tropical vines growing indoors for the winter. Water thoroughly whenever the top few inches begin to dry. Apply enough water so that the excess runs out the bottom of the container.

DECEMBER

Check potted vines stored in the garage and sheltered locations outdoors. Water whenever the soil thaws and the top few inches are dry. Add enough water to moisten all of the soil. Stop watering when the excess water begins to run out of the bottom of the pot.

FERTILIZE

ALL

Plants are in sleep mode and don't need fertilizer. Do not fertilize frozen ground. Winter rains and

HERE'S HOW

TO ATTRACT WILDLIFE TO THE LANDSCAPE

Birds and butterflies can add color and motion to the winter and summer landscapes. Planting shrubs that provide food and shelter is a great way to bring them into your yard. Nature takes care of stocking the feeder, allowing you more time to sit back, relax, and watch the birds.

Here are a few hardy (zones 3 through 5) shrubs to consider:

Arborvitae (*Thuja occidentalis*) BS
Bayberry (*Myrica pennsylvanica*) BF
Chokeberry (*Aronia*) BF, BS
Coralberry (*Symphoricarpos orbiculatus*) BF, BS, HB
Dogwood (*Cornus*) B, BF
Elderberry (*Sambucus*) B, BF, BS
Flowering plums and cherries (*Prunus*) BF, BS, HB
Juneberry (*Amelanchier*) BF
Lilac (*Syringa*) B, HB
Rose (*Rosa*) B, BF
Spirea (*Spiraea*) B
Viburnum (*Viburnum*) B, BF, BS
Yew (*Taxus*) BS

KEY:
B—Butterflies; BF—Food for birds
BS—Shelter for birds; HB—Hummingbird

melting snow can wash the fertilizer off the frozen soil surfaces and into our waterways.

Store fertilizers for the winter. Keep granular fertilizers in a cool, dry place. Liquid fertilizers should be stored in a cool (above freezing), dark location.

INDOORS

Plants are still struggling to adjust to their indoor location. The poor light and low humidity result in poor growth. Wait until plants start to grow before adding any fertilizer.

Apply a diluted solution of any flowering houseplant fertilizer to flowering plants that are actively growing and showing signs of nutrient deficiencies.

Herbs and indoor vegetables need very little fertilizer. Use a diluted solution of any complete fertilizer (10-10-10) for herbs overwintering indoors and windowsill gardens.

PROBLEM-SOLVE

ALL

Store pesticides in a secure location out of the reach of children and pets. Store granules and powders in a cool, dry location. Keep liquid pesticides in a cool (above freezing), dark location. Make a note of old products you no longer use. Next spring watch for community clean-sweep programs, which collect and dispose of old pesticides. Store the unwanted materials together, and plan on disposing of them at the next community clean-sweep event.

ANNUALS

Continue to check plants for signs of whiteflies, mites, and aphids. Try trapping whiteflies with commercial or homemade yellow sticky traps. Coat a piece of yellow cardboard with a sticky substance. Place them in and near the infested plants. This will not kill all the whiteflies, but it can reduce the damage to a tolerable level. Use insecticides as your last resort. Select one labeled for controlling whiteflies on indoor plants. Spray three times, five days apart, in a well-ventilated location. If you miss an application, you must start over.

Control mites and aphids with a strong blast of water followed by a treatment of insecticidal soap. It is a soap that is effective at killing insects, but it is safe for people and the environment. Repeated applications may be necessary.

BULBS

Continue to monitor and control animal damage. Check stored bulbs monthly for signs of rot and disease. Discard infested and rotting bulbs immediately.

EDIBLES

Watch for fungus gnats, whiteflies, aphids, and mites. These insects are commonly found on indoor plants, including herbs and windowsill gardens. See January, Problem-Solve for descriptions of the insects, their damage, and control options.

LAWNS

Winter, snow, and deicing salts have a major impact on our landscape. Identify any lawn areas that are killed each year by deicing salt, and then evaluate your snow-removal technique. Consider alternatives, such as adding a border of annuals, expanding the walk, or incorporating some other landscape feature instead of grass in these areas.

PERENNIALS

Repellents may discourage squirrels, rabbits, and deer. Treat before feeding and digging begins. Reapply repellents as needed. Check the label for more specific directions.

ROSES

Clean up roses before winter protection is applied. In mild years, gardeners in the southern part of the state may still be doing this in December.

SHRUBS

Secure fencing and animal barriers. Continue applying repellents to areas and plants frequently browsed by animals. Reapply after harsh weather and as recommended by the label directions.

TREES

Finish installing animal fencing. Apply repellents throughout the winter to new plantings and those favored by deer and rabbits. Continue to scout and destroy egg masses of tent caterpillars, tussock moths, and gypsy moths.

VINES & GROUNDCOVERS

Take a walk outside before the snow gets too deep. Note any existing and potential problems with vines and groundcovers to watch for in the future.

■ *A wreath from fresh-cut pine boughs can brighten any door.*

Planting a Tree

Remove transit guard, burlap, and wire baskets. Stake only if you must—bare root,

large canopy with small rootball, or similar situation.

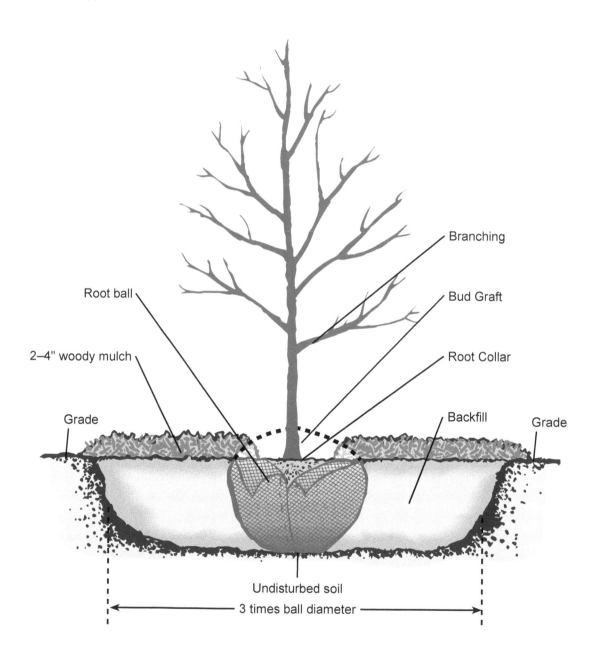

Branching

Bud Graft

Root ball

Root Collar

2–4" woody mulch

Grade

Backfill

Grade

Undisturbed soil

3 times ball diameter

Modified from the Wisconsin Department of Natural Resources
Call 811, a free underground utility locating service, 3 days before digging.

Pruning

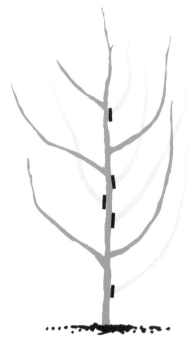

■ *Create a strong framework with proper pruning. The remaining branches should have a wide crotch angle and be well spaced in a spiral pattern along the trunk.*

■ *Renewal pruning is the process of removing one-third of the plant's growth each year.*

No other gardening chore evokes such a wide range of emotions as pruning. Feelings range from pruning paranoia (fear of killing or maiming the plant) to visions of a chainsaw massacre. Before breaking out the tools, make sure there is a reason to prune. My aunt pruned whenever she was feeling stressed, and her landscape looked it.

Prune your plants to create a strong framework and structure that withstands our adverse weather. Improve the look and ornamental appeal of your plants through proper pruning. Prune to increase flowering and fruiting, encourage new colorful bark, and maintain an attractive form. Remove hazardous and broken branches as they appear.

Minimize your workload by selecting the right plant for the location. You will prune often if you are trying to keep a 40-foot tree in a 20-foot location. This is hard on you and the plants.

I have compiled a few basics on pruning various plants. Be sure to check out the pruning recommendations in each chapter as well.

BASICS OF TREE PRUNING

As always, prune with a purpose in mind. Strive to maintain the plant's natural shape. Prune young trees to establish a strong framework. Use proper pruning to maintain a strong structure and healthy growth, as well as to improve flowering and fruiting on established trees.

- Wait two to four years after planting to start pruning for structure. The more top growth (branches and leaves), the faster the trees will recover from transplanting.

- Remove any branches that are crossed, sprouting from the same area on the trunk, or growing parallel to each other.

- Remove any branches that are growing straight up and competing with the main trunk.

- Remaining branches should be more horizontal (perpendicular to the trunk) than upright.

- Make sure branches are well spaced from top to bottom and around the tree trunk. See the illlustration on page 209.

- Well-trained trees will need minimal pruning.

- Consider hiring a certified arborist for large jobs. They have the training and equipment to do the job safely and properly.

- Start by removing dead and damaged branches.

- Next, prune out watersprouts (upright shoots on branches) and suckers (upright shoots at the base of the trunk) as close to their bases as possible.

- Remove any branches that are crossed, rubbing, or parallel.

- Only prune off lower branches for safety and clearance. The lower limbs are the tree's best defense against disease and old age.

flush with the trunk are slow to close and make a great entryway for pests and decay. Stubs left behind look unsightly and also increase pest problems.

- Remove branches where they join the trunk or other branches. This will help maintain the tree's natural form and encourage balanced growth.

- Larger branches (2 inches in diameter or greater) should be double-cut to prevent branch splitting and bark tearing.

- Make the first cut on the bottom of the branch about 12 inches from the final cut. Cut about one-fourth of the way through the branch.

- Make the second cut on top of the branch within 1 inch of the first cut. Continue cutting until the branch breaks off.

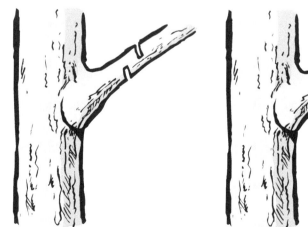

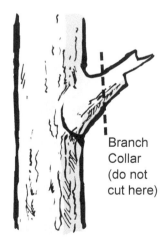

Branch Collar (do not cut here)

Limb removal

PERFECT PRUNING CUTS

How you remove a branch is as important as deciding which branch to remove. Improper cuts create perfect entryways for insects and disease.

- Make the pruning cut flush with the branch bark collar. See the final cut of the three-step limb removal illustration above. Pruning cuts

- The final cut should be flush with the branch bark collar. See the illustration above.

- Do not apply pruning paints or wound dressings to pruning cuts. Recent research shows that these materials actually trap moisture and disease rather than keeping them out.

■ *Renewal pruning*

■ *Heading back shrub*

PRUNING SHRUBS

Your landscape does not need to be filled with green rectangles, gum drops, and tuna cans. Instead, prune shrubs in their natural form to maximize their beauty and improve their health and longevity. Proper pruning can help you maintain size, improve flowering and fruiting and bark color, or remove damaged or diseased branches. When and how you prune is equally important. More details and specific plant recommendations can be found in the Introduction and monthly pruning tips of the Shrubs sections.

Prune spring-flowering shrubs, such as lilac and forsythia, in spring right after flowering. Spring bloomers flower on the previous season's growth. Pruning in late summer or winter removes the flower buds and eliminates the spring display.

Trim summer-blooming plants during the dormant season. Hills-of-snow hydrangeas, potentilla, and summer-blooming spireas flower on the current season's growth.

Remove dead, damaged, or disease-infected branches whenever they are found. Disinfect tools between cuts to prevent the spread of disease. Use rubbing alcohol or a solution of one part bleach to nine parts water as a disinfectant.

Make pruning cuts on a slight angle above a healthy bud, where a branch joins another branch, or where a branch joins the trunk. These cuts heal

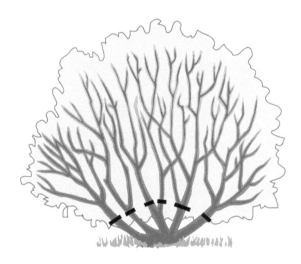

■ *Rejuvenation pruning*

quickly and reduce the risk of insects and disease entering the plant. The location of the pruning cut also influences the plant's appearance and future growth.

Use thinning cuts to open up the plant and reduce the size while maintaining its natural appearance. Prune off branches where they join the main stem or another branch. Thinning cuts allow air and light to penetrate the plant, improving flowering, fruiting, and bark color. It also helps reduce some disease problems.

Use heading cuts to reduce the height and spread of shrubs. Limit the number and vary the location of heading cuts to keep the plant's natural appearance.

Prune branches back to a shorter side shoot or above a healthy bud. Excessive heading can lead to a tuft of growth at the end of a long, bare stem.

Reserve shearing for only the most formal settings. This technique is easy on the gardener but hard on the plant. Shearing makes indiscriminant cuts, leaving stubs that make perfect entryways for insects and disease. Prune so that the bottom of the plant is wider than the top. This allows light to reach all parts, top to the bottom, of the plant.

Use renewal pruning to manage overgrown shrubs, contain growth, and stimulate new, healthy, and more attractive stems. Start by removing one-third of the older (larger) canes to ground level. Reduce the height of the remaining stems by one-third if needed. Repeat the process the next two years for overgrown shrubs. By the end of the third year, the shrub will be smaller, more attractive, and healthier. Continue to remove older canes as needed throughout the life of the shrub.

Use rejuvenation pruning to manage the size of some fast-growing and overgrown shrubs. Make sure the plant will tolerate this severe pruning. Cut all stems back to 4 inches above the soil line during the dormant season. The best time is late winter through early spring before growth begins. The plant will soon begin to grow and recover.

PRUNING POINTERS FOR A FEW SHRUBS

Get the greatest ornamental value from your shrubs through proper pruning. Match the pruning method to the shrub for increased flowering, improved bark color, and maintenance of its natural form.
• Barberry* (*Berberis* species) and cotoneaster (*Cotoneaster* species) are generally slow growing. Remove only damaged and diseased stems to ground level in spring before growth begins.
• Blue mist spirea (*Caryopteris* × *clandonensis*) is marginally hardy in northern areas and usually dies back over winter. Cut the plant back to 4 to 6 inches above the soil in late winter. Remove old, diseased, or dead stems to the main framework.
• Burning bush* (*Euonymus alatus*) needs minimal pruning, which can be done during the dormant season. Selectively remove vigorous growth to major side branches to maintain the desired size

*Consider replacing these invasive plants

and shape. Do not use renewal or rejuvenation pruning on this single-stemmed shrub. Consider replacing overgrown plants with a non-invasive shrub.
• Butterfly bush (*Buddleja davidii*) usually dies back over winter. Prune back to 4 to 6 inches above the soil in late winter or early spring before growth begins.
• Dogwoods (*Cornus* species) can be pruned during the dormant season. Remove old and discolored stems of the suckering type to ground level. Wait for Cornelian cherry dogwood to blossom before pruning. Pruning will depend on the desired form.
• Forsythia (*Forsythia* species) flowers on the previous season's growth. Wait until after flowering to prune. Finish pruning by early June so that the plant has time to set flower buds for next spring's display. Remove three-year and older stems to ground level.
• The honeysuckles (*Lonicera* species) are tough shrubs that can take severe pruning. Consider removing invasive species from the landscape. Renewal prune (remove one-third of the older stems to ground level) others to encourage new growth at the base of the plant. These tough shrubs will tolerate rejuvenation pruning back to 4 inches above ground level. Prune during the dormant season.
• The hydrangea (*Hydrangea* species), hills-of-snow, 'Annabelle', and other snowball types of *Hydrangea* should be pruned back to 15 inches above ground level each winter. Wait until late winter if you want to enjoy the dried flowers in the winter landscape. Panicle hydrangeas are often trained into small trees or specimen plants. Regular pruning is not needed but can improve flowering. Prune the plant to the desired shape. Yearly pruning cuts can be made back to the first set of healthy buds above this framework. Allow big leaf hydrangeas (*Hydrangea macrophylla*) to stand for the winter. Prune off only dead wood. Older varieties only flower on wood arising from last year's growth. Newer introductions like Endless Summer® and Twist-n-Shout are supposed to flower on old and new wood.
• The juneberry or serviceberry (*Amelanchier* species) can be trained as multistemmed large shrubs or small trees. Do minimal pruning once the main stems are selected. Prune suckering types of Juneberries the same way you prune forsythia and dogwoods. Remove one-third of the older

stems to ground level. Prune in late winter or just after spring bloom.

• Lilacs (*Syringa*) bloom on old wood and should be pruned after flowering. Remove old flowers after bloom to increase next year's floral display. Prune one-third of the older canes back to ground level to encourage fuller growth at the base of the plant.

• Potentillas (*Potentilla fruticosa*) are summer-blooming shrubs that can be pruned anytime during the dormant season. Prune plants back halfway, then remove the older stems to ground level. Or prune the whole plant back to several inches above the soil line. The plants will recover but tend to be a little floppier with this technique.

• Rose-of-Sharon (*Hibiscus syriacus*) is pruned in late spring. Remove dead branches and prune out dead tips to healthy buds or side shoots. Do very little additional pruning to established plants.

• Spireas (*Spiraea* species) are divided into spring and summer blooming types. Spring-flowering bridal wreath/Vanhoutte types should be pruned right after spring bloom. Remove flowering tips to improve next year's bloom. Remove one-fourth of the older stems to ground level on established plants. Older, overgrown plants may be slow to respond to rejuvenation pruning. "Anthony Waterer", "Japanese", "Bumald", and other summer-flowering spireas can be pruned anytime during the dormant season. Wait until late winter if you want to enjoy the winter interest provided by the chestnut brown stems and seed pods. Prune these the same as potentilla. Lightly shear these plants in summer after the flowers fade. This deadheading encourages a second flush of flowers.

• Viburnums (*Viburnum* species) grow at different rates. Slow-growing species need very little pruning. Remove old, damaged, and unproductive branches to main stem or ground level.

SHARING SHRUBS

Gardeners love to share special plants with friends and relatives. Tip cuttings, layering, and division can be used to pass along a piece of that special plant. Try propagating lilacs, forsythia, weigela, and other shrubs by the tip cutting method in late spring or early summer.

1. Gather all the materials needed. This includes a sharp knife or hand pruners, small containers, well-drained potting mix, sand or vermiculite, and

HELPFUL HINTS

Tired of shearing your shrubs? Undo years of shearing and improve the plant's health over the next few seasons. The goal is to remove the tufts of green at the end of the branches, open up the center of the plant, and regain the plant's natural form.

• Start by removing the thickest cluster of twigs back to a side branch in the spring. Thin shoots and trim stubs that were left behind.

• Wait until the following spring for the next phase of pruning. Continue to cut out dense clusters of old growth back to side branches.

• Continue thinning and opening the shrub. You should start to see it regain its natural appearance.

a rooting hormone for woody plants.

2. Remove several 6- to 8-inch pieces from the new growth at the tips of the stems. Remove the lowest set of leaves. Dip the cut end in a rooting hormone for woody plants. Stick one or more cuttings into a pot filled with a well-drained potting mix, sand, or vermiculite.

3. Store the rooting cuttings in a shaded location. Group with other plants or place under trees or shrubs to increase humidity. Keep the rooting medium moist.

4. Transplant rooted cuttings as soon as the roots develop. Plant in a container filled with a well-drained soil. Check soil moisture daily and water as needed. These will be ready for planting next spring. Try layering shrubs with long, pliable stems. Dig and divide rooted suckers to start new plants. Dogwoods and other suckering shrubs send out shoots.

1. Carefully remove the soil at the base of the sucker to see if it has roots.

2. Use a sharp spade to disconnect the sucker from the parents. Some gardeners prefer to leave it in place to develop a stronger root system. Others divide, dig, and transplant immediately. For greatest success, try this in early spring before growth begins.

PRUNING EVERGREENS

Prune evergreens to control size, remove damaged branches, and direct growth. Select the time and method of pruning that is best suited for the plants you are growing.

• Pines are terminal growers. They send out new growth from stem tips once a year. Control their size by removing one-half to two-thirds of the expanding buds (candles) in spring. More severe pruning on stems, removing all terminal buds, will kill the branch.

• Spruce can also be pruned in spring before growth begins. Prune stem tips back to a healthy bud. Make cuts at a slight angle just above the bud. Do not leave stubs that create an entryway for insects and disease.

• Arborvitae and yews can be pruned in spring before growth begins or in early summer after new growth has expanded. Both plants form buds on older wood and tolerate more severe pruning than pines and spruce. Prune back to a bud or branch for best results. Keep the bottom of formal sheared hedges wider than the tops. Avoid fall pruning.

• Junipers require little pruning when the right size variety is selected for the location. Prune to control growth and keep the plant within the available space. Remove selected branches in spring or early summer. Cut the branches back to side shoots to cover cuts. Tip prune in summer for additional sizing. Avoid fall pruning.

PRUNING APPLE TREES

A good harvest starts with a properly trained tree. Start early to avoid butchering overgrown fruit trees into productive scaffolds that look like tortured plants in the landscape. Spend a few minutes reviewing the training method for tree fruits before getting out the saw. It is easier to read and study the information in a warm house than try to remember when you are standing in front of the tree, cold wind blowing, and saw in hand.

Consider training your tree fruits in the Central Leader System. It is easy for you and good for the tree. Follow this step-by-step process:

• **At planting**: Prune whips (thin, unbranched stems) back to 30 or 45 inches at planting. Do minimal pruning on branched trees. Remove only the damaged or broken branches now.

• **First spring after planting:** Prune in late winter or early spring before growth begins. Evaluate the tree and branching structure. Look for evenly spaced branches with wide crotch angles (angle between branch and trunk). Leave four to five of the strongest and most evenly spaced branches with the lowest being 24 to 36 inches above the ground. These branches should be evenly spaced around the trunk and located within 18 inches of the lowest branch. Prune the other branches back to the branch collar. See page 210.

• **Second and third years:** Remove broken and damaged branches each spring before growth begins. Remove suckers (shoots that arise at the base of the tree) just below ground level. Prune off watersprouts (branches that grow straight up from scaffold branches) that interfere with growth and fruit development. Remove any drooping, crossing, and parallel branches. Remove branches back to the point where they join another branch. Prune flush with the branch bark collar (the swollen area at the base of the branch).

• **Third and fourth years:** Select another set of scaffold branches 24 inches above the first. This will allow light to reach the first set of scaffold branches. Keep the upper tier of scaffolds shorter than the bottom set, allowing light to reach all parts of the tree. Spurs (the short fruiting stems) will begin to form along the branches.

• **Fifth year and beyond:** Maintain the leader as the tallest branch. Prune back any side branches that are starting to reach the height of the leader. Cut the tip of the branch back to a side branch. Slow down tree growth once it reaches the desired height. Most gardeners like to keep dwarf trees 8 to 10 feet tall and semi-dwarf trees 12 to 16 feet tall. Prune the tip of the leader back to a weak side branch to slow upward growth. Repeat yearly as needed.

• **Yearly:** Remove watersprouts, suckers, broken, and damaged branches. Watch for and prune out crossing and parallel branches that will eventually rub. Remove all inward- and

- downward-facing spurs and branches. Do the heaviest pruning just before the bearing season on alternate bearing apples.

PRUNING OVERGROWN APPLE TREES

We often inherit, or due to inexperience or busy schedules, end up with overgrown apple trees. These need to be pruned to improve their productivity and make maintenance easier for you. Neglected trees tend to be too tall or too densely branched to produce a good crop of flowers and fruit. Take several years to get these trees back in shape. Heavy pruning stimulates lots of leaf and stem growth and discourages fruiting.

1. Start by reducing the height of tall trees. Take a close look at the tree's structure. Remove one or two of the tallest branches back to the trunk. Then remove any damaged or diseased branches. Wait a year to do additional pruning.

2. Open up the dense canopy. This can be done the first year on short trees or the second and third year on trees for which you have reduced the height.

3. Remove deadwood, suckers, watersprouts (stems that grow straight up from branches) and broken branches.

4. Next remove crossing, rubbing, or parallel branches that will eventually grow together.

5. Always make cuts back to the trunk or where a branch joins another branch. Make the final cut flush to the branch bark collar. This is the swollen area that occurs at the base of a stem.

6. Use the three-step system when pruning larger (2 inches in diameter or greater) branches.

7. Do not use pruning paints. Allow plants to naturally seal the wound and fight off pests on their own.

PRUNING BACKYARD FRUITS

Many other backyard fruits require special pruning and training systems to ensure a good harvest. Match the training system with the available space, landscape style, and your gardening goals.

GRAPES

Grow grapes on a fence, arbor, or a trellis built just for them. Select a support system strong enough to hold the weight of the plant and easy enough for you to prune and train the grapes. Pruning and training grapes is not for the weak at heart. You must be aggressive with the pruners and remove a large amount of growth each spring. Insufficient pruning will result in excessive, but less productive growth.

Late March is the time to start training and pruning grapes. Train your plants over an arbor, across a fence, or on a trellis constructed for this purpose. Select a training system for your grapes. The Four-cane Kniffen System is one of the most popular, though some of the newer systems allow more sunlight to reach the plants.

- **At planting:** Start training your grapes now. Cut the stem back leaving only two buds above the soil. These two buds will produce new stems and leaves the first summer. Secure the trunk to the trellis.

- **2nd year:** Get out the pruning equipment in late March. Select one or two straight canes to be your permanent trunk. Remove other stems back to the main trunk.

- **3rd year:** Select the four strongest and best placed side branches in late March. Attach these to the trellis. Cut these side branches back to 8 to 12 buds each. These will be the fruiting canes that produce this season's harvest. Select secondary side shoots close to each of the first ones selected. Prune these back to two buds. These are the renewal spurs that will be next year's fruiting canes. Prune off all other growth.

- **4th year and beyond:** Remove last year's fruiting canes. Replace them with the renewal spurs. Cut the new fruiting canes back to 8 to 12 buds. Select new renewal spurs close to the fruiting canes. Prune these back to two buds. Remove all other growth. See figure on previous page.

BLUEBERRIES

Prune blueberries like all the other fruit in spring—before growth begins. The first two years, remove only broken and dead branches. Once the plants are established, by the third spring, you will need to do a little more aggressive pruning.

- Start by removing any damaged or broken branches. Remove some of the smaller, bushy growth and a few young shoots. Leave the most productive shoots. These are thick, hard, and 3 inches or longer. The more pruning you do, the smaller the crop will be, but the bigger the fruit.

- Change your pruning strategy after the fifth year. Remove the weakest and oldest canes to ground level. Leave five or six of the healthiest, heavily budded stems intact. Prune back extremely tall canes to the height of the other branches.

CURRANTS AND GOOSEBERRIES

Train currants and gooseberries the same way. Prune when the plants are dormant in late winter or early spring. You can remove winter damage and train the plant at the same time.

- **At Planting:** Prune right after planting. Remove any broken or damaged stems. Prune remaining stems back to 8 to 10 inches.

- **Second year:** Remove all but six to eight of the healthiest canes. Always remove any canes lying on the ground or shading out the center of the plant.

- **Third year:** Leave three or four of last year's stems in place. Keep four or five of the new stems. Remove everything else.

- **Fourth year and beyond:** Keep three or four each of the two- and three-year-old canes. Repeat this each spring.

ELDERBERRIES

Elderberries are easy to prune and train. Remove any broken or damaged stems at the time of

planting. Prune the remaining stems back to 8 to 10 inches. The following year, in late winter or early spring, remove any weak or broken branches. Prune out any shoots rubbing other stems or growing toward the center of the plant. Leave six to eight healthy canes for the coming season. Repeat this each year in late winter or early spring.

RASPBERRIES

Train raspberries to keep the plants healthy and productive while making it easier for you to harvest. Proper timing is critical for fruit production.

- **The Hill System:** Place a wooden or metal stake at the center of each hill. Allow canes to develop within 1 foot of the stake. Loosely tie the canes to the stake after pruning.

- **The Narrow Hedgerow System:** Use a trellis made of sturdy posts and wire to keep the raspberries inbounds. Place posts every 20 to 30 feet for adequate support. Prune old and new growth to maintain narrow rows that are 12 to 15 inches wide.

- Summer-bearing red raspberries produce their fruit on second-year growth (floricanes). Fall-bearing raspberries produce the fall crop on new growth (primocanes) and the summer crop on these same canes the following summer.

- Consider planting both summer- and fall-bearing raspberries. Sacrifice the summer crop on the fall-bearing plants to reduce maintenance and increase fall production. You will still get two crops (summer and fall) of raspberries, just from separate plantings

Prune summer-bearing and everbearing raspberry plants right after harvest. Remove all the older canes that bore fruit that summer and any diseased or insect infested stems. Cut these back to ground level. Summer pruning improves light and air circulation that helps reduce pests problems and increase productivity. In winter thin the remaining canes to 3 or 4 canes per foot or 5 to 6 canes per hill. You can cut back long canes and side shoots. Remove no more than ¼ the total height. More severe pruning can greatly reduce fruit production.

Fall-bearing raspberries (pruned for fall crop only) can be cut to ground level any time during the dormant season. Remove only disease- and insect-infected first-year canes on fall-bearing red raspberries that were cut to the ground over the winter. All these first-year canes will produce fruit this fall.

Ordering Soils and Mulch Chart

GARDEN SIZE IN SQ FT	CUBIC YARDS OF MATERIAL NEEDED TO COVER GARDEN SPACE DEPTH OF DESIRED MATERIAL			
	2"	4"	6"	8"
100	½	1+	2	2½
200	1+	2½	3½	5
300	2	3½	5½	7½
400	2½	5	7½	10
500	3+	6	9	12
600	3½	7½	11	15
700	4+	8½	13	17
800	5	10	15	20
900	5½	11	17	22
1000	6	12	18½	25

PEAT MOSS	AREA THAT CAN BE AMENDED WITH	
BALE SIZE	1"	2"
1 cubic ft.	24 sq. ft.	12 sq. ft.
2.2 cubic ft.	50 sq. ft.	25 sq. ft.
3.8 cubic ft.	90 sq. ft.	45 sq. ft.

Or calculate what you need:
Multiply the area (length times width measured in feet) by the desired depth (in feet) of mulch or compost. Convert this volume from cubic feet to cubic yards by dividing by 27 (the number of cubic feet in a cubic yard). This is the amount of material you will need to order.

Late Planting Chart

Use late additions to fill in empty spaces or replant rows that have already been harvested. Allow enough time for plants to grow and produce before the first killing frost. Check the back of the seed packet for average days to harvest. Then count the frost-free days left in the season. Compare the two and decide if you have time to grow and harvest this crop. Allow at least two weeks for harvest. Keep in mind that some plants, such as broccoli and cabbage, can tolerate a light frost. In fact, their flavor improves with the cooler temperatures of fall. Use this chart for quick reference.

| VEGETABLE | FIRST HARVEST | LAST DATE TO PLANT WITH THESE FROST DATES | | |
		9/15	10/1	10/23
From Seeds				
Beets	50–60	7/15	8/1	8/15
Beans, Bush	50–60	7/15	8/1	8/15
Carrot	60–70	7/1	7/15	8/1
Chard	40–50	8/1	8/15	9/1
Chinese Cabbage	60–70	7/1	7/15	8/7
Cucumber	50–60	7/15	8/1	8/15
Kohlrabi	50–60	7/15	8/1	8/15
Leaf Lettuce	40–50	8/1	8/15	9/1
Mustard Greens	40–50	8/1	8/15	9/1
Peas	60–70	7/1	7/15	8/15
Radish	25–30	8/15	9/1	9/15
Spinach	40–50	8/1	8/15	9/1
Sweet Corn	65–70	7/1	7/15	8/1
Turnips	60–70	7/1	7/15	8/7
From Transplants				
Broccoli	60–70	7/1	7/15	8/7
Cabbage	60–70	7/1	7/15	8/7
Cauliflower	50–60	7/15	8/1	8/15
Chinese Cabbage	50–60	7/15	8/1	8/15
Collards	50–60	7/15	8/1	8/15
Kale	50–60	7/15	8/1	8/15
Kohlrabi	40–50	8/1	8/15	9/1
Onion Sets	40–50	8/1	8/15	9/1
Onion Plants	50–60	7/15	8/1	8/15

Plant Spacing Chart

Use this chart to calculate the number of plants you'll need. Divide the square footage of the garden by the spacing factor. The result is the number of plants you'll need.

SPACING (INCHES)	SPACING FACTOR	PLANTS NEEDED FOR SQAURE FT PLANTING BED			
		25ft²	50ft²	75ft²	100ft²
4	0.11	227	454	682	909
6	0.25	100	200	300	400
8	0.44	57	114	170	227
10	0.70	36	72	107	143
12	1.00	12	50	75	100
15	1.56	16	32	48	64
18	2.25	11	22	33	44
24	4.00	6	13	19	25
30	6.25	4	8	12	16
36	9.00	3	6	8	11
48	16.00	2	3	5	6
60	26.00	1	2	3	4

For example: If planting pansies 6 inches apart in a bed 25 square feet, you need 100 plants.

25 square feet divided by .25 spacing factor equals 100 plants.

Michigan Frost Map

Number of
Frost-free Days

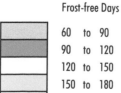

60 to 90
90 to 120
120 to 150
150 to 180
180 to 210

Bibliography

Brickell, Christopher and Judith D. Zuk, ed. *The American Horticultural Society: A-Z Encyclopedia of Garden Plants.* DK Publishing, Inc.: New York, NY, 1997.

Brickell, Christopher and David Joyce. *The American Horticultural Society: Pruning and Training.* DK Publishing, Inc.: New York, NY, 1996.

Browne, Jim, William Radler, and Nelson Sterner, ed. *Rose Gardening.* Pantheon Books: New York, 1995.

Coombes, Allen J. *Dictionary of Plant Names.* Timber Press: Portland, OR, 1993.

Curtis, John T. *The Vegetation of Wisconsin.* The University of Wisconsin Press: Jackson, MN, 1978.

Dirr, Michael A. *Manual of Woody Landscape Plants, 4th edition.* Stipes Publishing Co.: Urbana, IL, 1990.

DiSabato-Aust, Tracy. *The Well-Tended Perennial Garden.* Timber Press: Portland, Oregon, 1998.

Fell, Derek. *Annuals.* HP Books: Los Angeles, CA, 1983.

Martin, Laura. *The Folklore of Trees and Shrubs.* The Globe Pequot Press: Chester, Connecticut, 1992.

Reilly, Ann. *Park's Success with Seeds.* Geo. W. Park Seed Co., Inc., Greenwood: South Carolina, 1978.

Schneider, Donald. *Park's Success with Bulbs.* Geo. W. Park Seed Co., Inc.: Greenwood, South Carolina, 1981.

Still, Steven M. *Manual of Herbaceous Plants, 4th Edition.* Stipes Publishing Company: Urbana, IL, 1994.

Wisconsin Department of Natural Resources. *Wisconsin's Champion Trees.* 1998.

Wyman, Donald. *Wyman's Gardening Encyclopedia.* McMillan Publishing Co., Inc.: New York, 1977.

Glossary

Acid soil: soil with a pH less than 7.0. Acid soil is sometimes called "sour soil" by gardeners. Most plants prefer a slightly acid soil between 6 and 7 where most essential nutrients are available.

Alkaline soil: soil with a pH greater than 7.0, usually formed from limestone bedrock. Alkaline soil is often referred to as *sweet soil.*

Annual: a plant that completes its entire life cycle in one season. It germinates, grows, flowers, sets seed, and dies within one year.

Balled-and-burlapped: describes a large tree whose roots have been wrapped tightly in protective burlap and twine after it is dug. It is wrapped in this manner to protect it for shipping, sales, and transplanting.

Bare-root: trees, shrubs, and perennials that have been grown in soil, dug, and have had the soil removed prior to sales or shipping. Mail-order plants are often shipped bare-root with the roots packed in peat moss, sawdust, or similar material and wrapped in plastic.

Barrier plant: a plant that has thorns or impenetrable growth habit and is used to block foot traffic or other access to an area in the landscape.

Beneficial insects: insects or their larvae that prey on pest organisms and their eggs. They may be flying insects such as ladybugs, parasitic wasps, praying mantids, and soldier bugs; or soil dwellers such as predatory nematodes, spiders, and ants.

Berm: a low, artificial hill created in a landscape to elevate a portion of the landscape for functional and aesthetic reasons such as added interest, screening, and improved drainage.

Bract: a modified leaf resembling a flower petal, located just below the true flower. Often it is more colorful and visible than the actual flower, as in poinsettia.

Bud union: the place where the top of a plant was grafted to the rootstock; a term frequently used with roses.

Canopy: the total overhead area of a tree, including the branches and leaves.

Cold hardiness: the ability of a perennial plant (including trees, shrubs, and vines) to survive the minimum winter temperature in a particular area.

Complete fertilizer: powdered, liquid, or granular fertilizer with a balanced proportion of the three key nutrients—nitrogen (N), phosphorus (P), and potassium (K).

Composite: an inflorescence (cluster of flowers) also referred to as a head container petal and disklike flowers. They are often daisylike with a flat (disklike) center and petal-like flowers surrounding the outside.

Compost: decomposed organic matter added to the soil to improve its drainage and ability to retain moisture.

Corm: a modified bulblike stem. It is swollen, short, solid, and located underground. Crocus and gladiolus are two plants with corms.

Crown: (*a*) the point where the stems and roots meet, located at, or just below, the soil surface. (*b*) the top part of the tree.

Cultivar: a CULTIvated VARiety. A unique form of a plant that has been identified as special or superior and has been selected for propagation and sale.

Deadhead: to remove faded flowers from plants to improve their appearance, prevent seed production, and stimulate further flowering.

Deciduous plants: trees and shrubs that lose their leaves in the fall.

Desiccation: drying out of foliage, usually due to drought or wind.

Division: splitting apart perennial plants to create several smaller rooted segments. The practice is useful for controlling a plant's size and for acquiring more plants.

Dormancy: the period, usually the winter, when perennial plants temporarily cease active growth and rest. (The verb form is "dormant.")

Established: the point at which a newly planted tree, shrub, or flower has recovered from transplant shock and begins to grow; often indicated by the production of new leaves or stems.

Evergreen: perennial plants that do not lose their foliage annually with the onset of winter. Needled or broadleaf foliage will persist and continue to function on a plant through one or more winters, aging and dropping unnoticed in cycles of one, two, three, or more.

Foliar: of or about foliage—usually refers to the practice of spraying foliage with fertilizer or pesticide for absorption by the leaves.

Floret: a small individual flower, usually one of many forming an inflorescence considered the blossom.

Germinate: to sprout. Germination is a fertile seed's first stage of development.

Graft (union): the point on the stem of a woody plant where a stem or bud of a desirable plant is placed onto a hardier root system. Roses, apples, and some ornamental trees are commonly grafted.

Hardscape: the permanent, structural, non-plant part of a landscape, such as walls, sheds, pools, patios, arbors, and walkways.

Herbaceous: plants having fleshy or soft stems that die back with frost; the opposite of *woody*.

Hybrid: a plant produced by crossing two different varieties, species or genera. Usually indicated with a × in the name such as *Acer × fremanii*.

Inflorescence: a cluster of flowers occurring at the tip of a stem. This includes such arrangements as umbels (Queen Anne's lace), composite or head (daisy), spike (salvia), raceme (snapdragon) and panicle (coral bells).

Mulch: a layer of material used to cover bare soil to conserve moisture, discourage weeds, moderate soil temperature, and prevent erosion and soil compaction. It may be inorganic (gravel, fabric) or organic (wood chips, bark, pine needles, chopped leaves).

Naturalize: (*a*) to plant seeds, bulbs, or plants in a random, informal pattern as they would appear in their natural habitat; (*b*) to adapt to and spread throughout natural areas and appear as if native to that location (a tendency of some non-native plants).

Nectar: the sweet fluid, produced by glands on flowers, that attracts pollinators such as hummingbirds and honeybees, for whom it is a source of energy.

Organic material, organic matter: any material or debris that is derived from plants.

Peat moss: organic matter from peat sedges (United States) or sphagnum mosses (Canada), often used to improve soil drainage and water holding abilities.

Perennial: a flowering plant that lives over two or more seasons. Many die back with frost, but their roots survive the winter and generate new shoots in the spring.

pH: a measurement of the relative acidity (low pH) or alkalinity (high pH) of soil or water based on a scale of 1 to 14, with 7 being neutral. Individual plants require soil to be within a certain range so that nutrients can dissolve in moisture and be available to them.

Pinch: to remove tender stems and/or leaves by pressing them between thumb and forefinger. This pruning technique encourages branching, compactness, and flowering in plants.

Pollen: the yellow, powdery grains in the center of a flower. A plant's male sex cells, they are transferred to the female plant parts by means of wind, bees, or other animal pollinators to fertilize them and create seeds.

Raceme: an arrangement of single stalked flowers along an elongated, unbranched stem.

Rhizome: a swollen energy-storing stem structure, similar to a bulb, that lies horizontally in the soil. Roots emerge from its lower surface and stems emerge from a growing point at or near its tip, as in bearded Iris.

Rootbound (or potbound): the condition of a plant that has been confined in a container too long, its roots are forced to wrap around themselves and even swell out of the container. Successful transplanting or repotting requires untangling and trimming away some of the matted roots.

Root flare: the transition at the base of a tree trunk where the bark tissue begins to differentiate and roots begin to form just before entering the soil. This area should not be covered with soil or mulch when planting a tree.

Self-seeding: the tendency of some plants to sow their seeds freely around the yard. It creates many seedlings the following season that may or may not be welcome.

Semievergreen: tending to be evergreen in a mild climate but deciduous in a harsher one.

Shearing: the pruning technique whereby plant stems and branches are cut uniformly with long-bladed pruning shears (hedge shears) or powered hedge trimmers. It is used when creating and maintaining hedges and topiary.

Slow-acting (slow-release) fertilizer: fertilizer that is water insoluble and releases its nutrients when acted on by soil temperature, moisture, and/or related microbial activity. Typically granular, it may be organic or synthetic.

Succulent growth: the sometimes undesirable production of fleshy, water-storing leaves or stems that results from overfertilization.

Sucker: a new growing shoot. Underground plant roots produce suckers to form new stems and spread by means of these suckering roots to form large plantings or colonies. Some plants produce root suckers or branch suckers as a result of pruning or wounding.

Tuber: a thickened portion of underground stem used for energy storage and reproduction. Irish potato is a tuber.

Tuberous root: a swollen root with one point of growth where stem joins the root. Sweet potatoes and dahlias grow from tuberous roots.

Variegated: having various colors or color patterns. The term usually refers to plant foliage that is streaked, edged, blotched, or mottled with a contrasting color, often green with yellow, cream, or white.

White grubs: fat, off-white, worm-like larvae of Japanese and other beetles. They live in the soil and feed on plant (especially grass) roots until summer, when they emerge as beetles to feed on plant foliage.

Wings: (*a*) the corky tissue that forms edges along the twigs of some woody plants such as winged euonymus; (*b*) the flat, dried extension of tissue on some seeds, such as maple, that catch the wind and help them disseminate.

Index

Notes

Notes

Notes

Notes

Notes

Photo Credits

Liz Ball: pp. 7

Tom Eltzroth: pp. 22 (bottom), 54, 127 (top middle), 145 (top), 154 (middle)

Katie Elzer-Peters: pp. 27, 29, 31, 36, 39 (all), 44, 51, 57 (bottom), 59 (all), 68 (both), 69 (both), 76 (all), 77 (both), 81, 90 (all), 92, 96 (all), 102, 109 (both), 110 (all), 111 (all), 114, 127 (bottom), 129, 140 (both), 145 (lower), 163, 173 (all), 174 (all), 192, 205

Pam Harper: pp. 97

iStock: pp. 138, 150, 169, 186, 198, 204

Melinda Myers: pp. 20, 22 (top), 23, 33, 34, 40, 47, 57 (top), 88, 95 (bottom), 105, 108, 112, 124, 137 (both), 141, 147, 164, 166 (both), 170, 183, 185, 189 (both), 195, 201, 202

Jerry Pavia: pp. 64, 127 (top left, top right), 142 (both), 154 (left), 188

Shutterstock: pp. 28, 48, 66, 86, 89, 95 (top), 104, 106, 152, 154 (right), 200, 203, 207

Neil Soderstrom: pp. 36, 42, 71, 74, 131, 136, 155 (both), 179, 182

Lynn Steiner: pp. 37, 62

Meet Melinda Myers

Nationally known gardening expert, TV and radio host, author, and columnist Melinda Myers has more than thirty years of horticulture experience. She has written more than twenty gardening books, including Can't Miss Small Space Gardening, The Garden Book for Wisconsin, Minnesota Gardener's Guide, Month-by-Month Gardening in Wisconsin, *the* Perfect Lawn Midwest *series, as well as the* Midwest Gardener's Handbook, Minnesota & Wisconsin Getting Started Guide, *and* Michigan Getting Started Garden Guide.

In addition to authoring books, Myers hosts the nationally syndicated "Melinda's Garden Moment" segments that air on over 135 TV and radio stations throughout the United States. She is also the instructor for The Great Course How to Grow DVD series. Myers is a columnist and contributing editor for *Birds & Blooms* magazine and writes the twice monthly "Gardeners' Questions" newspaper column. She also has a column in *Gardening How-to* magazine and *Wisconsin Gardening* magazine. Melinda hosted "The Plant Doctor" radio program for over 20 years as well as seven seasons of *Great Lakes Gardener* on PBS. She has written articles for *Better Homes and Gardens* and *Fine Gardening* magazines, and was a columnist and contributing editor for *Backyard Living* magazine. Melinda has a master's degree in horticulture, is a certified arborist, and was a horticulture instructor with tenure. Melinda Myers' many accomplishments include starting the Master Gardener program in Milwaukee County and winning two Garden Media Awards (a Garden Globe Award for radio talent and a Quill and Trowel Award for her television work), both from the Garden Writers Association. She has also won the American Horticultural Society's B.Y. Morrison Communication Award for effective and inspirational communication. Melinda was the first woman inducted into the Wisconsin Green Industry Federation Hall of Fame.

Visit Melinda's web site at www.melindamyers.com.

CPSIA information can be obtained
at www.ICGtesting.com
Printed in the USA
LVHW01s0554200118
563216LV00008B/8/P